Nancy –
Thank You for
the Support
Alberta Sequeira
8/7/10

Someone Stop This Merry-Go-Round
An Alcoholic Family in Crisis
By Alberta H. Sequeira

INFINITY
PUBLISHING.COM

Copyright © 2009 by Alberta H. Sequeira

ISBN 0-7414-5415-7

Alberta H. Sequeira
12 Rounseville Road
Rochester, MA 02770
alberta@ahealingheart.net
www.albertasequeira.com

Cover Art:
Phil Sayer
www.imagebuy.co.uk

Editor:
Adele Brinkley
Adele@withpeninhand.net
www.withpeninhand.net

Published by:

INFINITY
PUBLISHING.COM

1094 New DeHaven Street, Suite 100
West Conshohocken, PA 19428-2713
Info@buybooksontheweb.com
www.buybooksontheweb.com
Toll-free (877) BUY BOOK
Local Phone (610) 941-9999
Fax (610) 941-9959

Printed in the United States of America
Published September 2009

"Forever in Our Hearts"

In loving memory of
Richard Lopes
1940-1985

Acknowledgements

With All My Love and Appreciation
Without family, my book wouldn't be complete

My heartfelt thanks go to my family for their support in writing this story. Many tears have fallen thinking back on our lives. There were times that I almost decided against telling these events. People think authors heal by writing about their tragedies. We don't really, but we manage to go on with life despite the hole left in our hearts from grief.

My daughter, Debbie Dutra, gave me support and confidence in having our private lives opened to the world. I'm very proud of her for endless reasons. She loved her father and was old enough to treasure the healthy years with him before his illness changed him into another person.

Our daughter, Lori was born four years after Debbie and her formative years coincided with the beginning of my husband, Richie Lopes', frequent and continuous drinking. It left her searching for answers all through her life.

Our memories of happy and fun times with him are many. He loved laughing at the old cartoons on television like Deputy Dog and the Road Runner. Our dearest memories will be his love of the sea, boating, and fishing.

We were an ordinary family with dreams of always being close and happy. Richie had been a man of ambition when he started his own television repair business. There were times when he was a proud and loving father and husband.

I'm grateful to the Lopes family for allowing me to use their names and private events in this memoir. They will forever miss Richie's wit and gentle ways.

Sonny and Anita Lopes supported me through my married years and after my husband's death. Their children Paula, Gilly, and Gary hold onto the fond memories growing up with their uncle.

This story is meant to show how alcoholism affects a family. I will always stand by my belief and hope to demonstrate that alcoholism is hereditary. Our families wanted to come forward with our sincere and private emotions to help other families who are fighting the same battle. It's my fervent hope that this book will aid in finding ways to help other families and their loved ones who are suffering from this killer.

A special thanks to my editor, Adele Brinkley, for her professionalism in editing this book.

I'm grateful to Phil Sayer, the photographer, for developing such a great picture for my cover.

Introduction

Alcoholism is a disease that affects millions of people along with heart problems, diabetes, cancer, and drug addiction. We hear and read about different diseases that kill people every day and how they leave broken-hearted families behind.

Who is considered an alcoholic and what are they like in behavior? We all have our own personal conception about what a person has to do in order to be considered an alcoholic. Usually, they're labeled as habitual drunks.

Most of us picture an alcoholic as a person, curled-up and passed out among the over-turned garbage cans and found on a hidden side street between buildings or someone under a torn, grimy blanket sleeping on a park bench with a newspaper over their face and wearing ragged, filthy clothes looking as though they needed a hot, sudsy shower. In fact, a large percentage of the public automatically assumes it's a man in this condition having the problem. Rarely does it enter our minds that a woman could be the alcoholic in these situations.

Our intellects come to the understanding and conclusion that the drinker has absolutely no desire to find a job or no wish to mingle with and contribute to society. We insist that many of them are living off the welfare system with no intention of bettering themselves. When we come in contact with the drinker, many of us lose patience with them or omit them completely in our conversations and social circles.

It's more comfortable for us to pretend that they don't exist. In other words, they're not getting their act together to think and do things the way *we* believe they should.

Because our own lives are structured and orderly, we believe that we're better than the alcoholic. We forget how blessed our families are to have jobs that pay well, three good meals a day on the table, independent lives, and the freedom to come and go as we like. This concept is what most people consider to be a healthy American life under normal living conditions.

The reality of an alcoholic's life won't hit us until we come in direct contact with a family member, friend, or a close acquaintance who's struggling to combat this disease. Then we develop the need to understand fully and to gain the knowledge of what alcohol is doing to the alcoholic and the people around them.

Once the abuser's actions start to affect *our* lives, we suddenly sit-up and open our eyes to what's happening to the individual. The desire to help them is there because we love the person and can see that the disease has changed his or her personality, morals, and ambitions. The devastating fact hits us that alcohol is slowly killing our loved one.

The alcoholics themselves can become acutely aware that they are drowning in drink and still don't feel the need or have the willpower to get help. For them, the battle to give up liquor has too many side effects, and it's too hard to combat the habit, especially if this life-style has been going on for years.

It's a struggle every day for an alcoholic to just get out of bed. Many spend their days sleeping. They skip meals because their appetite has disappeared, thereby causing more damage to their health because their bodies break down from lack of proper nutrition to keep them stable.

Many alcoholics who have tried to fight the disease don't relish the unpleasant physical effects of going without a drink; instead, they give in and turn back to drinking. In their mind, taking a drink is the only way to stop the effects of withdrawal. They fear going to any public place, and the drinking imprisons them in their own home behind closed doors.

Their lives and minds are constantly in a confused state. Alcoholics live in uncertainty that immobilizes them. They find it hard to do anything for themselves or their families. All confidence disappears. They make up all kinds of stories in order to avoid doing anything that makes them uncomfortable.

Doctors' appointments are cancelled because they fear what they may be told. Family events are ignored so they don't have to hear about their behavior or their broken promises. They live in denial that they have any problem at all and believe they can stop drinking at any time.

Getting sober for an alcoholic means they'll have to take the giant step of signing themselves into a detoxification center. There, they'll experience what they feared: the shakes, being confined, and taking medicine that will make them feel worse before they get better. They're subjected to answering personal, embarrassing questions and being cooped-up in a single room with strangers, whom they consider to be sicker than they are.

After weeks or months of drying out, they're pushed into the outside world again to face the same problems that brought them there. Depending on circumstances, they'll have to confront the people that they hurt, deal with job hunting, and return to having the responsibility of making family decisions. Some become paranoid, thinking that everyone is judging them and watching their every move to see if they slip. Some probably are being watched because the whole family becomes sick and confused from the disease.

If they don't continue to seek professional counseling after being rehabilitated, join an AA group, or find a sponsor, most alcoholics go right back to the bottle, which is always there to comfort them with no condemnation.

Going back to drinking, or *falling off the wagon* as the expression goes, doesn't mean that they want to—it means they're sick. Alcoholism is a disease that is highly hereditary. It would be so much easier if drinking could be cured by simply taking a pill. The first step to recovery for the alcoholic is for him or her to want the help. No one can help them if they don't want to be helped.

Alcoholics have the same wants and dreams as the rest of us. There was a time when they held a job, had a marriage, brought up children, owned a home and a car, and had a social life with their friends and families. Now, they have become frightened, misplaced human beings who have lost their dignity.

Alcoholism doesn't happen overnight. The reality of their lives being out-of-control came when catastrophes started to happen all around them. Some drinkers are fortunate to be able to keep their lives fairly normal, but others don't realize it's a problem until they lose everything.

Society needs to stop looking at the millions of alcoholics as bums or low-class individuals who don't want to better themselves. They have a disease that can reach the point of no return.

If a person has been drinking for years and wants to stop, the body may have reached the point where it *needs* the drink. The body craves it; then there's no stopping.

Someone Stop This Merry-Go-Round is based on the true story of my life living with and losing a husband to alcoholism. Slowly, our happy lives as a secure family started to fall to pieces at different stages. It seems completely incomprehensible to me now that I couldn't see the signs of serious drinking from this uncontrollable disease.

Chapter One
A Life Changing Call

RING... RING!

The emergency line flashed and lit up bright red.

"Dighton Police Department, may I help you?"

"Mom?"

"Lori, what's the matter? Why are you crying?" My daughter was hysterical and crying uncontrollably on the other end of the phone.

"Mom, Dad's dying! He's in the hospital, and the doctors say he's not going to pull through."

I felt a sudden rush of pressure go straight to my head.

"Oh, my God, Lori, where is he?"

"He's in the VA Hospital in Providence, Rhode Island. Dad's whole family is there now. Debbie and I are going to ride up together. Can you meet us there?"

"Calm down, honey." I could tell by her breathing that she wasn't in control of her emotions.

Richie and I had been divorced for six years. Through town gossip, I had heard that he was still drinking, but it never entered my mind that there was a possibility of him ever dying from it.

The years apart hadn't erased my emotional attachment to him. I held on to the hope that he would straighten out his life and seek counseling. Leaving him was the only way that I could have remained sane. No matter what I did or said, he never accepted help to fight this terrible demon.

"Of course, I'll meet you there. I have to see if I can get someone to take my place on such short notice."

"His room is on the fourth floor. We'll be waiting for you." Lori hung up without waiting for a reply from me.

I had been a dispatcher for the Town of Dighton for nine years and was used to handling emergencies, but this call threw me for a loop. This one concerned my ex-husband, and my daughter was in a state of panic. This catastrophe was happening to *my* family.

I was glad that my daughter, Debbie, was going with Lori. In a crisis, she was calmer than her sister. Debbie was four years older and always handled a bad situation in a mature way.

I worked the day shift from 8:00 a.m. to 4:00 p.m., and replacements weren't easy to find. Dispatchers on the detail from 4 a.m. to midnight and midnight to 8:00 a.m., however, seemed to have no problem.

All the emergency and routine calls for the ambulance, fire, water, police and highway departments came into my office at the police station. I had to log every transmission of the day.

The year was 1985, and the town didn't have computers to record proceedings. Everything had to be documented by hand with the precise time of each event and the conversations from the caller. The ambulance and fire departments were the only ones that used tape recorders on their phones. My job entailed a tremendous amount of stress.

Chief Karl Spratt's secretary, Janet, was in the next room; a sliding window separated our offices.

"Janet, I have to talk to Karl. Can you take the calls until I return?"

"Of course, is everything okay?"

"I'll tell you when I get back."

I rushed down the long hallway to the Chief's office. There was never a knocking formality, unless the door was closed. It was a small police force with two officers to a shift, a situation that gave us the chance to be informal with one another. I went straight to Karl's desk. My nerves started to take over, and I could feel myself hyperventilating.

"Excuse me, Karl, but I have to leave right away. Lori called and said that Richie has been admitted to the VA Hospital in Providence."

Karl bent his head down to stare at me over his thin, clear-framed glasses. "Is it something serious?"

"It's not good. She's been told that he's dying. It has to be from his drinking. I don't have all the details. I'll start calling to see if someone can come in for me."

"Hold off a minute. I think Bob is still in the back room." Bob was a reserve officer and a volunteer dispatcher.

The Chief yelled across the hall, "Hey, Bob. Can you cover the phones for Alberta? It's a family emergency."

"Sure. I'm free."

"Good…You're free to go, Alberta."

I couldn't believe the luck of Bob being in the office. It would normally take hours to get someone to cover my shift.

"Thanks, Karl."

He put his hand on my shoulder. "Drive slowly," he advised. I saw the concern in his eyes.

"I will."

There was a lot of unfinished work on my desk but I knew it was more important to meet my daughters. I grabbed the paperwork and flung it on top of the filing cabinet. *I'll deal with it later.*

"Janet, Karl will explain my situation. I really can't stay."

I grabbed my belongings and headed out to the parking lot. It was February and the cold, raw wind went right through me. The hood from my long, gray, wool coat flew off my head. I hated winter.

My heart was pounding and my hands started to shake as I fumbled for the keys in my pocketbook. I should have taken them out sooner. I unlocked the car door and sat to start the car. My hands were shaking so badly, I missed putting the key into the ignition several times.

I looked both ways before entering the highway. Suddenly, I heard a loud horn. An old, black pickup was right on top of me. I came within a second of colliding with it.

"Hey, watch it, lady!" The young man's face was red with anger as he screamed out his open window.

"I'm sorry. I didn't see you," I yelled back even though I knew he couldn't hear me.

By now, my insides felt like they were going to break into a million pieces. The driver made an obscene hand signal and sped away. His gesture upset me. I noticed that his truck had multiple dents, and I concluded they were probably caused by his driving too fast in the first place.

I've got to compose myself. I can't afford to have an accident. I tried concentrating intensely on my driving. The hospital was forty-five minutes away.

I drove along the back roads onto William Street, a path that would get me to Route 44 faster. The street had been in bad shape for years with many pot holes that caused me to slow down; however, I wasn't in the right frame of mind to be practical with speed.

I loved North Dighton. I had lived there for more than twenty years. It was a small town of just over 5,100 residents in a rural setting, much of it farmland. Every year, the Bristol Agricultural School had a long waiting list of applicants.

Growing up in this peaceful town, my daughters and I had been blessed with many friends. Lori was seventeen and in her last year of high school. She had long, beautiful, midnight-black hair in tight curls which she constantly tried to iron out straight. Her brown eyes were enhanced by her makeup and the deep summer tan which stayed with her even after summer ended.

Her mischievous ways made her the "leader of the pack." Her best characteristics were her personality and wit. Lori had never adjusted to Richie's and my separation and hid her problems with it more than I knew at the time.

Debbie was twenty-one and seemed more adjusted. If she were troubled, she never talked openly about what bothered her. Her light, brown hair was long with bushy curls. Her constant wide smile put everyone she met at ease.

Debbie was available to help anyone in need. She was always game for fun, but she seemed to be more a watcher than a doer. Her personality was more like her father's, quiet and thoughtful. She had the perfect life with the perfect man. Brian Dutra, her fiancé, was wonderful, and they had set a date in August to marry.

Once I got to Route 195 near East Providence, I was relieved that the traffic moved at a normal pace. I was fighting to control the desire to speed up to make better time, but the last thing I needed was a traffic ticket.

Suddenly, the traffic slowed to a crawl. All I could see were vehicles bumper to bumper with their brake lights on. Cars were merging from the side exits trying to squeeze into the jammed four lanes.

Oh, God, not now!

Drivers were edging in from one narrow line to the next, each trying to get into the fastest moving lane. I could see construction up ahead. The usual ten minute drive to the hospital from this point became twenty-five minutes.

I sat in traffic thinking back to our days together as a family; the good and bad. *Damn you, Richie, why didn't you go for help? Our poor daughters have to go through all the pain of witnessing you die in front of them.* I was angry one moment and then I'd feel sorry for him. He had a disease.

When I reached the hospital, there were no parking spaces out front. Rather than keep searching the streets, I headed straight to the parking garage. Luck was on my side and I found an open parking spot on the first level. I seized my pocketbook and hurried up the side ramp to the elevator.

The open elevator door was about to close. I ran toward it. "Hold the door!"

I stepped in and discovered three people with unresponsive faces staring at me.

"Thanks." I gave each of them a smile while panting from the short run. No one acknowledged my gratitude. They probably had their own problems to deal with.

The doors opened on the fourth floor. I wasn't sure if I'd be able to handle seeing Richie so sick and near death.

My first instinct was to find Debbie and Lori. I saw no one familiar anywhere so I went straight to the nurse's station.

"Could you please tell me what room Richard Lopes is in?"

A stocky, gray haired nurse looked me up and down for a few seconds and then asked coldly, "Are you family?"

"He's my ex-husband and our two daughters are with him."

"Sorry. You're not allowed to see him, only family. You'll have to sit in the visitors' waiting room around the corner."

The nurse had given the order with no sympathy whatsoever and turned back to writing on a patient's chart.

Why didn't I say that I was family? After all, I am.

Turning the corner, I saw a sign above a door: Hospital Waiting Room. Magazines were scattered throughout the room but the area was empty of people.

Everyone must be visiting him, I thought in amazement.

I couldn't understand how so many family members had been allowed to be in his room at the same time. No one was walking in the corridors when I glanced out the door. *God, maybe they're all with him because he's dying.*

I had no legal right to make any health decisions. From Richie's thirty years or more of drinking, he was now fighting the last stages of cirrhosis.

I sat with a knot in my stomach, thinking of the reality of what was happening to my world, to my daughters.

Please, God, give me the strength not to fall apart in front of the girls, when I go to his room. They need to see me strong so that they can lean on me for support.

It seemed like an eternity passed as I waited for my daughters.

Where's everyone? I'd been there for fifteen minutes, and no one appeared. I couldn't even spot a nurse walking in the hall. The surroundings seemed cold and gave me chills. The empty corridor was creepy and felt like death.

Richie's mother and two sisters, Lena and May, walked up the corridor toward the waiting area. What a relief, I would finally find out what was going on, and someone would take me to his room.

May looked in my direction and saw me sitting in the waiting area. She immediately turned her back to me and started talking to her family in the hallway. At first, I thought they were discussing Richie's condition privately. I assumed that once they were through talking, one of them would come over to me. After all, they did see me.

I looked outside the door and noticed a poster on the wall, right above where May was standing. The advertisement was about alcoholism with an Alcoholic's Anonymous telephone number written in bold, black letters.

Of all the people to be standing under that sign, I thought. May never accepted her brother's drinking addiction.

I took a deep breath and tried to compose myself. The stress was building up. I couldn't understand why everyone was ignoring me. I started to fear that he died. My head began to spin. *Why wasn't anyone coming over to me?*

Alberta at the Dighton Police Dispatcher's Office

Chapter Two
Sara Thompson

I could no longer control my emotions. I placed my head in my hands and burst into tears thinking about Richie's struggle with his drinking problem. I came to understand, more than anyone else, how his condition got to this point. I was the one who lived through it.

I was at the hospital to support my daughters, and I expected to see Richie. It never entered my mind that I would be cut out from the family and not be allowed to see him, especially at this final stage of his life.

A few weeks earlier Anita, Richie's brother's wife, told Debbie that he had been admitted to the VA hospital the month before, but he walked out of the hospital without being discharged by the doctors. They warned him that his health status was life-threatening and advised him not to leave. He couldn't stand the painful treatments and the thought that his death could be imminent.

I purposely stepped out into the corridor to be noticed. I was giving them the benefit of the doubt that maybe they hadn't seen me in the waiting room. No one made an effort to look my way. Whatever the problem was, I wasn't going to be acknowledged. It absolutely infuriated me knowing that they were openly ignoring me.

I wanted to call my parents in East Falmouth, but I decided to wait until a complete up-date on Richie's condition was given to me. Deep down I craved to hear a friendly and caring voice.

The last thing I wanted to do was to put the two families together. There was enough stress as it was. I knew my father would be wild beyond anyone's imagination if he knew how I was being treated. He wouldn't put up with it.

Dad would have confronted them face to face and demanded answers.

I wasn't one for standing up for myself. Through my teen years, it wasn't easy requesting things from my mother. If she said no, there was no more discussion about it.

She'd reply, "I told you no, and I don't want to hear another word." Her tone along with a firm look stopped me from asking any more questions. It was something that I carried through my whole life in relationships. A loud voice or one with authority would make me clam up right away.

I felt that all the years being a member of Richie's family were being erased. Everyone seemed on edge with me being there. It was obvious that no one was going to be pleasant toward me. They kept their distance for some strange reason. Occasionally, I would see one of them looking toward me and then turn to whisper to the group.

I had always been comfortable with his family but red flags flashed in my mind telling me to stay away for the moment. I was determined to not let them see the distress they were causing me.

By now a responsive person would have been welcomed. I couldn't piece it together. This action of putting a wall up between me and Richie came from someone in the family, but who would do it? It was bad enough that it was tearing me apart that he was dying, much less, his family giving me a cold shoulder.

I picked up a magazine, hoping it would take my mind away from what was happening. I couldn't concentrate and wasn't really interested in reading in the first place. There was nothing there to occupy my time or mind. I couldn't get past the anger inside me. Their cruel stares hurt me. They acted as though I was invisible. I reacted by being frozen in place.

No one showed me the simple courtesy of saying hello. I was stunned that they could be so heartless. Did they think there were no emotional ties between Richie and me, or that I didn't have any feelings for him?

I should have at least been shown some respect, being the mother of his children. I was always close to the family, and there were never any arguments or hard feelings. How could they let our daughters go through this horrendous time in their life and cut me away from them? They needed me by their side. We were family! I had no way of venting my frustration.

At last, Debbie walked toward the visitor's room.

"Hi, Mom, I'm so glad you're here," she said after giving me a hug.

"Debbie, what on earth is going on? No one is speaking to me. They're acting like I have the plague. It can't be something I said because no one has spoken to me since I got here an hour ago."

"I don't think it's a good idea for you to stay here, Mom."

"Why not?" I was angry. My own daughter was asking me to leave. Didn't anyone realize that this was tearing me apart? "He was my husband and your father. Why should I leave?"

"Dad's girlfriend, Sara, is here. She has demanded that under no circumstances, whatsoever; was anyone to allow you to see Dad. She's being very bossy and making all the decisions." I could sense that Debbie was afraid to confront her.

"You've got to be kidding!" I snapped back in disbelief. "Who does she think she is?"

"Mom, if she sees you here, she'll make an awful scene."

"For what reason? I'm your mother, and have every right to be here with you and Lori."

"I can't get into it now. I've got to get back to Dad, Mom. Lori's with him. He looks awful. I wanted to see you first and warn you. Are you staying?"

"Don't worry about me. I'll be right here if you two need me."

"I'll try to come back again," she called as she hurried down the corridor.

I stood there in shock. Six months earlier Richie asked me to go back to him. No one was aware of this, not even the girls. I couldn't imagine him not wanting to see me. I became sick inside thinking that he may want to say something private to me before he died. I needed to see him.

My blood started to boil. Sara, a stranger, was controlling the family. I couldn't fathom how they were allowing it, especially Anita. She and I had been so close for years. How could she sit back knowing that I was being treated so badly?

Anita had told me that Richie moved into Sara's home after our divorce. I was happy for him. I thought that maybe he was settling down. He hated to be alone. I'm sure he took advantage of having a place to take his shoes off, a roof over his head, and a meal placed in front of him.

Now, Sara Thompson was taking over and acting like a wife. I was enraged knowing that everyone was too weak to stand up to her in such a serious situation. How could they allow this woman to say that I couldn't be with him? After all, she was only a girlfriend. They weren't even engaged. She had no right making decisions about who could visit him. I was still family whether she liked it or not. I was the mother of his kids, and no one could take that away from me, especially her.

The moment was going to arrive for me to meet Sara. This wasn't going to be a happy introduction. She was now in complete control over his family and that made it a lot more difficult for me. Everything seemed to be working against me. Suddenly, I was the one on the outside looking in.

My mind raced, wondering how I was going to handle this uncomfortable situation. I felt trapped. Even my daughters wouldn't intercede on my behalf. I felt nauseated, and couldn't understand what was causing everyone to act the way they were toward me.

All I wanted to do was say goodbye to him and console my girls while their father was dying. I needed some comfort with this. There were feelings still alive in Richie and me, even if it was just mutual respect.

My God, I'm not going to be able to see him. How can they take this away from me? I hadn't done a thing for this to be happening.

Knowing Sara's attitude toward me led me to believe that she was a domineering person. There was no likelihood that the two of us would be civil to one another. It would be intense rivalry. Already, I didn't like her.

It did cross my mind driving to the hospital that she might be there. At the same time, I felt that it would be limited to immediate family. Who would have thought that a stranger would be considered family, and I would be left out? I never thought there would be any hostile feelings toward me. The situation stunned me. How could Sara hate me without knowing me? She couldn't have much security in her relationship with Richie.

I sat there trying to picture what she looked like. I imagined her as a tall blonde with a perfect complexion and a body to kill. I wasn't sure if I could handle seeing her look better than me on top of her having this power over me.

Richie had been such a handsome man before his drinking days that I automatically expected Sara to be a beautiful woman. Guilt hit me for having these thoughts as my ex-husband was dying somewhere down the corridor. Here I was mentally competing with his girlfriend. There was no reason for it in the first place. Why couldn't we be respectful toward each other and me be allowed to see him? Everyone else was given this opportunity.

I should have been proud of my own looks. At forty-four, I kept my body in good shape going to Gloria Steven's gym four times a week. People frequently noticed my green eyes and complimented me on them, especially if I wore colorful tops. My auburn hair had been cut in a short style with a new perm.

I was a confident person when it came to my attire, and today was no different. It was a pattern that I had kept, being in the public eye. My makeup was neatly applied. I wore black high heels with a sky-blue, silk blouse along with a black wool skirt and a black and white striped blazer. I took a lot of pride in myself. But as the hours went by, I was losing my self-assurance.

I paced back and forth in the visitor's room trying to calm down from the anxiety of all the pressure. I needed to be strong and not show the anger that I was feeling. No one needed to witness a scene with two women going at one another in a hospital.

The emotional strain exhausted me. The hour and a half drive to the hospital felt like three because of the heavy traffic. If only I could converse with someone to pass the time. I couldn't stand being isolated and not knowing Richie's condition. He was at death's door. Was I going to have time to see him? The thought of not being allowed to began to upset me more with every passing minute. My heart was racing faster than normal.

I sat in a chair and laid my head back to rest. My eyes were heavy and it was hard to keep them open. I decided to rest for a short time so I'd be mentally alert when my daughters came back to see me.

When I closed my eyes, my mind started to drift back through my life. *Whatever happened to Richie and me?* I started to reminisce about how I almost missed being married to him. I had cared very deeply for another boy when I was sixteen-years old. Alcoholism had never been mentioned or seen in our family. When I met Richie, I didn't see the signs that were in front of me until it was too late. There were many warning signs that I had overlooked or missed.

Chapter Three

A New Move

In the summer of 1956, my parents made a decision to move from West Springfield, Massachusetts, to North Dighton, a town located in the southeastern part of Massachusetts outside the city of Taunton. I was just six-years old when we moved to West Springfield and didn't remember all the moves my family made for many years while my dad was in the Army. I was younger then and not connected to friends.

In 1941, my twin brother Albert and I were born in Pocasset, Massachusetts. My parents weren't expecting two children. They didn't have the sonograms that they have today to foretell multiple births.

In 1946, my sister, Leona, was eight years old, when our brother, Walter, died from Polio at seven years of age. My parents were distressed by his death. It was an era when wakes were held in the family home. This practice was traumatic for the whole family. My mother was devastated by the loss of her first born son, and having to see his casket lowered into the ground, which was also part of the funeral ritual at the time, completely finished her. She stopped performing her normal daily tasks.

In 1951, Billy was born. Four years later, Joey arrived and Mom was already in her middle forties. She went through a period of Postpartum Depression and lost all confidence. Being alone caused her unreasonable fear and she had to have a family member with her at all times. There was also the fear of leaving her home, which is commonly referred to today, as Agoraphobia. My mother depended on Leona to help when she went through the breakdown.

Leona stepped right in and took over the roll of our mother. In her senior year of high school, she quit school to take over the responsibilities of the house and raise my younger brothers. She didn't have the time to spend with her friends or think about dating.

When we moved to North Dighton, Leona was nineteen-years old and excited, with hope of finding a job in this strange town. She kept her tightly-curled, black hair cut short. I envied her for being able to let it dry on its own without worrying about styling it. My hair, in contrast, was poker straight.

Albert was very independent and a dare-devil. He had no problem attracting girls at an early age. I assumed our moving would be no different for him to mix and make new friends.

Leona, Albert, and I wore glasses. They didn't seem to mind, but I grew to hate them. Boys were constantly making fun of me with the usual cruel remarks of "four eyes" or "specks." Nicknames that they gave me, like "birdie," short for Alberta, or "graham cracker," an alteration of our name, Gramm, didn't' help my self-esteem.

The innocent, jabbing jokes stayed with me growing up. To make it worse, one summer my father forced me to buy a pair of glasses with pink frames. The hot sun faded them into pure white. Add them to my freckled-face, and I wasn't Miss America!

My teen years were upon me and the news of our moving was devastating. I never heard of this town of North Dighton and the idea didn't excite me. All I knew was that I was leaving my dearest girlfriend, Carol, behind. I was fourteen-years old, and we had been friends since first grade. How was I going to survive without her?

I can still see Carol standing in our driveway as my father backed our station wagon out. Her hands hung by her side as she wept. She couldn't even wave goodbye to me. I sat in the back seat of our over-packed car, sobbing. I thought my world had ended.

Our family was making this new move because our father, Albert L. Gramm, had been offered a job as an assistant to the president of Anderson Aircraft, Inc. in North Dighton. Our father was an amazing man. In 1928, he enlisted in the National Guard. In 1941, with the start of World War II, all National Guard divisions were inducted into the Federal Service. His regiment was shipped to Europe. He was one of the commanding officers of the 26th Yankee Division which fought in the battles of Lorraine and Metz, and Bastonge, the famous Battle of the Bulge, and he had been awarded the Bronze Star. On leaving the service, he rejoined the National Guard and retired in 1956 as a One-Star Brigadier General.

He was a serious man who made all the decisions in the family. He was used to being in control of the men under him in the service and continued the same regimentation with his family.

My mother, Sophie, wasn't happy with the constant moves, but she went wherever Dad had to be. It was something she did all through her married life, especially during Dad's military years that forced us to move from one state to another.

Mom was a tall, slender woman, five feet, six inches with light, brown hair that hung half-way to her shoulders. She walked with her head held high and her long legs made her look like a model. Shorts complimented her legs. It was hard to imagine that this beautiful woman had no confidence in herself.

As Dad traveled out of West Springfield, Albert, Leona and I were squeezed together in the third seat of the station wagon. Joe was in his car bed and Bill was with him in the middle seat in case Mom needed to attend to them.

The three hour ride seemed to take forever. Dad made one stop for lunch and a restroom. We were exhausted from being cramped together for what seemed like an eternity until we finally arrived in the small city of Taunton.

Dad drove around the town green, a rotary. It was potted with colorful red, yellow, purple and blue flower beds and benches facing the traffic. I prayed that it wasn't all the entertainment that this cracker box of a town had to offer.

There were no skyscrapers that reached to the sky or huge department stores like Sears or Macy's. Compared to the City of Springfield with its tall buildings and large businesses, this city seemed like a ghost town. A ride down one main street, around a rotary, and that was Taunton.

I remarked, "This is it?"

"It's a quaint little town, but you'll come to love it. It'll be nice not having to deal with heavy traffic. They have the same things here, but not a large variety," my father said.

Maybe he knew something that I didn't.

"Okay, are we ready to see our new home?" Dad asked, excitedly. "North Dighton is only ten minutes away. You'll like this place."

As he drove, we left the business district and got onto Route 138, Somerset Avenue. The car shook when we went over the uneven pavement and the numerous pot holes, it seemed like the roads were never repaired.

We finally arrived at our new neighborhood. The homes in the area were well maintained with beautiful landscaping.

Dad stopped on School Street in front of a brown, two-story house with white shutters. My eyes lit up when I noticed that the front porch had a swing on it like our other home. Our family spent many evenings enjoying the swing on hot summer nights. There was a short frontage, but the yard continued around the side of the house to the back.

There was a common driveway that was shared with a neighbor, a single man in his early thirties. The garage was behind the house. I started to get excited after seeing the property; my sadness turned to anticipation.

Dad parked the car in the driveway and all of us scrambled out, pushing and shoving each other to be first at the front door. We couldn't have gotten out faster if the car were on fire. Billy was only five-years old, but he ran in hot pursuit behind his siblings. He wasn't quite sure what the excitement was all about, but something was going to be fun from the way everyone was running. Joey was only a year old, so Dad opened the car door and carried him out.

He handed Mom the keys so she'd be the first to open the front door to our new home. It was also a surprise for her to see it. When Dad accepted the new job, he did a house search one day on his own and fell in love with this one. Mom wasn't one for traveling and gave him the okay to make the final decision.

There were two living rooms, a den, kitchen, laundry room, and a pantry on the ground floor. Upstairs were four bedrooms and a full bath.

To our surprise, some of our furniture was already in place. Dad had worked with the movers a few days before. They arrived a half hour later and brought the rest of our belongings into the house. It didn't take long to get comfortable and feel like we fit in perfectly. We soon discovered that our neighborhood was full of kids our age. Albert found them around every corner. He quickly made friends with Julie and Roland Sousa and Jimmy Haywood. They became tight.

Slowly, I found my own friends: Barbara Andrews, Sandy Simmons, Cindy Broadbent, Roseanne Lavigne and Linda

Gunn. Within weeks, our home became the popular place to congregate. My letters to Carol dropped from weekly to monthly to, "if I had a chance."

My favorite time of day was in the evening when our chores were done and Leona and I sat on the porch swing. We talked about her new job as a bookkeeper for the Durgins Food Company inside the Raytheon plant down the street. It was a restaurant that was available for the employees who worked for different companies in the same complex.

The porch became our gathering place with my friends. Our main topic was Elvis Presley. We'd hook up the record player and dance until our feet hurt. We knew all the latest dances like The Slop, The Hand Jive, The Bop, the Stroll, the Circle and the Calypso.

Weekday afternoons were spent watching the kids on American Bandstand with Dick Clark. I knew all their names and about their personal lives. Everybody knew the names of the regulars: Kenny Rossi, Arlene Sullivan, Bunny Gibson and others. We were glued to the television set for the hour it was on.

The era was a time of memories with television shows such as Ed Sullivan, Lucille Ball, and the Honeymooners. Our interests were in going to drive-ins, drag races, Dairy Queens, and the A&W Root Beer stand in Raynham.

In the fall, I entered my last year of grammar school. I felt comfortable knowing that a few of my new friends would be classmates. The school year flew by, and I graduated with the excitement of entering high school in September.

Left – Joey, Alberta, Billy, Albert, Leona

Left – Mom, Alberta, Leona, Albert, Dad

Chapter Four
First Encounter with Richie

Mom did all the cooking, and it was up to my sister and me to set the table, wash and dry the dishes, and leave the kitchen spotless. We owned a dishwasher but were denied use of it. If company came, it was filled. Mom felt that doing dishes by hand gave Leona and me time to laugh and talk together.

Albert's strenuous job, besides cutting the grass, was to empty the garbage and burn the trash in a barrel in the backyard. That's if we could find him to do it. Usually, Leona and I ended up doing his chores.

If the house needed painting, Dad made sure that the two girls were included in the project. There were no special jobs for any of us. If one could help another with any chore, we did. My sister and I took turns pushing the manual reel lawnmower. Albert's turn came if he got cornered by Dad.

Little did I know in those days how much Dad's teaching of responsibility would help me later in life. Did we like our rules? No, but we survived, and became better grown-ups. Our father was a wise man in his thinking, making demands on us so that we'd become more responsible adults.

No one complained. There was such togetherness in our family that even our chores were actually enjoyable.

The only way that Albert and I got around the neighborhood was with our bikes or walking. Leona worked a block down the street so she walked. There was only one car in the family, and Dad used it. All the grocery shopping was done when he got home.

It was a great summer, and I couldn't wait to get up and spend time with my friends. I was a morning person. Nature was close to my heart. I loved waking to the sounds of birds and the sunshine coming through my open windows. I cherished the smell after a rainstorm and enjoyed walking in the street barefoot through the warm puddles left from it. Early in the morning, I'd watch the squirrels chasing one another up the huge elm tree in our backyard. They entertained me with their loud chatter and tails snapping back and forth like whips as I sat at the kitchen table having my breakfast.

We were a family of pet lovers. Dad's beautiful Irish Setter, Rusty, had full, soft, red fur. It felt like silk and shined from his constant brushings. Mom bought six tiny ducklings that roamed freely in the backyard.

One Saturday, I grabbed my record player and rummaged through the 45rpm records in my collection. My mother came out with her iced tea and sat on the swing to watch my girlfriends Cindy, Rosanne, Barbara and I dance. Once the jitterbug song *Tutti Frutti* by Little Richard came on, the group came alive. Mom's favorite was *I Want to Walk You Home* by Fats Domino. We'd be lined up across from each other on the long porch and do the slide. I noticed Mom's feet tapping to the beat.

"Come on, Mom, put that tea down and let loose," I said loudly.

She waved me off. "I just like sitting here watching you girls dance." Her smile showed that she missed her younger days.

Her sister, Helen, once told me, "Your mother had a lot of boys chasing her when she was single. She was a looker and loved dancing. Every week she'd get all dressed up and go to the dance hall. I was younger, and I'd sit and watch her get ready. How I wanted to join her, but she wouldn't let me."

It must have seemed so long ago to my mother, but young hearts never die. Her memories were locked away. Those were the days before she experienced pain from losing a child and lost her courage to face the world after her breakdown. Her chores consisted of preparing three meals a day for seven people and chasing Joey and Billy around all day.

Fun was fun, but my parents had rules. Whether we liked them or not, we didn't dare break them. I was fortunate that they were stern, even though I might not have thought so back then. I don't know what kind of a person I would have become without rules. I loved fun and was usually the daredevil of the group.

The same rules were made for our friends when they came over. Mom never allowed disrespect from anyone. I remember the day my girlfriend, Linda, was at my house and got a call from her mother. She was angry because she was told to return home for something. She banged the phone down hard and without saying goodbye to any of us, walked out the front door and slammed it behind her.

My mother quietly walked to the front door and watched her until she got to the corner and then she called out. "Linda, could you please come back here a minute?"

Not knowing what was facing her, Linda trotted back without questioning the request. I stood there waiting wondering what Mom's punishment would be.

When Linda entered the door, my mother looked her in the eye and sternly, but quietly said, "Go over to the phone, pick it up, and put it down the way it should be."

Looking shocked but not daring to refuse, Linda went and did what she was told, placing the phone down without a sound.

"I'm sorry, Mrs. Gramm," she replied.

"When you get another call from your mother that upsets you, don't ever show disrespect for her in my home again, and don't abuse the things that we own. Now, open the front door and close it behind you without slamming it. I don't want to hear it shutting."

I could see that Linda was still mad, but she respected my mother. She closed the door with only the sound of a *click* when it locked. That was the first and last time she ever showed her temper in our house.

After a while, the girls and Albert's friends thought nothing of doing a lot of things together. There was always a story to share or a viewpoint to get from the other gender. We decided one afternoon to group together and go into a tent out in the backyard and smoke cigarettes. The boys wanted us girls to try them.

It seemed like fun at the time. We knew Mom wouldn't come out to check on us. Maybe she'd call out the back door, but that would give us time to put them out. We didn't stop to think that the smoke needed to go somewhere—like out the top of the tent. It circled thickly into the outside air. Suddenly, the flap opened and Mom stood facing the group. There we sat on the ground with our laughter and smiles frozen in place as the cigarette butts hung from our lips. That took care of the gatherings for a couple of weeks.

In 1956, the summer went by faster than we wanted. I was entering Dighton High School. Albert was a sophomore already. When we were in first grade, we developed rheumatic fever from so many bouts of strep-throat. We were hospitalized but my recuperation took three months longer than his. The Catholic nuns at school thought I should be held back a year to catch up. It bothered me for years watching Albert and my friends advance ahead of me.

In my sophomore year, Albert and I started taking our driver's education classes through the school. On September 5, 1957, we turned sixteen. During the school year, we took our driver's tests and happily passed. We now had licenses. Albert worked part-time at the Raytheon Plant, and a year later he bought a 1955 red Chevrolet Impala convertible with a 3 speed stick. It was rare that I asked to borrow it. Not being used to a standard shift, his car stalled out a lot on me, especially when I stopped on a hill. If there was a desire to go out, I used the family car which had an automatic transmission.

I loved the high school. It was an old building and the floors creaked when we walked on them. The teachers were great. I was the class clown and delighted in getting the kids to laugh during study period. Once they got caught, I'd put on a straight face and look innocent. I did my studying but enjoyed the social aspect of school more.

Boys loved me as a friend but not a *girlfriend.* They included me in all their activities. Like teen boys, they searched out the popular girls like the cheerleaders, majorettes, the knock-outs, and the "friendly" ones to date.

Wearing glasses, I felt like I had no sex appeal. The teasing diminished as I got older and pretended it didn't bother me, though it did.

One day, a classmate and I were walking to our geography class when a loud racket above the gym floor caught my attention. The kids, who were changing classes, opened their lockers to change books and caused a commotion. I stopped and looked up.

My attention went directly to one couple. The girl was absolutely beautiful! Her long, black, curly hair flowed past her shoulders. Her olive skin tones reminded me of Sophia Loren, a beautiful and popular actress. The boy with her had short, black, wavy hair, and extremely handsome with his dark, ruddy complexion. They were perfectly matched. As they walked away, he put his arm around her tiny waist.

"Who's that couple?" I asked.

"Which one?"

"The boy in the white jersey and the girl with the red blouse," I said, pointing them out.

She smiled and acted surprised that I didn't know. "That's Judy Fisher and Richie Lopes. They've been a twosome for years!"

"What a nice looking couple," I replied.

I tried to imagine how Judy felt with such a handsome boyfriend. I searched day after day to spot them again. They were seniors and their classes didn't coincide with mine.

The only other time I saw them was in a picture on the back page of my year book. My eyes strained to focus clearly on a shaded snap-shot of the seniors at their prom. There they were in the front row as the couples marched down the gym floor toward the stage. They had been voted king and queen of their senior prom.

They stood out from their classmates. Judy looked like a queen in her flared, pale-pink gown. Her dark features against the pink made her look immensely sexy. Richie wore a black suit and matching tie and looked as proud as a peacock holding her hand.

They had graduated two years before me, and I never gave Judy or Richie another thought. I was more fascinated with their looks than anything else.

There weren't many boys that I had been attracted to in school. One classmate followed me around every day. He was chunky with red hair and freckles, and he always smiled at me. I seemed to bump into him no matter where I went. He had asked me out a few times, but I had no interest in him, other than being friends. Funny how we seem to get attention from the ones that we don't want, and the ones we do, don't even notice that we're breathing.

Left – Albert & Alberta

Graduation Picture

Chapter Five
Meeting Danny

In my sophomore year, I met a special boy from North Carolina when Leona and I took a Saturday afternoon to travel the streets of Newport, Rhode Island. It was a beautiful, clear July afternoon with temperatures in the high eighties and a light breeze. We walked the cobblestone streets and went in and out of the quaint stores. A few side streets led to the piers that docked expensive sailboats and cruisers that looked to belong to millionaires.

We walked by one that caught my eye. It looked to be about 70 feet long. I peeked in a window to see the inside and saw rich, tan leather seats and a bar nestled in the corner of the room. There was a grand piano in the center, and I imagined wealth beyond my dreams.

Christie's Restaurant was the most popular place to dine. The scenery was breathtaking sitting by the water where the yachts lined-up like trophies. As people ate, they were entertained by the activities of the owners passing by the large, full length windows going to and from their boats. There were many smaller boats in the 20-30 foot range which stood in sharp contrast to the large yachts.

In the late fifties, Newport Rhode Island had a large Naval Base, and Fall River, Massachusetts were had been a Naval Reserve Center. No matter where people went in either town, sailors crowded the streets. The officers walked proudly in their dark navy dress uniforms while the enlisted men wore their white uniforms with the white sailor caps. Seeing servicemen thumbing along the roadside was a normal sight and folks were happy to give them a lift. They took my breath away and made my knees go weak. There was something about that Navy uniform!

After hours of shopping and strolling along the shoreline, we stopped at a small café. Two sailors sat at a table facing us. We ate our lunch slowly and stayed longer to relax with a glass of iced tea. The sailors approached our table.

"Hi girls, do you mind if we join you?" Sailors were always looking to meet girls, but it wasn't often that they stayed in port long enough to start a serious relationship.

Their appearance was timed perfectly, just as our desserts arrived. Knowing it was a public place, we felt safe being in their company. We agreed to have them sit with us. Besides, I had my eye on the blonde boy. He had a warm smile that attracted my attention. They pulled up two chairs and joined us.

The tall, thin, sandy haired boy didn't seem to have the charisma that the blonde did. He spoke first. "Hi, I'm Bob Waltman and this is my buddy, Danny Cook."

Danny—I like that name. It fits him, I thought.

"Hi. Where are you two from? Are you stationed in Newport?" I asked.

Bob answered quickly, "Yes, but I'm from Punxsutawney, Pennsylvania."

"I'm from Raleigh, North Carolina," Danny said. He had a hint of a southern accent. I loved the sound of it. "We're stationed in Newport. Where are you girls from?"

"From North Dighton, which is about an hour away," Leona replied.

"We're not too familiar with any towns around Newport. We don't get the chance to tour the area that much. We don't have our cars with us either."

"How do you get around?" I asked.

"Usually a buddy will drop us off somewhere. Otherwise, we thumb," Danny said.

Bob sat next to Leona, and I was excited that Danny chose to be near me. I loved listening to him talk with his deep, rough voice. His laughter was hearty, and he had a great sense of humor. His eyes were emerald green, and I couldn't help looking at them as he spoke. His blonde hair was messed-up from the light wind outside. His jaw line was square making him look more masculine. I could tell that he was comfortable with conversation, and we seemed to be relaxed together. I felt an instant magnetism.

They asked to see us again and wanted our telephone number. We gave it to them but said that our parents would have to be asked first if we'd be allowed to meet once more.

"What does your father do?" Bob asked.

"He's a retired Brigadier General," Leona said with ease. His military background was a normal thing for us.

"A Brigadier General!" he remarked with distress on his face.

Our father couldn't have had a more powerful position to them.

"No wonder you have to ask first, "Danny remarked.

"Do you need a ride back to the base?" I asked. I wanted an excuse to be with Danny a little longer.

"We'd love that. It's a long walk back," Bob said sounding relieved.

They sat in the back seat as we drove them to the base about five miles up the road. There were no hassles as we said goodbye. Neither of them tried to get a hug or kiss. They acted like gentlemen.

"How do we know it's all right to call you?" Danny asked me.

"Give me a call next weekend."

When we arrived home, our parents had their bedroom light on as they did every time we were out. I believed they wanted us to think that they were reading, or by coincidence just happened to be awake in bed. The reality was that they wanted to know that we were safely home.

The next morning, the family sat together for breakfast. It was Sunday morning and Dad was rushing off to church.

"Why aren't you girls dressed? Aren't you going to church?" he asked.

"We're going to the next Mass, Dad," I replied.

"Make sure you do."

Leona thought it would be best to wait until after we came back from church to mention the boys to our parents.

Dinnertime arrived, and we couldn't wait for Mom to put the meal down.

"You girls are sure quiet today. Have a good time last night?" she asked.

"We'd like to ask you something," Leona blurted out.

Since she was the oldest, I always let her ask for things while I stayed in the background. If I had met Danny alone, it might have been a different story but they thought I'd behave in Leona's company. She went through the whole story of how we met them.

Dad floored us. "You can see them if they come to the house and you stay here."

We were thrilled. It was a fair deal.

My parents made us stick to the rule. They made it clear that Danny and I couldn't go out alone. They considered me too young at sixteen to be dating. Leona was considered more mature at twenty-one years old. There wasn't a time the four of us didn't have fun together.

When Danny entered my life, he was a young man who touched my heart strings right from the beginning. I didn't realize the impact he was going to have on me. We dated for three years.

He became part of our family, and I couldn't have asked for a more family orientated boyfriend. He was a warm, funny, lovable guy, and he adored me. His gaze would make my heart skip. I knew he was special and that we'd marry once he got out of the service.

Bob and Danny hitched rides every chance that they could to be with us. Even with the cold, bitter winter storms, they arrived with snow covering them from head to toe. I felt sorry for Danny when I'd see the ice on his dark, navy pea-coat. He always walked in with a smile and hug. Nothing stopped him from coming to see me.

Leona and I spoke about the four of us getting married and living next door to one another. Bob and Danny thought nothing of taking Billy and Joey with us to the drive-ins or on fishing trips. They came to love our brothers. It was rare that Danny ever traveled home. He wanted to be with me every weekend.

Summer nights, Danny and I would sneak out to the porch swing to be alone and just hold hands. He loved it as much as I did. We'd quietly sit and listen to the spring peepers. There was wetland behind our house and the tiny frogs filled the area. Now and then we'd sneak a romantic kiss. We played records and danced for hours in the dark on the porch.

My girlfriend, Cindy, graduated a year ahead of me and married her boyfriend, Ernie Atwood. Danny and I became close friends with them and went to their home a lot. My life couldn't have been more perfect.

Danny informed me that he was being shipped out to California for a year. Depression hit us both knowing he was leaving. The day before he left, my parents gave us permission to go out alone. I looked forward to Saturday night with excitement. Danny was going to be mine without sharing the night with Leona and Bob.

I told Mom that we were going to a theatre to see a movie. I didn't dare tell her that I had plans to go to a drive-in, or I wouldn't have been allowed to leave the house.

I planned to take the family car and meet Danny at the bus station in Taunton. He had to be back at the base Sunday since they were pulling out of port that morning. He couldn't depend on thumbing back in case he was late.

As I left the house, I tried not to act any differently than any other date night. I didn't want my parents to see the thrill that was over-taking me. I couldn't wait for the evening to start.

I thought I was putting something over on my mother. I didn't look at her as being young once herself with the same emotions of being in love. I soon found out differently.

Before I could put my last foot out the door, she came up to hug me and stopped me in my tracks. She whispered, "Be a good girl tonight."

It was a short but *powerful* remark. It put a damper on my private plans being alone with Danny. Reality hit me on what could happen between us on this hot, summer night. The setting was perfect for romance, and it took my breath away.

I left the house feeling guilty with the thoughts that were going through my mind. My mother took all the enjoyment and relaxation out of me. It left me uptight about any actions that might be facing me.

Danny was standing outside the bus station in his white sailor uniform and white cap. I felt like I did when I first laid eyes on him. My heart leaped in my chest. He was so handsome. I took him for granted too often.

He got into the drivers seat and kissed me before we drove off. We were both thrilled about being alone for the first time.

"I thought about you all day, and I never thought that the time would come," he said.

"Me, too," I said pushing so close to him that a pin couldn't have come between us. I wrapped my arms through his and laid my head on his shoulder.

Since it was a weekend, we had to drive around a few times at the drive-in to get a good spot. It wasn't easy finding a speaker that worked. Danny finally got a location in the middle row on a high slant behind the concession stand.

The first hour was spent talking and laughing. It was so easy having fun with him. His hearty, deep laugh became catchy. *The Apartment* was playing and we weren't spending time watching it. We really didn't care about the movie. We were looking for a night alone.

It began getting dark and the conversation got to the topic of him leaving. The mood dropped to sadness between us. He looked directly at me and held my hands.

"I can't stand knowing that I'll be without you for so long."

I looked into his eyes that were filled with tears. My fingers pushed his blonde hair back from his face. I kissed him softly. The kiss lasted longer than it should have.

It felt good and I didn't want him to stop. My emotions that had been held back for years were exploding. I tried to just hold him tight but his soft kisses were on my face and his hands held my breasts. His actions made me crave more. His touch was sending wonderful vibrations all through me, I didn't want to stop.

"Oh, Danny I want you. Now, please."

Tears were coming down my face. My love was deep and strong. All I wanted was to make love and holding back was becoming painful. My mind was racing with what was right and what I desired.

Someone suddenly leaned on the horn next to us and it snapped me out of my passionate trance. It brought me back to reality because, for a few minutes, I wasn't even conscious of my surroundings.

I was now aware of someone next to us. We could have reached out and touched them since we were sharing the same stand for our speakers. I wanted to tell Danny to drive to the very back of the parking lot, but I knew if we did, there would be no stopping. My mother's remark put a guilt trip on me, and I couldn't go any further.

"Danny, I don't want to stop," I cried squeezing him tightly.

He kissed me, "Its okay, Honey."

It was late and we couldn't stay to see the whole movie. I needed to get him back to catch the bus. We drove in complete silence. Once we reached the bus station, I sat with him waiting for it to arrive. He brought no luggage so we talked while the passengers boarded and the bus driver placed packages in the bottom compartments.

"I'll write every day, Danny."

"You won't be able to because we won't be pulling into any port. I'd like you to write to a friend of mine back home. She's only a friend. Her name is Jenny. I'd like her to get to know you. Here's her name and address."

I took it, "I'd like that. Maybe she'll tell me some secrets about you," I said laughing.

"I love you so much." He hugged me until I thought my ribs would break. His kiss was soft and firm. I loved the way he kissed me.

Danny didn't have to tell me to wait because I loved him. He was everything I ever wanted.

I stayed at the bus station until he boarded. I raced from window to window, until I spotted him. I waved as the bus pulled out and I couldn't see him any longer. My heart broke in pieces wondering how I was going to make a year without seeing or holding him.

Chapter Six
Introduction to Richie

Bob was excited about being discharged from the Navy in a few months. He and Leona were ecstatic about scheduling a date to get married. My sister started filling her dreams of having the perfect wedding. I was asked to be her maid of honor and was so happy for both of them. Danny dreaded the two years that he had left to serve, and I couldn't wait for the day to come for us to make our engagement announcement when he was ready to be discharged.

I was in my last year of high school and couldn't wait to graduate. A few months passed with Danny being gone. I tried filling my weeks by writing to Jenny once a week. We became good pen pals, and I loved hearing things about Danny. I could tell they had been good friends for years, and she wrote about how much he loved me. I looked forward to her letters.

I was lost without Danny, and I started to feel cooped up in the house. Albert tried to get my mind off the emptiness that I was feeling. He offered to take me out one night in his convertible.

"Come on, Alberta. We can find the gang and go check who's hanging around the Taunton Green. There's always something going on there."

He loved using his car to get the attention of girls as he'd spin-out. The convertible had been kept in tip-top shape and always had a highly polished shine. You could see your reflection in it. Albert had a slim build and everything he wore looked great on him.

The main streets in town were packed nightly, especially on weekends, with boys leaning against their hot rods wearing tight jeans and loafers. They kept their cigarette packs folded in their rolled-up t-shirt sleeves. Smoking back then was a very hip thing to do. It made you fit in with the crowd and look "cool."

"Thanks, Albert, but I'm going to see if Dad will give me the car for the night. It's a Friday night, and I'd like to see a movie. I haven't been out for a fun night with a friend since Danny left. I desperately need to get out of the house."

"Okay, but if you change your mind, let me know. I'm leaving here about seven."

To my surprise, my father handed me the keys without giving any long speech on where I could go or what I couldn't do.

I called Roseanne and we decided to see *Love Me Tender* with Elvis Presley. I spent hours playing his records and wondered how they never wore out. I would close my eyes and daydream about meeting him and falling madly in love. What teenage girl didn't feel the same way with all his sexy moves?

Roseanne and I loved doing things together. She was eighteen-years old with long blonde hair, hazel eyes and perfect curves.

We tried to arrive at the movie early to get our popcorn and sodas and have time to talk. The seats were already taken-up with wild teenage girls. The ushers searched hard with their flashlights to find two seats together.

As soon as Elvis came on the screen, the theatre echoed with deafening screams. I felt too mature to join in the uproar but it didn't stop me from sighing silently each time he came on the screen. The movie lasted two hours with girls yelling and crying the whole time. It was a relief to leave the theatre and start for home.

"I'm starved," Roseanne said holding her stomach. "Let's take a ride to the A&W Root Beer stand in Raynham. I can taste a cheeseburger, fries and a cold root beer."

"That does sound good," I replied.

That was the one place where people had to search hard to get a parking spot, it was always jammed. It was the hottest spot to go to when the evening ended. The guys loved the young car hops in their uniform shorts, bobby socks, and saddle shoes. It was known as a pick up spot.

A tiny blonde girl chewing gum came up to us. "What'll you have?"

"Two orders of the cheeseburger special with the works, chips and two root beer sodas," Roseanne said faster than lightning.

It was twenty minutes before she returned and placed a side food tray on my window. We checked out the cars to see who was there while we ate.

After finishing, I was getting uptight because it was close to midnight. Dad wasn't too keen on me coming in late. On our way home, we passed the depot parking lot. It had been a train station at one time but was empty now. It was around the corner from Roseanne's house.

"Stop, pull in there!" she said all excited pointing to the parking lot.

"Why, what's over there?"

I tried to see what she noticed. It was completely dark but I got a glimpse of two cars.

"I think I know the guys in the parked cars near the building. I want to say hello to them." She strained her neck to look in the direction.

"I'm not too keen going over to two strangers," I said.

41

"Oh, you know one of them," she said without looking at me as we pulled in.

"Hi, Eddie, how are you?" Roseanne said with a huge smile.

"Hi, girls," he replied as he started to stroll over to where we parked.

I realized that it was Eddie Pierce. He graduated from Dighton High School with us. Eddie leaned into Roseanne's window to hug her.

From out of the shadows, the other guy started to approach us. I couldn't believe who I was seeing. Richie Lopes was standing by my window. It had been years since I'd first seen him in school with Judy.

He smiled and introduced himself. "Hi, I'm Richie."

He was inches from my face and gorgeous. He took my breath away. When he spoke, his manner was polite, yet flirtatious.

I was glad it was dark because I could feel myself blush. *Lord, if he ever knew how my heart was racing.* Being Danny's girl, I hated these feelings. For a girl who had no problem communicating with boys, I was suddenly lost for words.

It wasn't long into the conversation when I became aware that both guys had been drinking. They weren't drunk, but the longer Richie spoke, it became obvious that he was slurring his words. It was enough to be noticed.

Eddie offered an invitation. "Why don't we all go for something to eat?" he asked.

"Thanks, but we already stopped at the root beer stand. I have to get back home." I jumped right in before we were locked into a commitment. I didn't want Richie to get the wrong impression and think I was available. "Besides, it's late and my dad has rules."

We left after fifteen minutes of conversation, and I headed for Roseanne's house. Before she got out of the car, I remarked about the drinking.

"Boy, you could smell the liquor on them!"

She laughed, "Guys will be guys, Alberta. They all drink now and then. It's their way of having fun and being *macho*."

"Do you know Richie?"

"I know of him. He lives with his sister, May Rapoza on Route 138. She and her husband, Vic, own the vegetable stand around the corner."

"You've got to be kidding? I take my mother there all the time. I didn't know they were related. May and Vic are great people. What a small world!" I remarked.

"His family is nice."

She opened the car door and leaned back in the window, "Don't let the drinking bother you. He's a nice guy."

Pulling out of her driveway, I tried to put the drinking out of my mind. I drove down our long driveway to the garage. I locked up and walked to the front of the house. Coming home late always made me nervous, especially being alone. It was pitch black and every noise caused me to jump with fright.

Neighbors had complained to the police that a peeping-tom had been seen in the area. Hearing the news made me go from walking to running to the house. My heart pounded in my chest until I reached the door. I feared that someone would come out from behind a tree and grab me. I took a deep breath when I entered the house.

As I climbed the stairs to my bedroom, I heard my parents talking across the hall.

"Alberta, is that you?" my father called out.

"Yes! I'm back."

"Okay, get a good night's sleep," my mother said with relief in her voice.

I was uneasy after having met Richie. I prayed it was the end of seeing him. It would be hard resisting him after seeing him in person. My attraction to him made me uncomfortable.

I stayed up and wrote a letter to Jenny. It was the closest I could get to Danny. I didn't dare tell her about Richie. She wouldn't understand. How could she? Why was I making a big deal out of this? It was just a meeting.

I longed to hear Danny's voice. It was impossible since he was out at sea. Nothing had ever threatened our relationship, but meeting Richie was different. I didn't know why or how, only that it would.

Being introduced to Richie was going to leave a powerful impact on me. It was about to open the doors to confusion, uncertainty, and abuse. Little did I know that my peaceful, secure life with Danny would soon disappear.

Richie

Left – Charlie, Richie, Syl (Army Buddies)

Chapter Seven
A Bad Decision

Roseanne called, energized about having met a new guy. "His name is Ray Costa and a friend of Richie's. He works for the Dighton Highway Department. They want us to double date. What do you think?"

"I don't know. It's not worth seeing him if it confuses things with Danny."

"Oh, come on, it's only a date. You can stop seeing him when Danny comes back. It's no big deal. He doesn't have to know."

"I would know. I'm not one for lying."

I felt my interest rise thinking about seeing him.

"Tell him I'm too involved with someone." I hung up hoping that would be the end of it.

I couldn't push Rosanne's conversation out of my mind. I couldn't imagine why Richie wanted to date me after being with such a beautiful girl like Judy.

A few weeks went by and Rosanne called again. "Well, Richie won't let up. He wants to see you."

"Whatever happened between him and Judy?"

"After high school, he went into the Army. It wasn't long before her family moved to South Carolina. While down there, she met another knockout! The distance and Richie's service years put a gap in their relationship. No one ever thought they'd break up. He was totally crushed when he found out that she got married."

"I knew there had to be a serious reason."

"If he didn't go into the service, they'd be married."

I didn't realize that my situation was on a similar path.

"He isn't going to stop asking us to go out."

"I can't lose what I have with Danny. Tell him no."

The following Saturday afternoon while I was sitting out on the porch, Richie pulled up in front of the house. Roseanne and Barbara were in the back seat.

"Hi, Alberta," Roseanne said as she jumped out and came over to me. What are you up to? We thought you'd like to go for a ride to Frates for an ice cream."

I was in a state of panic seeing Richie sitting in the car.

"I don't think so, Roseanne. I have things to do," I replied.

"Come on. We won't be gone that long," she pleaded.

My mother was weeding around the front porch. I didn't tell her about meeting Richie. I knew she could hear the conversation. I started to feel excited and cornered at the same time.

I walked around the side of the porch. "Mom, the gang wants me to go for a ride to Frates. Is that all right?"

"I think that would be okay. Be home for supper."

I walked up to Richie's immaculate 1957 white Chevrolet convertible. The leather interior was a bright red and the top was already down. *It's the perfect car for a guy like this,* I thought. Albert's idea of having a sharp car to get a girl's attention was right on.

Roseanne jumped into the back. The empty passenger seat faced me.

"Hi, Alberta," Richie said with a warm smile. He was more gorgeous in the daylight.

"What a day for a ride," Barbara yelled.

Guilt gnawed at me when I slid into the reserved passenger seat.

"If the breeze is too much for you girls let me know, and I'll put the top up," Richie yelled back at them.

A radio station blared away with the song *Lucille* as we drove from the house.

"Turn it up, Richie," Barbara said while she held her hands up high.

Deep down, I knew that he planned this unexpected visit to throw me off guard. Having the girls tag alone was to make me feel secure.

I innocently wanted to get to know him. If he was conceited, I'd be able to walk away very easily, but he didn't act that way, he seemed like a nice guy. At the time, I didn't know if the gentleman side was just an act.

We pulled into the parking lot of Frates Ice Cream Stand, and the girls pushed through the open doors to go inside.

"Want a hot fudge sundae?" he asked me.

"That's a lot so close to supper. I'll take a small chocolate chip sugar cone."

"That's all? Are you sure?"

"Yes, thanks. I can go inside."

"Sit here. I'm going in to give the girls the money. It's my treat."

He returned shortly and sat with me, and we made small talk. I couldn't get my eyes off him.

He finally sent out the invitation himself. "I would love to take you out. I've been calling Roseanne, but I never did get a direct answer from her."

"Didn't she tell you that I have been seeing someone?"

"She mentioned something along that line," he answered. "Are you engaged?"

"Not officially, but I'm sure that we'll get married when he gets out of the Navy in a year."

"Did he ask you?"

"No, but I know he will when the time is right," I replied. It was a statement that I tried to defend. "It's something that you feel after dating a long time."

Being determined he replied, "Since you're not engaged, maybe I can come by now and then or call. There shouldn't be any harm in that."

I was getting mixed feelings sitting next to him. He wanted to date *me*. I was the plain Jane. I was teased through the years growing up with name calling about wearing glasses. Boys just wanted to be my friend, and here was the catch of the year wanting to date me.

I shouldn't have knocked myself so much. Danny was handsome and loaded with personality. I never felt plain with him. He made me feel like the luckiest girl in the world. So, why was I sitting in a convertible with someone else and liking it?

The girls piled in with our cones and their sundaes. "Don't drip it all over the car," Richie pleaded as he passed out the napkins they brought out.

We all joked back and forth until we finished our treats.

"What do you say I take you girls for a spin through the city? Maybe there will be some excitement."

An hour later, he pulled up to my house. "Thanks for the treat," I said smiling back a him.

"I'll call you," he replied back as I started to go up the walkway."

I waved without looking back and heard the girls yelling goodbye.

Richie started calling, and I tried to keep it friendly. There was nothing that I could find bad about him. I broke down and went on what I considered innocent rides with him on the weekends.

To lighten the guilt, I convinced myself that double dating with Ray and Roseanne was not *really* cheating on Danny. We went to beaches and drive-ins and did a lot of parking by the dam on Elm Street. We walked through farmer's fields at night and stole huge tomatoes from their gardens: we considered it innocent fun.

I learned that Richie was a quiet guy with a lot of ambition. He talked a lot about an electronic school that he was attending in Boston. He wanted to start his own business when he graduated.

I grew more confused dating him as the months past. I wondered how I was going to feel when Danny came home. I truly believed that when the time came to see him that I'd realize that the feelings for Richie wouldn't last. After all, there wasn't any physical relationship between us. We were just friends.

Chapter Eight
Meeting Richie's Family

One Friday night I was returning home from a drive-in movie with a few of my girlfriends. After dropping them all off at their homes, I traveled by the depot parking lot. As I passed, I saw Richie standing by his car waving to get my attention.

I pulled up next to him; Eddie was sitting in his own car. Richie walked over to me, and as soon as he leaned into my window, I could smell the strong stench of liquor on his breath.

"Why do you find it so important to drink while you're out?" I asked.

"You make me drink," he remarked losing his balance.

"How's that?" I asked.

"Well, if you broke it off with Danny, I wouldn't be doing this. All I want is for you to be my girl."

I was stunned seeing how much he drank. All the times that we dated, he never touched it in my presence. I had no knowledge of the danger that this could cause in my life.

I should have taken the signs more seriously and ran. The thought had raced through my mind, but my feelings were hard to turn off by now. My foolish, young, immature, unknowledgeable mind thought that he must really love me to be drinking this much because he was upset about me seeing Danny.

I slowly allowed him to push his way into my emotions. He knew it, and grabbed onto it. I had no idea that this was the beginning of a serious problem and a bad relationship. He was drinking too much, and it wasn't normal. I kept making excuses that it only happened when he was out with his friends.

Richie and I rarely socialized with other people besides Ray and Roseanne. If we went out alone, we spent time parking, riding around town, or we traveled to Cape Cod. I still hadn't met his family.

I was blind to these differences with Danny. My time with him had been spent with my family, relatives, and friends. He loved my brothers, Joey and Billy, and spent hours playing with them, and he was comfortable talking to my parents.

Richie spent no time mixing in with my family. He talked politely to my parents if he had to wait for me to get ready. I allowed him to take up all my spare time. My girlfriends were pushed aside, and I made myself available each and every time he called. I didn't stop to think about the situation. We hardly laughed or got silly together, everything was serious.

I didn't take the time to analyze whether or not we had anything in common, I thought it was touching that he wanted me all to himself. I wasn't aware that being a loner could be a sign of an alcoholic as much as over-drinking on occasions is.

How did my life change so much in eight months? For a girl with a good head on her shoulders, I was making poor decisions. My feelings for Richie were real, and I knew this wasn't just a fling. I couldn't understand how I could love two men at the same time.

One Friday night in June, he finally took me to meet his sister May and her husband Vic. They were working at their vegetable stand. Their only child, Marie, was thirteen-years old and worked every day with them.

"May, Vic this is Alberta," Richie said smiling back at me.

"Well, hello, Alberta. How's your mother," May asked. She had recognized me from my frequent trips to the stand with my mother.

May was a beautiful woman who had long, jet-black, tight, curly hair that she kept pinned up. The curls fell and encircled her face as she bent down to fill the baskets with tomatoes, lettuce, or corn from the fields. Her cheeks were rosy-red from being out in the sun all day long.

Her arms were muscular from carrying the heavy, large baskets of plants. She worked in the fields when it was time to pick the vegetables or sort the flower baskets that they had for sale in their greenhouse.

May was quiet toward me but polite. It was hard for us to get to know each other since they moved non-stop waiting on people arriving at the stand. Their business was one of the most popular places to buy produce and flowers in the area.

Vic may have been a short man, being only 5 feet, four inches tall, but he was very strong. He was in his early forties and did all the planting himself each spring. At the end of the season, he'd use his tractor to level everything clean in the fields. They rented property from other relatives throughout the town to grow the crops. Vic had a great sense of humor, and I enjoyed being in his company.

A few weeks later on a Friday evening, Richie took me to meet his brother, Sonny and his wife, Anita at their home in North Dighton. I was comfortable with them from the very first. Anita kept her auburn hair short in a perm. Her light, brown-framed glasses complimented her complexion.

It was obvious to anyone that Anita took care of her husband's every need. She was French but said that she cooked only Portuguese meals for him. She informed me that it took her years to learn to put the right ingredients together. Their home was always filled with the wonderful aroma of herbs and spices.

Anita was devoted to her family. Their daughter, Paula, was seven-years old and their son, Gilly, was two-years old. Her home was spotless. I could see that Anita took great pride in her housekeeping.

She never put on airs; she was down-to-earth and I felt comfortable with her, and we bonded right away. We both had a sense of humor and were at ease being ourselves from the beginning.

Sonny was a few inches shorter than Anita with thinning, light, brown hair. He was much quieter than Richie when it came to talking, which shocked me. He didn't contribute to family conversation much. Now and then, a grin came across his face if he found something funny.

He was just starting his own trucking business, which he named Lopes Trucking. When conversation involved his business, he participated more with information about himself. His only piece of equipment was a dump truck, and he'd bid on any job that opened up in the area.

It was after 7:00 p.m., and I watched as Anita folded a tablecloth in half and positioned it in front of her husband. He was eating late because he had just come home. Anita had already fed the rest of the family, and Richie and I had eaten earlier, he thought I'd be more comfortable just visiting the first time. Anita placed marinated roast beef in Sonny's plate and topped it with red, hot peppers and spiced tomato sauce. My eyes widened as he added more black pepper in the already seasoned meal. He dunked thick slices of Portuguese bread into the sauce, saying nothing as sweat beaded on his forehead. He didn't mind eating a meal with hot spices.

A while later, their sister, Lena, dropped by to meet me. Her husband, Ben, was with her. They lived in Fall River, Massachusetts, a city about thirty minutes south of North Dighton. They brought Richie's mother with them. She was also named Lena and lived in Fall River. I had the feeling that everyone was eager to meet the new girlfriend. Of all of Richie's siblings, I felt that Lena was the most outgoing once we began talking.

Lena's dark features resembled May's. Lena wore heavy makeup, which May omitted completely. It gave her a hard look. Her long, black hair was teased in a high, wild, puffy hairstyle.

Richie's mother sat quietly in a kitchen chair against the wall, staring at me. She was a full-blooded Portuguese woman. Her attire was dreary and plain, consisting of a pair of worn-out black slacks with an over-sized black shirt that hung over the pants. She hardly spoke at all; studying everyone with her deep, sunken, brown eyes as she sat in a distant corner. She was only 5 feet, two inches tall with short, straight, black hair, and the same dark complexion as the others. I was uncomfortable when I tried to be friendly and smile at her. She had no reaction except to give me a blank look. Her husband had passed away years before.

It was a long stressful day meeting everyone. I tried to be myself, but being the center of attention, made it hard for me to relax with the whole family at the house. May and Vic were at work. It was rare that they took a day off from the stand to attend any family gatherings, unless it was absolutely necessary.

Nothing changed in my relationship with Richie during the following few months. He never mentioned a future with us. In fact, there wasn't a time that he said he loved me. He wasn't a man with romantic notions or words. We were just considered a couple. Like most women, I longed to hear how deeply loved and cherished I was. Danny said it a hundred times and showed it every chance he got. I couldn't understand why I was clinging to this relationship with Richie. I didn't take the time to think about the most important aspects of my future.

My mother used to say to me, "Marry a man who loves you more, Alberta, because you're a giving person. The rest will fall into place."

I was blinded by the fact that Danny and I had that connection already. Richie and I weren't in that kind of relationship. I couldn't have time with Danny, so I was spending it with Richie. My parents were giving me the freedom to go anywhere with him alone; something they never permitted with Danny.

We took a drive one Sunday to our favorite parking spot along the Cape Cod Canal. We cuddled as we watched the sun go down.

"This'll always be our private spot," he said, putting an arm around me. "We have so many memories here."

"It's beautiful and peaceful, isn't it?" I sighed, feeling relaxed.

I leaned into his arm and looked up at him. He kissed me. The moment got heated with passion. I was holding back my desires with his touches. He wanted more. I felt my strength leaving my body. My breaking point was showing.

I made no resistance while he tested me. I let his hand slip into my blouse and go under my bra. A hot sensation rose way beyond my imagination. I allowed his other hand to travel under my skirt and up my thigh. My skin started to feel sweaty. I wasn't mindful of our surroundings, and I was swallowed-up with passion. It was the furthest that I had ever gone with anyone.

I let out moans and kept kissing him back hungrily. I wanted to make love now and didn't care at this point about safety or rules. My body was in high gear and I didn't want to stop. He was now in complete control and I loved it. I was going to give whatever he wanted.

He slowly took my blouse off. Gently, he unsnapped my bra and placed me flat on the front seat of the car. He started to undress himself and then put his naked, hard body on me. I reacted by pushing my lower body up against him. I never knew anything could give me so much pleasure. The feel of skin on skin drove me insane.

Suddenly, the car lit-up as though a flood light shone on it. A car was approaching in the distance. We jumped-up and started to get dressed before it reached us. It was a police cruiser patrolling the area.

"Hi, kids. Staying out of trouble?" Two officers were staring back at us. The cruiser moved slowly along side our car. Suddenly, they flashed their flood light in our faces and we blinked from the brightness.

"We're just talking," Richie replied.

The driver became stone-faced. "I think you should move on. It's getting late. There's no parking allowed in this area."

"We're about ready to leave officer."

The cruiser started to back up slowly as if they were debating about checking us out.

"Boy, that was close," Richie said.

"I want to go home," I replied almost in tears.

"Alberta, don't carry any guilt over this."

"There's no guilt. I just want to leave," I answered not looking at him while I completed buttoning my blouse.

When we reached my front door, he kissed me. "I'll call you tomorrow."

"We'll talk later." I replied and got out of the car.

I opened the front door and prayed that my parents weren't waiting up for me. They would have known that something happened. I climbed the stairs and went quietly into my bedroom. The light in my parent's room was off.; which was rare. Leona was in a deep sleep in her twin bed next to me.

I knew that I would have given in if the police didn't show up. I hungered for the intimacy. How long was I going to hold out?

Left Back – May, Paula (baby), Vic,
& their daughter, Marie

Left – Gilly, Sonny, Paula, Gary

Chapter Nine
Danny's Return

The next weekend came, and I had made plans on Saturday afternoon to go with the girls to Lincloln Park. I tried to keep in touch with my friends to vent. It wasn't unusual for us to go the amusement park in North Dartmouth, Massachusetts; it was our favorite place to spend time. During the winter months, we went to the roller skating rink there, a popular feature of the park. In the summer, we enjoyed the rides.

After a few hours of going from one ride to another, we headed home so there'd be time to stop for an ice cream. I came home at 10:00 p.m., and it was still an early night. Usually, I'd be strolling in about midnight.

I came through the front door and discovered my mother waiting in the kitchen. I knew by her wild eyes that she was upset.

"Where have you been?" she asked in an angry but quiet tone through clenched teeth.

"I told you that I was going out with the girls. What's wrong?"

"I've been sitting all night, entertaining Danny. He has been here since eight o'clock. Why did you go out? That's not like you."

"I didn't know he was in port. He was supposed to be gone another month!" I was shocked.

"Well, goodnight. You take care of this situation and don't ever put me in the middle of it again." She started toward the stairs to go to bed.

"Goodnight, Danny," she said politely as she passed by the living room.

"Good night, Mrs. Gramm," he answered softly.

I was frozen in the kitchen. I'm sure he heard the conversation with my mother and knew she was upset. His arrival was unexpected, and I wasn't prepared to greet him.

I rounded the corner and saw him sitting straight up on the couch in the low-lit living room when I entered. I knew by his serious expression that he was upset because I wasn't home when he arrived. He didn't get up to hug me as he usually did. My heart sank.

"Danny, I'm so sorry. I didn't know you were in port."

"I wanted to surprise you but instead you surprised me. I thought a call wouldn't be necessary. You're always home. I didn't think it was important to call first."

He took a moment and then apologized. "I'm sorry. You had a right to go out. I know that you would have been here if you knew that I'd be coming?"

How was I going to tell him that there was someone else in my life? *Do I have to tell him? Did he have to know tonight?* After all, I didn't even know if I loved Richie.

He stood up and walked over to me and gave me a kiss. "Why do you seem nervous? Has something been going on since I left?" I think he was praying that his imagination was running away with him.

Why was I holding back my feelings for him? I loved this man for three years; he was my world, I wanted to marry him. I should have been clinging to him with kisses.

Instead of not bringing up Richie, my guilt was taking over making me think that I should be completely honest. Danny and I never had anything to hide from each other. This was the first time that anything had come between us. I was hoping that he would understand and help me work this dilemma through.

If I could have looked into the future and have seen what this honesty was going to do, I would have lied without blinking an eye. I wanted time alone with him to sort out my feelings.

"Danny, I have been seeing someone else for a short time. Nothing has happened between us," I just blurted it out.

The shock hit him hard and left him standing there staring at me with a blank look on his face for a few seconds. "Why? What happened? Did I hurt you without realizing it?"

"You've done nothing wrong. I don't know why I started seeing him. He became a friend."

After seeing his eyes fill with tears, I realized the serious damage that I had done to our relationship. I felt that I had just made the biggest mistake of my life.

He sat down on the couch and leaned over and hung his head in his hands, "I felt there was something going on. I don't know why? You weren't excited to see me. You didn't even kiss me."

"I'm sorry," I said placing my hand on his shoulder. "I swear nothing happened." I meant it from the bottom of my heart.

"Of course, something happened," he said looking up at me with fire in his eyes. "You were cheating on me. Is this serious?"

He was no longer hurt, he was mad. I knew at that moment that I couldn't say anything to soften the blow. The deceit was now out in the open. The trust was gone.

I got on my knees in front of him and held his arms. "I don't want to break up. Give me time to work this out. I swear nothing physical has happened with him."

He didn't care by now. He looked at me and stated, "Nothing physical has to happen. It's the emotional connection that I worry about. I can't sit back after three years of loving you, knowing that someone else has been dating you. Don't ask me to wait it out. I'm not strong enough to do it." He was in disbelief about what was happening.

"Please, give me time to sort this out," I begged.

He got up from the couch and looked coldly at me. "There's nothing to sort out. You either want me or him. If you can't decide that with me standing here, then there's nothing more to say."

I wanted to tell him that I'd break it off with Richie, but I still wasn't sure what I wanted. *My God what's wrong with me*? I could see he was crushed.

Danny gathered his things together and headed straight to the front door. I walked behind him trying to get him to stay and talk.

"Please, Danny, don't go like this. Stay and talk to me. Lets' go out for a ride."

He continued walking without turning around to look at me. He wasn't going to answer me. Our perfect life together fell to pieces within minutes.

He opened the front door and I was devastated by what I had done.

"Let me give you a ride back to the base," I pleaded.

"Don't bother. I got here alone, I'll go back alone."

He went out the door without saying goodbye. I watched him leave and wondered how I could have been so heartless. It was as if time had stopped; I was traumatized. All my actions while he was away caught up with me.

Why didn't I stay home? I stood there stunned that our love wasn't strong enough to handle this catastrophe.

God, why did I tell him? Why am I so damn honest?

I put my head against the door and cried my heart out.

It's ok. He'll call me. He would never let pride ruin our relationship.

I climbed up the stairs to my bedroom, feeling like my world ended. Bob and Leona had gone out so I couldn't talk to her. I had pushed my relationship with my sister on the side and stopped sharing my emotions with her.

I got undressed and crawled under the covers and lay there thinking of Danny hitchhiking down the dark streets all alone. It was an hour drive back to Newport, and I couldn't imagine how long it would take him trying to hitch a ride. Why didn't I run after him? I didn't realize at the time the profound affect that day would have on my life.

Things will all work out tomorrow. He'll call.

Chapter Ten

The Damage Path

Months flew by with no phone call from Danny, and I continued on the damaged path of dating Richie. Pride kept me from driving to the Newport Naval Station. I suddenly realized that I did the same thing to him that Judy had done to Richie.

August 5, 1961, Leona and Bob married. I watched as they said their marriage vows in St. Joseph's Church in North Dighton. Our dreams of having a double wedding disappeared forever. My parents went all out with a sit-down dinner and an open bar; it was the talk of the town. I hung onto hope that Danny would walk into the reception hall, but he didn't.

The following spring, Dad surprised the family with the unexpected news that we were moving again. This time it would be to Hull, Massachusetts. It was an hour's ride from where we lived. He was offered the position of President and CEO of the Pyrotector Company in Hingham, a manufacturer of smoke detectors. Our new home was about fifteen minutes from the company.

I hated the idea of moving. I was now nineteen and all my friends were here. My worst fear was moving too far and Richie wouldn't visit me.

The movers arrived and the house was emptied. Leona and Bob relocated with us. As we pulled out of the driveway, I panicked leaving the town that I loved.

When we arrived in Hull, Dad drove down the main road in front of Paragon Park. We could hear the screams as people rode the amusement rides. It brought me right back to the fun I had with my friends at Lincoln Park.

Instead of continuing down the main drag, he took a side road and drove along Nantasket Beach. He opened the windows; the ocean view was beautiful. The smell of the salt air was refreshing, and we could see and hear the waves crashing against the shore.

Some people were in the water, and others were on blankets or sitting in beach chairs. We could hear the children yelling as they played in the water. They leaped, trying to jump over each wave coming toward them.

We left the beach area and came upon the quiet, private section where there were no bathers. Couples were holding hands while walking barefoot along the flat sand in their bathing suits or shorts. A man was playing Frisbee with a black Labrador, throwing it so that the dog would run and leap in the air to catch it. There were many children on the beach making sand castles or filling their pails with seashells and other treasures they came upon.

My tensed muscles started to relax as I took in the tranquil scenes. It was like therapy.

Dad drove to the end of the ocean area and turned up Beacon Road where the house was situated. It was a tremendously steep hill, and I wondered how we would manage it in a winter storm.

The house sat on top of the hill. It was a beautiful estate with French doors on the second floor, which opened onto a small, rounded balcony facing the street. The home was surrounded with a wall of perfectly shaped hedges that hid the property and the driveway.

The front door took us directly into the living room. It was so large that it contained our ten-seat sectional, a pool table, a fireplace, and our piano. There was a half bath downstairs.

The dining room was off the living room which was open to the kitchen; a closed-in porch ran along the front and one side of the house.

On the second floor, there were five bedrooms, two full baths, and the upstairs porch which faced the street. The French doors and windows along the whole front had a spectacular view. When we opened the doors, we were so high up on the hill that the beach and amusement park could be seen from the house. At a right angle you could see the yacht club with the bay full of sailboats and cabin cruisers. It was a place for beach and ocean lovers.

It didn't take long to settle in and enjoy the beautiful area. Months went by and Richie rarely called, nor did he travel to Hull very often to visit. Albert tried getting me out of my rut by taking me to meet his new friends. They belonged to a bowling league and wanted me to get involved. Not me, I lived and breathed to go back to North Dighton and gave nothing or anybody new a chance to fill my life.

I used excuses so that I could go back and visit Roseanne. I took the car and stayed with her on weekends. My trips made it easy for Richie. We'd continue to double date with Raymond and Rosanne.

One night Mom made me sit with her in the living room. "I'm tired of you constantly traveling to see Richie. Why don't you let him run after you?" she asked angrily.

"Mom, it's hard for him to travel because of his job and going to school in Boston," I answered trying to defend my chase.

"I don't care. If he loved you, nothing would stop him from seeing you," she replied. "Besides, he can come on weekends."

Dad approached me and cut in. "You can go tonight, but your mother's right. I believe in the man doing the chasing. I don't like you traveling so far by yourself."

I was too blind to see what they were trying to say to me. Danny had thumbed in all kinds of weather, including the dead of winter in snowstorms, to see me. He did the chasing, not me.

There were a few times, Richie brought Roseanne to my house and they spent the day with us. She loved the area; it was like a resort to her because of all the activities nearby.

The convenience of staying with Roseanne came to a sudden and abrupt end; a tragedy befell her family. Her mother suffered a massive and fatal heart attack; she was thirty-eight years old. Roseanne was only eighteen at the time, with six siblings; George was seventeen, Charlie was fifteen, Bill was eleven, Jim was ten, Claire was six, and John was just a year old.

Because her father had to work to support the family, Roseanne's life changed dramatically. She gave up her job and started caring for her sister and brothers and took on full responsibility of the household. There was no free time for personal enjoyment. She became the mother figure, similar to the role Leona had in our family.

Backyard in Hull with Pool

Front View of Our Home in Hull

Chapter Eleven
Our Wedding

On my last trip back to Dighton, I confronted Richie, "Where is this relationship going?"

"What do you mean?"

"I mean, is there a future in this for us? How do you feel about me?"

"I care very much about you."

"*Care* for me? Do you love me? Is marriage in the picture?"

He hesitated and looked at me without an answer.

"I can't keep dating forever. I want more, I want a family."

I despised being the one having to bring up marriage. It didn't make me feel loved by any means.

"If you don't feel the same, I'm moving on."

"I don't see why we can't make plans and set a date," he finally said.

That's how we decided to get married. I admired what a hard worker he was and the future plans he was developing for his own business. I knew he was quiet, but he was a sincere and gentle man. There had been no obvious drinking in over a year, not while I was in his company.

I wanted to be a wife and have a house full of children. That was another topic that we never talked about. Nothing was discussed about my wants, needs or hopes for the future, only his. I knew he was Catholic since it was information that was needed in planning our wedding.

We set the date for August 11, 1962. I would turn twenty-one in September. I didn't feel any great excitement while making plans, no imaginary bells ringing or my heart racing. It just seemed like the thing to do.

I asked Leona to be my matron-of-honor, Sonny was the best man, Roseanne and Richie's niece, Marie, were my bridesmaids, and the ushers were Ray and Albert.

The night before the wedding, Roseanne was invited to sleep over instead of having to travel early in the morning. We talked into the early morning hours, and it felt more like a sleep-over than the day before my wedding.

I went to bed and lay there thinking of Danny. This was supposed to be us. I wondered where he was and if he had married. Jenny stopped writing once she heard we broke up. We had been writing to each other for over a year. I couldn't help thinking what my life would have been like if I hadn't started dating Richie.

The morning of my wedding arrived, and there still were no butterflies. I felt like I was going through an event with no emotion. It was my dream to be married but nothing was pulling at my heartstrings.

Roseanne helped me get into my wedding gown. My Aunt Frannie let me wear her gown; the same one Leona had worn. It was still gorgeous with all the pearl beads in the design and the wedding dress clung to my tiny figure, I weighed only 108 pounds. I looked in the full length mirror and saw a stranger. I didn't take time to have my hair or makeup done professionally. There was no glow showing in my eyes or on my face. A bride was supposed to beam.

I tried to picture Danny waiting for me at the church. I'd be on cloud nine taking my vows facing him. My heart skipped thinking this could have been *our* special day. There would be a different, radiant woman looking back at me in the mirror. I would have done everything in my power to look beautiful. That's what was missing. My eyes filled up from sorrow knowing it could never be with us.

Damn, Danny, why did you let me go without talking? Did I mean that little because I dated someone? How could our love not have withstood something so minor?

My parents went all out, renting a hall at the Heritage Golf Course in Hingham with a very expensive sit-down dinner. Guests were already sitting in church in anticipation of seeing two happy people being married.

I started to walk down the long stairway to our living room to meet my parents at the bottom step. I tried blowing off my insecure feelings from being the one having to ask Richie to get married. I prayed that once I saw him, my doubts would go away. I really wanted us to be happy together.

"Alberta, smile, look happy. This is your day!" Roseanne remarked, bringing me back to reality.

"You look like you lost your best friend," Leona added.

Little did they know that I had. What would they think if they knew the thoughts and emotions that were going through my mind and heart about Danny? I let him go, and he was beyond reach now.

Everyone got into the cars to go to the church. My parents looked as proud as any parents could be. My mother was dressed in a multi-colored cranberry, tan and white printed dress with the same printed belt. Her dress fell just below her knees. She topped her outfit with a tan pillbox hat with a short veil that covered her bangs. Dad looked sharp in his black pants, white shirt with a black bowtie covered with a white jacket. He gently folded my wedding gown into the car before closing the back door.

I waited at the front of the church door with my father for the music to begin. The organ began *The Wedding March* as we strolled down the aisle together. All eyes were on us. Richie was standing at the altar, white as a ghost. I could tell that he was uncomfortable with all the attention.

When we came to the altar, Dad lifted my veil and gave me a kiss and hug before taking his seat. I turned and went up a few steps to stand next to Richie. He looked so handsome, but he was jittery and stiff as a board as he tried concentrating on what we learned at practice the night before.

When we said our vows, he looked so serious and never smiled. His hands shook putting the ring on my finger. The priest pronounced us man and wife, and he kissed me fast from nerves. I felt he couldn't wait to get off the altar and exit out of the church. He was so relieved the ceremony was over. When he found out that we had to stay on the church steps to be congratulated, he wasn't enthused, but he did put a smile on for the guests.

"How long do we have to stand here? Can't they do this at the reception hall?"

"It'll only take a minute. Relax the worst is over." I tried to be understanding of his shyness, but his discomfort made me feel like he had no joy in us just becoming man and wife. My heart broke seeing no emotion from him.

We drove to the reception and went directly outside to have pictures taken of the families and the wedding party. Richie's mother didn't mix in or make any conversation and stood in the background when she wasn't needed. Richie tried to be patient with being told where to stand and how to be positioned for pictures. I kept looking to see some expression of enjoyment on his face since it was our day.

"God, how many pictures are they going to take?" he said fussing like a child.

It seemed like hours before we were paraded into the hall and announced as husband and wife. I felt like it was a play instead of my own wedding.

"I thought we'd never get to the hall," he whispered as we sat at the head table with the wedding party.

"Richie, can't you *act* like your happy?" I snapped. By now, I was beginning to lose being patient.

A knot started in my stomach. My nerves were bad enough getting up in the morning with fear of making a mistake, but not getting any affection from my new husband increased my doubt. He didn't kiss me unless he heard a spoon clank on a glass. My insecurity engulfed me.

We ate quietly without much conversation between us as I watched everyone at our table laughing and having fun. I plastered a smile on my face hoping to hide my disappoint- ment in my husband's actions and remarks. I tried to be pleasant hoping that our guests would think I was happy. Behind all the smiles, I was fighting to hold back a flood of tears.

My parents had an open bar and the drinks were flowing freely. People were getting loud and some men were strutting around after a few drinks trying to get the attention of the women.

Once the dinner was served and the tables were cleared, the bride and groom's first dance was announced.

"I hate dancing," Richie said as he forced himself to go onto the floor.

I came to see why he made the remark. There was no rhythm in him at all. It was hard trying not to step on his feet. I didn't dare remark about his clumsiness on the floor.

After our dance ended, the band switched to fast dance tunes. The tables emptied as the dance floor filled up.

Richie and I went back to sit. By now, we were the only ones sitting at the long head table.

"Lets get up and dance," I pleaded.

"I told you, I don't like to dance," he replied in a panicked tone.

Of all times to discover this, I thought. I had never asked him if he liked dancing. Me, who loves to dance my feet off! I came in second place in my senior year as the best female dancer in my class, and my husband hated to dance.

"What do you mean you can't dance? Just move around. No one will notice what you're doing. The floor is packed." I was trying to be calm, but I was burning inside.

"I'll pass on this."

Albert grabbed a girl and never left the dance floor. There were many single women who had been invited so he had his pick all day. They seemed to be lined up waiting for him. He loved dancing as much as I did. Roseanne, Raymond, Eddie and my girlfriends mixed right in. It was the kind of wedding reception that I would have loved to attend. Instead, it was mine, and I wasn't participating in it at all.

Left – Dad, Mom, Alberta, Richie, Mrs. Lena Lopes

Richie & Alberta

Chapter Twelve

Who is this Stranger

Everyone, young and old, was kicking-up-their-heels. My out-going, fun-loving personality suddenly fell out of me. I became exasperated watching Richie sulk and thinking of ways to get him to mix in. I felt completely apart from everyone. I was usually the life of the party.

A jitterbug played, and Albert waved me over, "Come on out and boogie, Alberta."

I just smiled back.

"Richie, we can't just sit here and show how miserable you're feeling. Why are you doing this?"

"I just want to sit and watch people," he said looking upset.

"We aren't *guests*! We're the bride and groom who should be beaming with excitement."

My Uncle Joe suddenly appeared at my side and grabbed me.

"Come on, Alberta, let's swing. We'll show them what dancing is."

Joe St. Onge was a hellion. He was in his forties and very handsome. He wasn't related to us, but we had been brought up to call him uncle. He and his wife, Anita, were close and dear friends of my parents.

To me, he was the best dancer in the world. I always thought the world of him growing up.

As he pulled me onto the dance floor, I remarked, "Don't twirl me too fast, Uncle Joe. I have no slip under this hoop."

It was the wrong thing to say to a joker! If my clothes were more comfortable for dancing, it would have been fun to let loose with him.

I could see that he didn't care about my hoop. He not only swung me around, but lifted me off the floor like a feather. I was light on my feet. All eyes were on the two of us, and it was obvious that we impressed everyone.

When we got off the dance floor, people clapped. It was the first time that I came alive and acted like myself the whole day. I could hardly catch my breath when I got back to the table.

"She's all yours, Richie. If she moves like this is bed, you're a lucky man," he said joking with a large grin. He gave me a tight hug and a warm kiss.

"Boy! That took a lot out of me." I said sitting in the chair gasping for air.

"I know one thing, I don't have to wait until tonight to see what you own," he remarked sarcastically.

"What do you mean?" I asked.

"I mean, when your uncle twirled you, I saw your underwear pants."

"Oh, no, I told him to be careful of that!"

After the event, he showed no intention of moving from his spot at the head table. No one in the bridal party returned to sit with us because the fun was anywhere but with us.

After a half hour of just sitting, I started to get angry. To make matters worse, we couldn't find anything to talk about. By this time, I was so upset that I couldn't speak to him. Not once did we smile or laugh with each other. We looked about as unhappy as a couple could be. I thought divorced people must have been happier than I was feeling.

"Richie, we should be walking around thanking our guests for coming."

"You go. I hardly know anyone," he said.

"It's something that we are *supposed* to do together, whether you know them or not. They came to celebrate with us and brought us gifts. It's the polite thing to do."

I looked at him and wondered who this stranger was that I had just married. I knew he was shy, but this was ridiculous. It was causing me embarrassment. He refused to mix in. I couldn't understand why he wasn't even interested in sitting with his buddies.

"We can't sit here until the wedding ends. We look stupid." I wanted to get up and walk out of the hall. *Oh, my God. What have I done?* Since I walked into the church, I hadn't felt a moment of happiness. Were those feelings I had at the house a warning?

He sat while I went around the room alone thanking people. *How can this man be in love with me? How can he degrade me like this?* I didn't want to talk to anyone about his actions, not even our friends. I was so depressed with his refusal to participate. I should have known then what I was in for. My fears quickly multiplied.

My relatives started throwing the questions at me that I dreaded. "Is Richie feeling ok?" I knew they were taken aback with his behavior.

No matter what I gave for an excuse, I knew deep down that everyone was aware that I was covering up for him. I was fuming about being put in this situation. He was acting like a spoiled brat, and worse, a man with no excitement about being married.

Along with everyone else, my mother was now ready to add to my discomfort. "Alberta, you two look like the most miserable couple that I have ever seen getting married. What's wrong with that boy?"

"That boy—Richie—will be fine, Mom," I snapped trying to defend him. I became angrier knowing how noticeable his behavior was becoming to other people. I could picture everyone talking about us.

Inside I felt the same as my mother did, but I wouldn't give her the satisfaction of admitting it. Now, I knew what she and Dad were trying to tell me about chasing a boy. If I had told her what I was really feeling, she would have had a hysterical daughter on her hands and possibly witness her running out of the hall, and the marriage. I thought about women who have probably done such a thing, and admired them, but I had too much pride.

I started to think back to how Richie never sat and mixed in with my family when we dated. We never spent an evening just talking to my parents. A sudden reality hit me that this was the first time that we socialized with family and friends at a large gathering. All our time had been spent alone or with very few friends. What a time to notice this!

I couldn't wait for us to cut the cake and have him throw the garter. Getting changed to leave for the honeymoon couldn't come fast enough. I went through enough stress and wanted out of the most hurtful and awkward time of my life. It was the worst experience. I didn't feel married. There wasn't a moment of happiness.

I felt bad for my parents knowing that they must have been questioned by relatives about what was going on with us. All the money they worked hard to save was spent on a foolish charade.

Richie wasn't concerned about manners or doing the right thing; the day was a nightmare. I was worn out from putting on an act for everyone.

81

My dream of having a beautiful wedding and marrying a man who was totally and madly in love with me was gone. I knew deep within my heart that this marriage was a big mistake, but I couldn't admit it out loud.

If only we could fast forward our lives to see the mistakes that we are about to make. Of all times for me to see a side of him that I didn't know existed. Why didn't it show dating him? Or did it, and I just ignored it?

We said our goodbyes and left in a hail of confetti thrown by well-wishers. Instead of going off with my prince on a white horse, I rushed to the car to end a disappointing event that should have been the most memorable day of my life.

Chapter Thirteen
Our Honeymoon

Richie informed me weeks before that he made all the arrangements for our honeymoon and wanted to surprise me. I had never traveled anywhere and was glad that he planned the itinerary. All he told me was that we were going to Canada.

I hoped that he would make up for the uneasiness that he showed all day and would start to unwind with me. I needed to see an out-going, fun-loving person. By now I was drained from the torture. It was a relief to be away from people who attended the wedding. I didn't want to face anyone else that day.

"Where are we staying?" I couldn't wait for the surprise.

"I don't know. I thought that we'd just ride until we saw a motel around New Hampshire or Maine."

"You didn't make arrangements?" Why was I surprised?

"Don't worry, Alberta. It's not a problem."

We traveled for three hours with little conversation between us. There was no laughter shared with this man I had just married. He never put his arm around me to pull me close to him. No soft kiss was placed on my forehead with a smile.

We reached Old Orchard Beach in Maine, and I noticed an amusements park all lit-up. Richie drove in front of a small motel right on the beach. I could hear the low waves softly hitting the shoreline.

"You sit here, and I'll go in and register," he said as he opened the car door.

It wasn't long before he returned.

"Richie, let's walk around and go on some rides, it would be fun." I got a burst of energy being amid all the action with the lights, hearing the noise from the rides and everyone laughing and screaming. The dust flying around reminded me of Nantasket Beach and Lincoln Park.

"I'm bushed, Alberta, from the long day and the drive."

"We can just sit on a bench and smell the salt air for a few minutes."

It was only ten o'clock, and I couldn't believe how he was ready to call it a night. I feared that he didn't know how to have fun. Maybe he wanted us to be alone. This would be my first time making love. I wanted it to be special.

We got inside our room, and I pulled the drapes back so we could see the beach. I wanted to open the screen door, but it started getting chilly.

I picked out a soft, pink gown from my suitcase. Leona had given me a shower with my closest girlfriends. I brought beautiful nightwear to choose from for the week. I stepped into the shower and felt my muscles tense up. When I finished, I slipped on my matching robe. I walked back into the bedroom and sat on the edge of the bed.

I waited for Richie to comment on my outfit. I wanted him to walk over to give me a kiss, a touch, a smile, any act of affection or to see excitement in his eyes. I wanted some sort of connection with him. He never looked my way.

"Guess it's my turn," he said as he walked toward the bathroom.

There were many heated moments dating, and I thought this night would be the same. I expected him to be an expert with love-making. Instead of relaxing, I started getting severe cramps in my stomach. I doubled up in pain.

Not now, I thought. *What's wrong with me?*

They came out of nowhere. At first I thought I was getting sick. My first reaction was fear of how I was going to make love if I was uncomfortable. I started to rationalize that it was nerves. I never experienced physical pain from being scared or uptight. By now, I just wanted us to sleep next to each other and wait for tomorrow to make love.

Between the bottled-up emotions at the wedding and the anxiety from the long ride, it was hard for me to be excited. There was no attention from him all day. I felt the pressure of *having* to make love.

He walked out of the shower with pajama bottoms on and it made me calm down. In fact, he looked sexy. I was too embarrassed to tell him about my cramps. My privacy in personal matters was now going to be open to someone else. I didn't like it.

We got into bed and he came over to me. I longed for him to hold me so that I could unwind. I wanted to hear how happy he was or maybe how sorry he was for his actions at the wedding. That wasn't the case. I should have felt comfortable enough to explain what I was feeling. I didn't know how to say it.

There was no conversation or much foreplay to make me comfortable before making love. I longed to hear how he felt about us being married, but it never happened. He was gentle, but I felt empty. I saved myself all these years for this man, and there was no emotion involved. I didn't know what it was supposed to feel like, but knew it should have felt better than this...I felt nothing.

Where was the romance that was there when we were dating? Or had there been any? Where was the excitement of being married? I felt completely alone lying in the darkness. How could I say this to him on our wedding night?

He gave me a light kiss goodnight. He turned over with his back toward me and went right to sleep. There was no conversation about the day, or about our becoming man and wife or our first moments together.

Our honeymoon was spent getting up each morning and driving all day long, only stopping to eat. We traveled straight through to Canada deep in the wilderness roaming the barren highways. It was a sight-seeing trip with no agenda; it was so boring and long. The only entertaining thing that we saw was a black and white Shepherd dog leading a flock of sheep all by itself down a road. It amazed me to see how an animal could have the intelligence to control them.

As it got late in the day, we'd look for a motel to spend the night, only to be continue what I felt was aimless wandering the next day. When Richie said he planned the honeymoon I thought he had included some specific destinations. We cut the week down to five days. I couldn't wait to get home. I kept all my frustrations inside so that I wouldn't "rock the boat." After spending a week together, I felt a strain keeping conversation going between us. Dating for a few hours was one thing, but going home together was a different story. Our life was not a fairy tale, it was now reality.

Chapter Fourteen
Making a Home

I was determined to make my marriage work. I could change him. It would just take time. I could teach him to enjoy other people and find things that were fun. Why do we think this?

Richie found a small apartment in North Dighton for us to rent before we got married. It was tiny, but cozy. It was a cottage-style home nestled deep in the woods. The woman who owned it lived alone downstairs, and she was hardly ever around. Richie would give her the rent each week after getting his paycheck.

He worked midnight till 7:00 a.m. at the Raytheon Plant. I never experienced being totally alone at night. There was always someone home when I lived with my parents. It was scary living in the woods, and I took it as the perfect place for a murder mystery.

We climbed outside stairs to get to our second floor. The door opened into a comfortable sized living room. The kitchen faced the backyard and the roof slanted to four feet off the outside walls; it was probably the attic at one time and been converted into an apartment. The three long kitchen windows went to the floor. There was one bedroom and a bath. It was big enough for a couple starting out and I was excited having my own place.

The furniture that we had bought a few months before just squeezed into our rooms. On a cloudy day, it was dark and gloomy in the apartment because of the trees that leaned over the house. The backyard had a thick cluster of trees that went back into the woods.

At night, I'd be frightened to go to sleep and stayed up to watch Johnny Carson or the Steve Allen show till 1:00 a.m. I waited until exhaustion took over, and my eyes could no longer stay open.

Richie didn't want me to work. Instead of learning to be independent, I gave in. He would arrive home at 7:30 a.m. and jump into bed after I made his breakfast. I'd take advantage of my freedom and use the car to visit my friends. Cindy, Roseanne, and Anita didn't work so I enjoyed visiting or going shopping with them. Back in those days, a woman staying home was a normal thing.

Richie developed a closer relationship with my family after we were married. Some weekend nights, we'd drive down to the Cape Cod Canal with Bob, Leona, Sonny, Anita, and Richie's cousin, Dot and her husband, Tony. The men would fish while the women would catch the lobsters. Once their claws grabbed onto our bait of chicken wings, which we tied to a line, we'd shine a flashlight on the lobsters to see where they were. When the lobster backed away with the bait, one of us would scoop them up in our net from behind.

When Richie and I went to Hull to see my parents, the four of us would play Pinochle for hours. All of us loved the card game. If my siblings and their families visited the same weekend, we'd team up for a game of pool in the living room. None of us were experts at the game, but there were hours of fun and laughter. There was a Playboy Club on the strip, and we took it in one night with Bob and Leona. It was my first time in a nightclub, and I found it exciting seeing the girls in their bunny outfits.

Not long after our honeymoon, I became pregnant and was sick every day. I'd make Richie his breakfast and disappear outside to sit on the top step until he finished eating; the smell of food upset my stomach and the coffee's aroma made it even worse.

During my third month, my doctor tried to ease my nausea. He tried giving me shots weekly, but they didn't help me. The next step was for me to rest in bed, eating chocolate candy bars and drinking coke, and nothing else. What a dream come true! Who wouldn't want to go on a chocolate binge? But it didn't help. Finally, he told me that I would have to tough it out. It took seven months before the nausea disappeared.

Being sick for so long didn't help Richie and I get close physically. A large chunk of the day was taken up with him sleeping after work. After awhile, we went through the motions of being married. The fun things and getting to know each other were pushed aside. We didn't sit and have long, private conversations about ourselves when he came home. He and I had surface talk; his job, my day or where I went, but nothing about us.

Our feelings, likes, wants, or dreams were forgotten. It wasn't that we didn't care for one another; there wasn't the deep intimacy of opening up with emotions. We were more like best friends. Joking around, grabbing each other, or doing wild things together wasn't in our lives.

Our days became routine because of his work schedule, working nights and sleeping days, we began to by-pass one another. We'd have supper together and relax for a few hours before he headed back to work. We watched a lot of television instead of getting out of the house and going places. Weekends we tried to visit family. He continuously accepted work on Saturdays until it became another work day. I spent time trying to find ways to entertain myself.

In a way, it had been a good decision for me not to apply for a job since I was so sick with my pregnancy, I dragged all day. When Richie left for work, my evenings alone started to become enjoyable. Cuddling up with a good book on the couch, writing a letter, or having a friend over gave me a feeling of independence. By then, I didn't worry about not hearing the mystery woman downstairs walking around or seeing her outside.

Cindy lived a few miles away, and many mornings I looked forward to going to her house for coffee when Richie fell asleep. I'd stay for hours and we'd have girl talk. We spent almost every day together. She had a daughter and was expecting a second child a few months before me. I went to her with all the questions about my pregnancy. I felt closer to her than my own husband. Being women, we talked about anything and everything on raising children.

Cindy's husband, Ernie, had his own carpentry business, and it was becoming a normal routine for him to come home late from work. He started to hang out with his drinking friends and came in at all hours of the morning. Ernie and I graduated from Dighton High School the same year. When he dated Cindy, they came to my parents' home often.

They were close friends with Danny when I dated him. It was after my marriage that Cindy informed me that they kept in touch with him. He was still single with a few months left in the service.

One morning, I arrived at her house and she remarked, "I'm glad you didn't come an hour ago."

"Why?"

"Danny was here for a visit. You just missed him."

It would have torn my heart out facing him with me being pregnant. It was something we would have wanted to share together. Knowing he had just left her house was extremely painful. As much as I would have wanted to see him, I wouldn't have been able to handle him seeing me in maternity clothes. I let a wonderful boy slip away from me. While Cindy and I talked over a cup of tea, I couldn't shake the thought that Danny had been sitting at her kitchen table just a few hours ago.

Roseanne was still working hard taking care of her siblings. After a few years, her father met a nice woman and remarried. She was now finally free to make her own wedding plans to marry Ray. We kept in touch more often since she had her life back.

My days were spent with friends; it was my time, and I was completely enjoying myself. I'd go home to make supper and spend my nights with Richie. I felt as though I had two lives.

One night, Leona called and we started talking about our past.

"I can't understand why Danny walked out so easily?" I mentioned.

"Alberta, Danny has kept in touch with us. He even phoned the night before your wedding."

"What! Why didn't you ever tell me?"

"And, what would you have done, stopped your wedding? I don't think so. What purpose would there have been in telling you?"

"You mean all the time that we've been broken up, he's kept in touch with you? Why didn't he ever call me?" By now, I was angry at him. "My God, all I did was *date* someone. I can't believe you never told me."

"You were so determined to marry Richie that you never would have changed your mind."

"We'll never know. At least, I would have had a chance to see him and decide. I've lived a year thinking his feelings stopped."

"Things happen for a reason. You're married and about to have a baby; something that I wish Bob and I were experiencing."

Leona had serious female health issues and couldn't conceive. Because of her problems, she had to have a full hysterectomy in her early thirties and couldn't have children. I felt she would have been a wonderful mother.

I hung up, shocked, thinking that all the time that I was thinking of Danny, he might have been thinking of me. How we let pride ruin our lives.

I brushed these feeling aside and thought of all the good qualities in my husband. I knew there were a lot of things about him that I respected. Because he didn't know how to show affection, I resented him, and acted the same toward him. It was as if he locked his heart and threw out the key. Weekdays were completely occupied with his work, and I couldn't wait for weekends so we'd have time together. He helped May and Vic a lot at the vegetable stand when he could, especially helping Vic get his fields ready for planting.

Chapter Fifteen
The Birth of Debbie

With a baby due in a few months, we needed to move to a larger place because our bedroom was too small for a crib. Richie asked his aunt, Mary, if we could rent one of her empty homes. It was located in North Dighton and there were two bedrooms on the first floor and two unfinished rooms upstairs. She had a large piece of property out back. The house wasn't occupied so she agreed to rent it to us. We made plans to move into the house within the month.

May 14, 1963, I went into labor and our daughter, Deborah Ann Lopes, was born weighing six pounds and nine ounces. She was beautiful with perfect tiny features. I did what all mothers do. I opened the pink receiving blanket that was tightly wrapped around her. She looked like a mummy. I sat and counted all her toes and fingers and kissed each one. What a precious gift from God, she was in perfect health.

The morning I was leaving the hospital, I dressed Debbie in her new pink and white one-piece stretch suit. I wrapped a pink plaid receiving blanket around her. When we got in the hospital elevator, she had already discovered her thumb and was sucking on it. I smiled wondering if it was something she did while I carried her.

While I was in the hospital, Richie and a few buddies moved everything out of the apartment into our new house. The furniture was in place when I came home. I was relieved at not being involved with the ordeal of moving.

Like all men, Richie hoped for a son, but once he saw Debbie and held her, he was so proud having a daughter. He carried her in the house with his out-stretched hands.

"Richie, hold her close to you so she feels safe."

"I've never held a baby before."

"Well, now you're holding your daughter."

As the months went by, it became obvious that he wouldn't be much help with Debbie. He was uncomfortable handling an infant. The fear in him showed whenever he tried to take care of her even with me close by. He enjoyed talking to her or holding her hand, but he wasn't the kind of father who would change or feed her. Walking the floor with her when she fussed or was sick was out of the question. He felt that was my department. I didn't have the comfort of two parents sharing in this special blessing. I brushed the thought aside and just assumed that all men felt that way.

The Raytheon Plant closed its doors in North Dighton and relocated to Newport, Rhode Island. Richie didn't want to transfer even though they offered him good money. It would have been an hour ride for him, not allowing for traffic tie ups. I didn't want to move away from my close friends, whom I had been with most of my life.

Richie wanted to further himself with his electronic schooling so he took a job at a television shop in Somerset. He became a repairman and loved the challenge. The shop was only fifteen minutes away from our home. He worked six days a week, and I was suddenly feeling alone. Having a baby so soon in our marriage gave him the freedom to go his own way.

There was only one pay coming into the house so I didn't argue about the schedule. The hours were good and he was home at 5:00 p.m. About a year after, he began coming home later and later. I never knew what time to have supper ready for him.

His excuses always revolved around how busy his day was and the stress it put on him. After the shop closed, he and his boss, Tom Pimental, stopped at the Elbow Room for a drink.

It was next door to the television store so it was very convenient.

His calls were always the same. "Hi. Tom and I have a few problems to discuss. Don't hold supper up."

I'd sit with an overcooked meal and too many leftovers. I'd try to make Debbie's mealtimes into a game. I didn't want her to sense my stress. She'd sit in her highchair smiling and laughing while I filled the tiny, baby spoon with her dinner. Vegetables weren't her favorite so I'd mix them into her mashed potatoes. I'd turn her spoon into an airplane. It would be high in the air and I'd drop it with a few loops before entering her mouth. She'd giggle and the food would splatter all over me as I made the loud sound of the propeller turning.

Debbie brightened my days, and I loved to bathe her and watch her take her first steps with unsteady legs on the plush, tan living room rug. She'd bend down looking backwards at me between her legs. I'd bend down with the same gesture only to have my face turn red. I'd be dizzy when I stood up.

I loved putting her into warm pajamas. I'd sing songs rocking her until she'd fall asleep in my arms before putting her in bed. It was comforting holding her close. She was the best thing that came out of our marriage.

Anita's third child, Gary, was born a few months before Debbie. She asked me to baby-sit a few hours each day while she worked part-time. Her three kids loved being with Debbie, and they entertained each other. I baby sat Paula, Gilly, and Gary for only six months, until Anita found it cheaper to stay home.

My emotions with Richie were up and down. First I'd respect him for working so hard, and then I'd be boiling inside waiting for him to come home. All I did was wait to see what he did or planned to do. I sat in the dark and watched television after putting Debbie to sleep, and by midnight, I'd crawl into bed alone. I needed my sleep so that I'd be able to keep up with the baby the next morning.

I went to bed and pulled the quilted cover over me, and turned to face our bedroom window. The dark sky was filled with twinkling stars. Sadness filled my heart and made me think back on my life; *Danny was somewhere out there. Was he thinking about me? He wouldn't be leaving me home alone.* I knew deep down that if Richie was giving me the love and security that I craved, I wouldn't be thinking about Danny.

I stayed awake remembering back to an older friend who warned me not to leave Danny.

"Someday you'll regret leaving him," she said. "How can you leave a guy who is so nuts about you?"

"I hurt him, and he walked out without talking about it. He couldn't forgive me," I answered.

She sighed. "Someone would have to be blind not to see the deep love he showed for you. You'd walk across a room, and his eyes followed you. He smiled when you laughed at anything. I had that with someone special and can see you are doing the exact same thing. Don't be blind like I was or let pride stop you from running back to him."

She sat down next to me at the kitchen table, "I want to tell you about a decision that I made when I was nineteen-years old. I was crazy about this boy that I had been dating for years. He treated me like gold. I became infatuated with a gentleman who came my way and impressed me with his good looks and fancy talk. I left the other guy because I was blind to what real love was all about. Don't get me wrong, I'm happy being married, but I'm not deeply in love. I settled for a hum drum life and still think about that boy who I let slip through my fingers."

How right she was. I loved Richie, yet, I wasn't feeling a connection in our marriage. Richie's drinking put a wall between us. I wanted to reach out to him, but I held back my emotions from him staying out so often. Everything was automatic; getting up, kissing my husband goodbye as he left for work, taking care of a baby, grocery shopping and living a life alone. He wasn't sharing in our marriage. When he wanted my affection, he welcomed my attention. His life was being spent at work and at a bar at the end of the day.

Am I going to end up like my friend? Am I going to look back in twenty years still thinking about that boy I let slide through my fingers?

Please, God, let my husband turn his life around and let us become a happy, normal family. Let my nights of being alone stop.

Luckily Debbie was so active during the day, because taking care of her exhausted me, and it didn't take long for me to fall asleep most nights.

Chapter Sixteen
Time Together Fades

Richie wasn't violent when he came home after drinking, and we didn't argue; of course, it helped since I didn't make an issue of it. When Debbie was a year old and past the infant stage, he felt comfortable taking her with him to see Vic and May at the vegetable stand. He loved showing her off.

He never drank when he was home so we enjoyed good times on the weekends. He'd sit and watch Debbie amuse herself with her toys. At night we'd cuddle on the couch with a huge bag of popcorn. The weekends were mine with him, and it was so relaxing with the three of us that I'd forget about the long and lonely week nights.

When Mondays arrived, my stomach would be tied in knots. I could have played a recording instead of waiting for his call. Our normal supper hours went from 5:00 p.m. to sometimes ten at night. Debbie wanted to stay up and see Daddy, but it was always too late. I hated our life; we weren't a family.

Anita and I did crazy things together to entertain ourselves during the day. We'd be in tears of laughter watching our children do or say silly things. We kept each other's spirits up because Sonny was a workaholic and Richie was never home at night. With Ernie staying out all hours drinking, Cindy's lifestyle was the same as mine. Sonny was the only one who was actually *working* late, the others would be out drinking. Cindy and I filled our emptiness in our marriages by sharing our marital problems. Crying on each other's shoulder gave us the emotional support we needed.

Ray and Roseanne came over often when Richie was home, and I looked forward to us getting together. The four of us played the game of cribbage for hours. If the guys teamed up, we joked about them cheating if they won. One night, I had invited them for supper and Richie never came out of our bedroom; he made no excuse, he just didn't join us. I was totally embarrassed and our friends were deeply hurt. Our good times as couples dwindled because of this one night and we drifted apart.

I clung to my girlfriends, and we did everything with our kids. I'd put Debbie into the carriage and take her for the mile walk to Anita's house. It was all back roads and it was enjoyable walking by the wooded areas. The roads were empty, and the sounds of nature were comforting as I strolled along the edge of the road.

One afternoon, while I walked the stroller to Anita's, a guy in a bright, red pickup truck stopped to say hello to me. At first I didn't recognize this boy who looked like a knockout movie star with blonde hair and a deep tan. He introduced himself and turned out to be that chubby, freckled-faced boy who followed me around in high school for four years and had a mad crush on me, the one I didn't give the time of day. He smiled and drove off after a short conversation. I guess we all have a part of us that wants to show the person who had ignored us what they missed. That made me chuckle. *Leave it to you, Alberta.*

Three years went by, and I got to like the old farm house. Debbie was an angel and gave me no problems with either her bedtime or her behavior. She was a joy.

On weekends, Richie helped Vic plant the crops and plow the fields on the property where we lived. He'd give Debbie tractor rides when he'd finish and then take her with him to the vegetable stand to put the equipment away. She'd be thrilled coming home with some sort of treat.

Richie's drinking increased, and my patience with it wore thin. He came home later each night. I couldn't solve the problem by talking to him when he'd been drinking, so my desire to do so was useless.

Catching him before he left for work in the morning was hard because I had to attend to Debbie's needs. He wanted to get out of the house as fast as he could so there would be no confrontation.

One evening, I made sure that I was awake when he came in after midnight. I needed to open up, or I'd burst. Things seemed fine to him because I didn't bring up the topic of him staying out late. I didn't look forward to standing up for myself; I actually feared confronting him.

"Richie, this has to stop. There's no need for you to be staying out this much and coming home late every night of the week. You're spending too much time drinking."

"I'm too tired to talk about this now, Alberta, who am I harming anyway? I need to unwind. You don't know how it is having customers call for their television sets when we're still waiting for the parts and they can't understand the delay. You're not helping with the stress when you're nagging me."

"When have I nagged you? This is the first time I've brought this up. If you came home and we had some sort of family life during the week, I wouldn't mind. Debbie's three-years old and you spend no time with her. She's sleeping when you come through the door. If you were honestly working late that would be one thing, but you're not, you're using customer complaints as an excuse to drink."

"Oh, for God's sake, you don't know what you're talking about."

"I know that it's not normal for me to be alone this much. I don't feel married doing everything alone."

"I'm working hard to bring money home so we can pay the bills."

"Not while you're sitting in a bar!"

"I don't need this," he stated and stormed out of the kitchen. "Forget about supper. I'm showering and going to bed."

I sat there in the kitchen, disgusted. Did he really think that I was going to give him supper at midnight? Amazing how he thinks. I'm important to him if I wait on him hand and foot.

I was stunned that we couldn't talk about his staying out and drinking. I came from a family that was always open to discuss any situation. My parents would sit down in a quiet fashion and speak about ways to help us. This way of living was new to me. My dream was to be happily married and sharing all problems and children's issues. I wanted a solid marriage.

As I crawled back into bed, the anxiety built-up inside me. I could feel pains in my stomach, and I didn't like the feeling of the two of us lying next to each other in bed with no words between us.

I couldn't shake the feeling that I was alone, even when he was with me. I started to question if maybe I was the one doing something wrong, and that was why he was out so much. For an instant, my mind went as far as to wonder if he was having an affair. All I knew was that he didn't want to be home. *Could I be blind to the possibility of someone else being in his life?*

I was sick of hearing the other wives of his drinking buddies give stupid excuses. "Oh, Alberta, they're all doing it. Let him get it out of his system, he always comes home."

I continued to live the same routine day in and day out during the week. I didn't know how to bring him home. One moment he was a good father and husband, and the next, he wasn't with us. It wasn't as if he came home drunk and caused a scene. Every night, I held a bomb inside of me. I didn't want Debbie to grow up hearing fights. I also didn't know how to handle making demands on my husband. Instead, I allowed his actions to continue.

Richie & Debbie on Vic's Tractor

Chapter Seventeen
Drinking Buddies

Richie and his boss, Tom, became close friends. Since Tom owned the business, money was no problem in giving lavish house parties. His wife, Nancy, continuously made remarks about counting her husband's drinks during the evening and wasn't afraid to talk about it.

She looked at me disgusted, "How can they drink so much? They don't even drink slow enough to enjoy them. The drinks go down so fast, and then they're filling their glasses again?"

Another woman, Trish, remarked, "Well, they've all downed about three drinks so the party should get rolling soon." She proved to be right.

Soon the men began telling off-color jokes and flirting openly with each other's wives. A few wives in the group laughed at the obnoxious scenes and joined the men with their flirtatious actions. From all the drinks that the husbands would down, we'd wait for someone to get out of hand.

After awhile, the men started to slur their words. I sat quietly and watched some of them lose their balance and spill their drinks. I didn't find any humor in their behavior, it was pathetic. I was tired of the get-togethers going this route; it seemed to happen every time we came to these parties. Richie drank one drink after another. I couldn't understand why he drank when he was out, but never did at home. I started to think that it was a social problem with him. It never hit me that he might be an alcoholic.

If drunks could only see what fools they make of themselves, I thought. When he was drinking, Richie changed from his normal quiet ways into a talkative, funny guy, but then, as he drank more he became unpleasant. Sober, he would die if he could hear the stupid things that came out of his mouth when he drank.

One evening, Tom set-up a screen in the living room and brought out his movie projector. Chairs were placed in the living room and the couples sat to watch a movie. I was a gullible person and got excited, thinking it was a comedy. Maybe the movie might take an hour away from the drinking.

Instead, it was an X-rated film. I didn't know how to act in front of everyone. I never watched one and became relieved when the lights went out.

I leaned over to Richie and whispered, "You've got to be kidding! I'm supposed to sit and watch this with other men in the room?"

"Alberta, we're all adults. What do you think we're all going to do, grab each other?"

"I don't want to find out!"

Tom clapped his hands and yelled, "Hey, quiet. Let the entertainment begin," as he tried to balance himself and hold his drink. His knees gave out from having too many, his drink flew across the room, and his shirt was soaked and so was the dining room tablecloth. Everyone laughed.

I sat there wishing that I could sneak out and disappear; I didn't want to watch such trash. When the movie got to a part with two girls having sex, I wanted to die. I could feel my face burning beet red.

It was so embarrassing sitting there, I only knew these people from the few parties we attended. I felt frozen in my chair and couldn't figure out if the other women liked it or felt the same discomfort. I didn't dare look around and make eye contact with anyone. You could hear sly remarks the men were making to their wives, which made it worse. I could only imagine what the women were in for that night.

When it ended, the lights came on, and no one said a word. Suddenly, everyone wanted to end the evening and the men joked about the fun they were going to have when they got home. I couldn't wait to just get out of that house.

The parties started to dwindle down because of everyone's busy schedules with vacations or planned events, I was relieved. About eight months later, Tom died of a massive heart attack in his home. He was only in his mid thirties, and all our friends couldn't believe the news. Because of his death being so sudden, Nancy didn't know what to do with the business. Marty, a friend of theirs, bought the shop, and Richie continued to work for him.

One Friday night, Marty invited us out the next evening to take in a movie with him and his wife. I wanted to get to know him so Richie would see that I wanted to share time with his friends. We were going to see *Midnight Cowboy*, a pretty risqué film at the time, and I had no idea what it was about. I soon found out.

Marty sat on my right, Richie on my left. My eyes were glued to the scenes, and I didn't dare look to either side of me. I started to think that I must be a prude; no one else seemed embarrassed, and I didn't dare bring it up after we left. Was this what married couples did for entertainment? Here I was hoping for a funny or romantic movie. Were they still making them?

Chapter Eighteen
The Birth of Lori

When Debbie was three-years old, I became pregnant again. The two bedrooms in the house weren't going to be enough space for two children. Richie asked his aunt if we could buy it. If we were able to purchase it, we'd have to fix the upstairs. It would be easy to get three bedrooms and a full bathroom up there, but it needed serious renovations. We didn't want to put the money out, if we didn't own it. She was firm on just renting, so we were forced to search for another place to live.

In my third month of pregnancy, I developed stomach cramps and almost miscarried. Dr. Wood, my gynecologist, told me to rest and avoid any strenuous activity for a few months until the danger passed. After the birth of Debbie, I didn't exercise to build strong stomach muscles; not doing so almost ended my second pregnancy. It was hard finding any time to rest with another child to care for, but Debbie entertained herself and never demanded too much of my attention, which helped a lot.

"I think it's time for us to look for a house," Richie said one night during supper. "If we're going to put money out, I want to get something back from it. Besides, I want to see if I can get a place where I can open a small repair shop."

"I'd love that." My hopes went sky high thinking that he would take his marriage and family more seriously. It would also get him away from the Elbow Room.

Both of us wanted to remain in town. We found a home in North Dighton on Old Somerset Avenue with weeping willow trees that offered privacy to the front and backyard and they gave a lot of shade. There were two large bedrooms, a dining room that opened to a living room and another room off the kitchen. The disadvantage was having only one bathroom and one long closet in the whole house. There was a door off the master bedroom that contained stairs going up to the attic which stretched across the full length of the house. It could have easily been made into three bedrooms and a full bathroom. We kept that in mind while looking at it.

There wouldn't be a problem with needed space until the two kids got older. A heated sunroom was attached off the living room; there was a garage below the kitchen, which faced the street, and there was a full cellar. A stairway came upstairs from the garage into an entry way to the kitchen. Richie could use the cellar for his television business.

We signed papers, and when we were ready to move in, I was in the hospital in labor. On July 29, 1967, Lori was born weighing five pounds three ounces. She was beautiful and had smaller features than her sister. I counted her toes and fingers as I had done with Debbie.

Children weren't allowed in the hospital rooms, so Richie brought Debbie outside below my window. I was a few floors up but I could still see her and wave. I couldn't believe how big she looked in his arms after holding a newborn. Until that day, I thought our four-year-old daughter was still a baby.

I was due to go home when Dr. Mealy, my obstetrician, came into my room. "Your daughter has jaundice and we may have to give her a blood transfusion. That's why her skin is a deep yellow. You can go home, but we will have to keep her a few days."

"I'm not going anywhere without my daughter. I'm nursing her." I sat on the bed firmly, with arms crossed, emphasizing my decision.

"You can always pump the milk, Mrs. Lopes."

"I refuse. I want to be here if she cries."

"Give me a few hours, and we'll make a decision," he said shaking his head with a smile.

Within four hours, Dr. Mealy came in with good news. "I'll let you take her home only if you call my office tomorrow morning and make an appointment in a few days for me to see her."

"I'd be happy to do that. Thank you, Dr. Mealy."

"See you in a few days," he said with a soft hand on my shoulder.

My husband's dream of having a son was not to be. Because of the jaundice, the doctor told us that another baby might need the blood replaced. He scared us by saying that the difference in our blood type could cause another baby to have a serious health problem.

Once again, Richie moved everything out of his aunt's house into our new home while I was in the hospital.

"Richie, I have to stop having babies. We keep moving," I joked.

With our new home and two beautiful daughters, he acted differently. We were talking about our future with the new business that he wanted to start. The setup was perfect. He decided to work for Marty a few months more until we got settled.

We were both excited for the first time in our marriage, and I felt that there was something special for us to share. He invested in a used Ford van for his business and it became our second vehicle.

He named the company the Southeastern Electronic Company and had the name printed on his white truck. The renovations began for his television repair shop in the cellar. He bought the main equipment for testing and repairs and ordered all the tubes and electrical parts that were needed. It was a huge room with only two small well-windows with two 8 foot fluorescent lights that were installed to brighten the room. A cement-block firewall with a door separated the garage and our washer and dryer fit perfectly beneath the stairs in the garage.

Our relationship grew more intimate. We talked every night for hours about our future. His list of customers came right away, and they loved him. I helped as much as I could. He'd take Debbie with him when he delivered television sets to close friends.

With a second child, he lost his fear of holding Lori and helped get Debbie into her pajamas at night. There wasn't too much to do for her since she was able to do most things for herself. She always acted grown up.

Debbie loved to watch cartoons on television, especially the Road Runner, and would sit on the couch with her blanket and suck her thumb. I wasn't sure if she loved the crazy bird or if she was scared of it. Richie enjoyed watching it with her, and since her father laughed when the Road Runner traveled with propeller legs, she lost her fear of it

When we were outside cleaning the yard, our neighbors, Bill and Effie Ferreira, came over to introduce themselves. They lived across the street and their oldest child, Kevin, was a few years older than Debbie. Their daughter, Donna was four-years old, the same age as Debbie.

Their youngest, Diane, was a few months older than Lori, and we all looked forward to bringing our kids up as friends. Effie was also a homemaker so we both thought nothing of taking each other's children for a few hours if either of us had to go somewhere alone. All five kids bonded. Bill was a plumber and helped us with anything that we needed to have done in the house.

Chapter Nineteen
Richie's Childhood

After three months, Richie had organized his business and finally quit working for Marty. We talked about how big he hoped the repair shop would become. I offered to take his telephone calls when he was out on the road. He finally felt good about himself.

"I want a good life for all of us, Alberta. I don't want the life I had as a kid."

"Why, what happened?" I asked.

"When my father was alive, my parents were well known in town, and the people loved them. We worked hard on our farm growing and selling vegetables. There was my brother, Sonny, my two sisters, Lena and May, and me.

My father died from pneumonia, and our family life fell apart. My mother had an awful time adjusting without my father and didn't take on any responsibility with raising us. She and my sister, Lena, started drinking and there wasn't anyone taking over the household. Sonny was the one who kept us together after he got a job.

When I was twelve-years old, May and Vic took me in for awhile. It was getting to be a lot for Sonny to watch all of us. I was taken into another drinking atmosphere."

"Who drank, your sister?" I asked.

"No, Vic did. I remember one night he was drinking heavy and was yelling so loud that it scared me. I went outside and hid behind the hedges. He'd be cursing while he was outside looking for me. "

"I didn't realize you lived that kind of life," I said with compassion.

I listened to him open up, and it was the most that I knew about him. When we dated, we never talked about ourselves or our lives, and we certainly hadn't done so since we married.

"You'd never know that about Vic. He seems like such a great guy," I replied.

"He is now after fighting years to give up drinking. I swear to God, I'll never drink like him, or my mother and sister."

I put my arm around him and held him tightly to me. I started to understand him a little more. That's why he was shy and quiet without confidence and not wanting to mix in with people. I couldn't imagine what it must have been like for him not having any love or security growing up. Thankfully, Sonny became the man of the family.

I started to be more patient and understanding of Richie; our life turned around, and we were communicating. I wanted to know more about his life so I went to visit Anita a few days later. She knew his family when she was a teenager.

"Anita, I didn't realize that Richie had such a hard life. He started to talk to me about it. How old were you when you met Sonny?"

"I was sixteen, and he was in the service. We married when I was eighteen."

"I heard that his father died from pneumonia."

"He was working in the fields one night and came in complaining about a terrible headache. He suffered three days with it until he couldn't stand the pain anymore. The family took him to Charlton Memorial Hospital in Fall River."

"What did he have?"

"The doctors found a blood clot in his brain and sent him to Boston. They operated on him, but there was no chance that

111

he would be normal again. The surgery was a success but there was too much damage to his brain. After a few days, pneumonia set in and he died."

"How old was he?

"He was somewhere between forty-two and forty-five, I can't remember."

"That's so young. His mother must have been devastated."

"She lived a sad life. Their son, John, died at the age of twelve from Spinal Meningitis. Another son named, Ernest, died at nine months old. I can't remember from what. He was a beautiful baby; judging from pictures I saw. She got pregnant again, and one day, while her husband was painting the house inside, the fumes made her very sick, causing her to abort twin girls."

"I can't imagine losing that many. Is that why she turned to drinking?"

"Her husband died in August, and she lost John the following January. To make it worse, her father died in February; she couldn't handle all those deaths. His sister, Lena, started drinking when she was in her early teens."

"Richie told me that."

"His mother was lost and had drank through her remaining years. She depended on her husband for everything. It was Sonny who took care of the family after he died."

"What a shame not being able to care for her kids."

She took a deep breath and continued, "Sonny was underage but worked at night in a foundry so there'd be money to feed the kids and make ends meet. He lied about his age when he was only fifteen. He would go out and buy Richie new clothes because he only had a few and no one kept up with the washing.

"What a lot of responsibility for someone so young."

"A truant officer came to the house one day because Sonny wasn't going to school. They were going to take all the kids away from their mother. Sonny threatened them with a BB gun while he sat on the roof of the porch. He told them, 'If you take another step, I'll shoot. My brother and sister aren't going anywhere. I'll take care of them.'

"Today, he'd be arrested for that, he's lucky he wasn't. He must have lived under constant stress. Were Richie and Lena going to school?"

"They both were, but they didn't look very presentable in class. Neither of them wore nice clothes. Lena's hair was so curly that he'd try combing it out but he couldn't style it. She went to school looking a mess."

"How old were they?"

"I think Richie was around twelve and Lena was my age—sixteen."

"Did the kids graduate from high school?"

"Richie did, but Lena went to work because the mother stayed home drinking. To make matters worse, a friend of the family came and offered to buy the house. It was way below the value, and the mother signed off. Sonny wanted to buy the house, but he didn't have the money. From there they moved to an apartment in Fall River. Months later, she regretted selling it."

"Where was May through all this?"

"She had married Vic and moved to North Dighton."

"Now I can understand why Richie doesn't know how to show affection!"

"They didn't have any, Alberta. The mother was always drinking. Their grandparents weren't like grandparents today. When we were kids, we'd meet a lot of grandparents, and they'd be lovely people. You'd be able to see the love that they showed toward their grandkids, but not Sonny's family. Richie didn't know how to show love because he never saw it. "

"I can't imagine growing up in that kind of environment. My parents were stern, but there was love."

We talked for hours, and I learned through Anita what happened to Richie. He never talked about it. I didn't ever tell him about my conversation with Anita.

Richie

Chapter Twenty

Hope Returns

For a few years, the television business was going well. His customers stayed with him, and the phone rang off the hook. Having the shop in the garage gave the girls time to be with him, and they loved it. Richie was home for suppers, and before Debbie and Lori went to bed, we both spent time playing with them. We had the desire to get close, and it was great being a family. There was finally fun in our lives.

We spent weekends in Hull frequently with my parents. Anita and I made trips when Richie couldn't go. The five cousins never left the swimming pool, giving the adults time to have conversations with no interruptions. Mom would walk around the yard watering her flowers.

Many Sundays were spent at Sonny and Anita's house. Her side of the family came often and all the kids played together. Richie and I looked forward being invited, and we joined the fun and laughter that echoed throughout the rooms.

Winter set in and Christmas arrived. Shopping together for the girls' gifts was a pleasure. We acted like kids trying out the toys before purchasing each one. The excitement built as we waited to give them a spiral-wired tunnel made with a cloth siding, which we had purchased for them.

Debbie was six-years old and knew what Santa was all about. She jumped into our bed.

"Mommy, Daddy, wake up. Santa came!"

I woke Lori, changed her, and took her into the living room. She was only two-years old, but her eyes became big saucers watching Debbie tearing the paper off the packages. She wanted to join right in since it looked like fun.

"Debbie, wait for us," Richie said as he put his arm around her.

Her eye caught the package with the tunnel and started to open it. "What's this, Mommy?"

"I don't know. Why don't we take it out of the box?" I teased.

Once Richie cut the box open, it popped open and the tunnel came out like a Jack in the Box with the wired spring expanding. It traveled down the rug looking mysterious.

Richie was the first one to inch his way into it. Lori crawled at top speed and followed behind him. Debbie pushed her way in-between the two of them and the girls ran through it on their hands and knees for hours; they thought it was the best thing ever. Richie lay down on his side and leaned on his elbow reading a book to them, with one story after another inside their hideaway place. It was wonderful seeing him play with the kids.

Lori was a clown even at her young age. She saw me taking movies of the three of them and started doing crazy motions. Trying to be the center of attention, she'd bend down looking at me from inside the tunnel and continuously stuck her tongue out. She was so silly that we couldn't help laughing.

We took our first summer vacation together and booked a cabin at the Jack O'Lanten Resort in Woodstock, New Hampshire. It was known for its beautiful golf course, but we stayed there because it was close to all the surrounding sites. It was a wonderful place for families. There was Santa's Village, train rides, moose trips, and Clark's Trading Post.

The sun would start to set, and we'd wait for the golf course to close. We had walked through the green to a path that led to a small stream. The girls collected crazy-shaped and colorful rocks and anything else their tiny fingers could hold. The best part was when they ran in the open fields until they were exhausted. Richie and I sat on the grass holding hands and laughed as we watched them being silly. It was the best time of our marriage. My family became normal with no arguments or waiting for Richie to come home.

We had spent a weekend in Provincetown at the tip of Cape Cod where we rented a cabin right on the beach. The town had rows of small, quaint stores side by side to rummage though. The restaurants were personable and offered a choice of meals that the girls liked.

It was fun sitting on the benches with ice cream cones and gazing at the people walking by in their colorful outfits. You could tell the residents of the small town by their clothing. Women wore long, vibrant, printed skirts with sandals and floppy hats. The men had cut-off shorts and sleeveless t-shirts. They didn't worry about matching colors or prints. The tourists stood out because their shorts and tops were coordinated.

During the day, we spent time climbing the sand dunes barefoot. Richie brought his fishing rod and fished off the beach while the girls made sandcastles. I sat on the blanket enjoying the peace and counting my blessings that our family life changed for the better. I had everything I wanted; just a simple life with Richie spending time with us.

After a few weeks of contentment, my security came to an end.

Left – Lori & Debbie with Leona's dog

Debbie & Lori climbing the sand dunes in Provincetown

Chapter Twenty-One
Frustration Creeps Back

A few months later on a Wednesday afternoon, Richie kissed me goodbye and left to deliver a television set. "I'll see you about five."

Five o'clock came and went, and he still wasn't home. I set the table and waited, but when it got to be seven o'clock, I realized that he wasn't out working. The same old familiar, nauseating, gnawing gut feeling came over me.

Oh God, don't let him be drinking. It's been so good.

I was upset that he was so inconsiderate knowing that I would be worried. By 8:00 p.m., I put both girls to bed. Debbie started with questions, "Can I wait up for Daddy—I want to stay up longer—I don't want to go to bed."

"Daddy's working late tonight. You'll see him in the morning." It was exhausting, lying as I defended him. She was just a child, and I didn't want to involve her in parents' problems. I tucked her into bed and walked into the living room. I felt so alone. With the happy life we were leading, I had stopped looking at the clock every half hour, and I wasn't worried about him walking through the door drunk.

I went to the phone and called Cindy. "Hi, Alberta, what's up?"

"I'm in a state of panic. Richie hasn't come home. Cindy, I hope he's not starting to drink again. The later it gets, I fear that he is. I can't imagine where he'd go."

"Right now you can't change the situation so try to stay calm."

"That's easier said than done."

"I know. I'm living the same way, remember?"

"Why are we going through this?'

"There's no answer except that our husbands aren't taking their marriage seriously. They're too wrapped up in themselves.

We talked about a half hour, and I wondered what I'd do without her? Both our lives were upside down one minute and then calm for weeks. We were always on a rollercoaster ride because of our husbands drinking pattern.

"Call me tomorrow."

"I'll let you know what happens."

At 9:00, Lori woke up crying. I felt her head, and she had a fever. The poor girl was teething. I picked her up and walked the floor with her, but it wasn't comforting her. Her cries turned into screams. I rocked her in the rocking chair until my arms ached.

The phone rang at 10:00. I tried balancing Lori with one arm while picking up the receiver. "Hello?"

"Hi, Honey. I'm at the club with a few guys. I'll be home soon."

"I've been worried sick. What club are you at?" My fear became a reality.

"I'm at the Dighton Golf Course. I should have called you, I'm sorry. I'll be home in about an hour."

"Richie, I could use some help with Lori. She's so sick. I've been holding her so long that I'm worn out."

"I'll take over when I get there."

I knew it wasn't going to happen because he never took over if one of the girls was sick, but I wanted so badly to believe him. After an hour, my patience completely left me. Lori was having one of her worst nights from the pain in her gums. I walked tapping her buttocks slightly and rubbing her back.

"It's ok, Sweetheart. Shh go to sleep."

At 11:00, Richie still wasn't home. I became furious that he found another place to drink. This place was only five minutes down the street.

I was in tears from complete fatigue and frustration. I picked up the phone and tried to hold my anger as I dialed the club.

"May I please speak to Richard Lopes?" I asked politely. Lori continued with ear-piercing screams as I held her in my arms.

"Let me see if he's here," someone replied.

I was no stranger to the ritual of the bartenders at the Elbow Room. He didn't have to check first to see if my husband was there. He was checking to see if he *wanted* to speak to me. *Did he think I was stupid?*

"Hi," Richie answered. His tone was friendly as if it was 5:00 in the afternoon, and there was no reason for me to be worried about him.

"I'm at my wits end with trying to calm Lori. Can you *please* come home to help me?" I hated to beg, and I wanted to scream at him. I knew that action would give him the excuse to stay out longer.

"Sure, give me a minute to finish my drink. I'll be there shortly." He answered slurring his words.

Another hour went by, and I was actually shaking from nerves trying to take care of Lori. Nothing that I was doing would bring her relief. *God, if someone could only take over.* I rubbed her gums with paregoric, a numbing medicine, and gave her a baby aspirin. She was worn out, and so was I. It was a miracle that Debbie was sleeping through all this commotion.

I picked up the phone again with such anger and redialed the club.

"Dighton Golf Course," the bartender answered with a happy tone.

I couldn't imagine how anyone could sound so happy at midnight waiting for drunks to go home to their families.

"RICHARD LOPES?" I replied through my teeth.

"I'm not sure if he's still here. Hold on."

I wanted to shout, "Stop playing games. We both know he's there."

Wives have to play these mind games with their drunken husbands; having to go along with them, made me wild. It felt like I was on hold for ten minutes before he picked up.

"YES?" he replied, in an obviously disgusted and embarrassed tone because I was still calling him.

For that second, I wished that I had no kids. He would have come home and found me gone. I was so angry that he was back to drinking, and I had to walk on eggshells so no one would get upset.

"I NEED your help." I yelled. Now, I lost it and my tears started. "What's wrong with you? Don't you know that I have to be desperate to call you?"

"Things came up, Alberta."

"Important issues don't come up at midnight unless it's an emergency in your family!"

"OKAY, I HEAR YOU. SEE YOU IN A WHILE," he yelled and hung up.

I finally got Lori quieted down. I held her close to me and wrapped a blanket around her. I sat in the rocker and cuddled her against me, softly singing the same song that I had sung to Debbie when she was younger. My mother taught it to me, and it became their favorite. It always comforted them.

"Down in the meadow in a little bitty pool, Swam three little fishies and a mama fishie too, "Swim" said the mama fishie, "Swim if you can" And they swam and they swam all over the dam, Boop boop dit-tem dat-tem what-tem Chu! Boop boop dit-tem dat-tem what-tem Chu! Boop boop dit-tem dat-tem what-tem Chu! And they swam and they swam all over the dam."

I kept repeating the first lyric because I never took the time to learn the other lines. Her body started to relax, and she laid her head on my shoulder. I felt guilty having been so upset with her. It was too much, emotionally, being livid with Richie and trying to stop her crying. Maybe Lori sensed my tenseness.

My shoulders and arms ached by now. I looked down and saw how swollen and blotchy her little face was from the hours of sobbing. I kissed her gently on the forehead.

I finally placed her in bed and covered her up. I looked down and saw how peaceful she became. I prayed nothing would wake her. Richie still wasn't home and it was after 1 a.m. Instead of crawling into bed, I made one last call to the club. I knew deep down that I shouldn't because I was still mad.

The phone rang once, and when the bartender picked up, I didn't give him a chance to say hello. I demanded, "I want to speak to Richie, and I know he's there." By now there was no need for giving his last name.

After the bartender returned, he stated in a trained speech, "Sorry, but he left a few minutes ago."

I went into the bedroom and undressed. When I tried to lie down, my body felt as stiff as a board. My heart was racing and it pounded in my chest from frustration.

It wasn't long before the front door opened. When he entered the bedroom, I made off that I was in a deep sleep.

He shook my shoulder hard. "I want to talk to you."

"I'm exhausted, and I don't want to talk right now. We'll talk in the morning, let me sleep. Besides, I don't want the kids to wake up; I just got Lori down ten minutes ago."

I forced myself to be nice so he wouldn't make a scene. If he did, the girls would get scared. I wanted to jump up and start pounding him for what he had put me through.

"I want to talk NOW!" he snarled.

"No, Richie. You want to argue, and I'm not going to."

My insides were shaking trying to stay calm.

"Okay, if that's how you feel about it," he said and started to take his clothes off to get into bed.

He smelled of liquor and the room filled up with the sickening odor. He hit his pillow and went out like a light. I tried to do the same, but I was mentally a mess. My mind was racing with thoughts of all the nights he had stayed out late drinking with his buddies. I couldn't help the fear that was overtaking me that he was falling back into the same habit. I didn't know how I could live that way again. I loved my husband and I longed for the gentle, caring man he had been for a few years. I didn't know how to stop his desire to drink. He needed help. Our families didn't know about our problems, and I didn't want to inform them. I still had hope that he would quit on his own, then I wouldn't have to deal with explaining his behavior to them. I stayed awake thinking, for what seemed like hours.

Somehow, by the grace of God, I fell asleep.

Chapter Twenty-Two
Trying to Hold Us Together

The next morning Richie got up and acted as if nothing had happened. Instead of sitting down and talking calmly about the previous night, we ignored it. He took his coffee and headed down the stairs to his shop. By afternoon he was on his way delivering the television sets that were repaired. I sat, emotionally drained, with no energy to do anything.

Later that evening, he came straight home after his deliveries. I didn't bring up the fight, because it would have led into another night of stress. I tried to hide my anger in front of the kids, but my insides were racing.

He was home for supper, and we sat in silence, except when we talked to the girls. The silent tension was just as bad as an argument. The strain between us was so thick you could have cut it with a knife. I couldn't find anything nice to talk about because I was still fuming. I became an expert at holding my hurt and resentment in to keep peace within the house. My first concern was to not let Debbie and Lori feel the hostility between us. I wasn't facing the reality that they were aware something wasn't right with Mommy and Daddy because we were always upset.

After what seemed like hours of silence, Richie spoke first. "I have a few buddies who are taking their wives out Saturday night for dinner at Georgio's Restaurant. Think we could join them?"

I swallowed hard, holding my bottled-up rage. I wanted to tell him what he could do with his night out. It took everything in me to act interested. There was no desire to talk to him. If the girls weren't around, I would have had a rip-roaring argument.

"Do I know any of them?"

"You know Frank and Wendy. I introduced you to them at the shop in Somerset a few years ago."

A hello and goodbye was our introduction; as though I'd remember them?

"Bill, Cathy, Pete and Joan will be there. I don't think you've met them."

I sat there thinking how honored we should feel that our husbands were acknowledging their wives on a Saturday night. It's a compromise they make for leaving us home all week with the kids and coming in smashed so many nights. I couldn't help feeling bitter.

"I'd have to see if Anita can watch the kids."

"I'm sure she will," he said in a friendly voice.

After a night of drinking, he always reverted back to the man I once knew. By then, I'd be too upset to enjoy his niceness.

Lori and Debbie were so excited that their father was home and giving them attention. They were grabbing their games and toys, placing them in front of him. While he entertained the girls, I decided to call Anita after I cleaned the kitchen

"Daddy lets play Chutes and Ladders," Debbie said as she took the cover off the game.

"That should be fun," he said hugging her as he knelt down on the rug.

Lori crawled on top of his back and sat there. They treated him like a king. Watching him play with them, I felt myself becoming jealous. *He stays out, comes home late, disrupts the family, and they're falling all over him.* That's what I wanted, but I couldn't control my resentment. I hated these feelings.

I went to call Anita, "Do you and Sonny have anything special going on Saturday? I'd like to leave the girls with you for a few hours. We've been invited to go to Georgio's Restaurant." It was extremely rare that we went anywhere without the girls.

"We have no plans as of yet. I don't see any problem."

"Thanks, Anita." We spoke a few minutes, catching up on what was going on with our kids. I never mentioned the problem with Richie and his drinking. I didn't want Sonny to think less of his brother.

When I hung up, Richie leaned back and looked up at me from the floor, "Sounds like we're set to go."

"They have no plans," I stated coldly.

It wasn't easy getting the girls away from him to get washed and into their pajamas.

"Get going and do what your mother says," he insisted as he playfully tapped them on their bums while they ran to the bathroom giggling. All of a sudden, he was acting like a father. So easy, one night out of a month!

It was another hour getting them settled, especially with Lori. She constantly used excuses to stay up longer. Either she was thirsty or didn't feel good. When I was alone with her, I'd stand on my head to please her in order to get time to myself. Her game started to wear thin after awhile.

I started to feel smothered; keeping the children occupied all day long and trying to deal with a marriage that seemed non-existent. I could handle the everyday problems but not the added stress from my husband. I felt totally used.

When is my time going to come? What happened to me? Where did I disappear to? Where is the marriage that I dreamed of with happy times and proud parenting? Where's the togetherness? I felt like I was drowning in quicksand and losing my identity.

I gathered my nightwear and went to take my bath. I let the hot, scalding water run until the steam filled the room and the bathroom mirror fogged up. Richie was home and I didn't have to watch the clock waiting for him.

While I was locked behind the bathroom door all alone, I wanted to be taken on a long voyage away from my family. I took a magazine from the shelf and laid my head back on the bath pillow to read. My body sank until the hot water reached the top of my shoulders. The heat was uncomfortable at first. Slowly, I forced my body to immerse in it and enjoy the pleasure of being completely and absolutely in an atmosphere of tranquility.

I could hear Lori crying out, "Mommy?"

"Mommy's taking a bath, go to sleep," Richie yelled.

"I'm thirsty, Daddy."

"No, you're not. You just drank a glass of milk. I don't want to hear any more from you."

I closed my eyes, took a deep breath, and blocked Lori's whining from my mind. I told myself that he was going to handle whatever was on the other side of the door.

If it wasn't for the fact that I craved silence for serenity, I would have been ecstatic to hear the girls screaming at the top of their lungs. I wanted him to feel what I went through all day long—alone.

Within a half hour the water cooled off. I pulled the chain on the plug with my big toe and stayed in the tub until the water got low. A chill went through me when it started emptying out. I stood up and dried myself off with an over-sized, brown, fluffy towel. My fingers were wrinkled from staying in the bath so long and my skin was red as a lobster.

"Your turn," I said to Richie as I headed for the bedroom.

"Any hot water left?" He joked.

"Should be," I said shrugging my shoulders.

Why couldn't he be like this all the time? I thought as he passed and hugged me. His sign of affection didn't make me melt, because I couldn't erase what happened the night before. How can I be turned on by a husband who hurts me?

I crawled under the blanket with my magazine. The room still contained the stale smell of liquor from the night before. He was home, and I had mixed feelings. I complained when he was out, and then when he was home, I wished that he wasn't. How did that make sense?

I desperately needed time alone to separate myself from everyone else's problems; I wanted to just worry about me. My mind was tired of trying to find ways to bring my husband home and acting cheerful with the kids when I didn't feel it.

After a fifteen minute shower, Richie came in and threw back the covers on his side to lie next to me. I was praying he didn't want any intimacy.

What's wrong with me? I want us to get close and put our marriage together, and yet, when he comes to make love, I tighten up. Letting my guard down wasn't easy on top of being loveable to a husband who made my days and nights miserable. It was asking too much of me. Everyday, my feelings were being turned off and on with his drinking getting out of hand.

He leaned over and put his arm around me. "I'm sorry about last night."

It was agonizing. I couldn't say that it was okay because it wasn't; I couldn't get mad because we would have had a big argument, I couldn't scream at him because the girls would have heard us. I didn't know how to talk about it. It was either days of silence or walking out. I felt the pressure deep into my chest; it was building up like a huge volcano waiting to erupt.

Instead of answering him, I put my hand on his, desperately wanting to love him. It was like he was asking me to put my hand on a hot stove after being burned so often. I was petrified to reach out again.

We avoided what was needed the most—to talk. He had taken the first step by mentioning the event and admitting to being in the wrong. I should have voiced my feelings in a calm manner. That's how I could have reached the intimacy that had been missing. Since the problem wasn't discussed, it could get easier for him to stop saying, "I'm sorry," and he might think that it was okay to repeat the drinking. Mixed vibrations would continue, and neither of us would know what the other was thinking or feeling if we didn't mention our needs. Our desire to get close would fade.

I didn't want to bring up his pattern of drinking and staying out late through the years, so I avoided the subject completely. I was afraid our talking would lead into a fight.

Instead of focusing on his drinking, this was the perfect time to tell him how good it felt having him home spending time with us. I should have concentrated on his positive actions. I wasn't expressing what the kids or I needed. He wasn't sharing what he was going through mentally and physically. After awhile, we lost the perspective on what was important as a family. Our confusion and battles became our normal life style.

I'd prayed daily for God to give me the strength to keep the marriage going. I knew that it was me keeping us together, but who was going to keep me together? I was afraid that if we separated, our relationship wouldn't be the same, and the kids would be devastated. My heart broke knowing how much the girls loved us both; they were so innocent.

He gave me a kiss, and I could smell the liquor on his breath. How I grew to hate that stench, it became the biggest turn-off. I pushed my emotions aside and embraced my husband. We made love, and I felt empty. I desperately needed the emotional part of our relationship which we both omitted to express.

I put my head on his shoulder and hoped he might open up and tell me his feelings. Instead of waiting for him to tell me, I should have been forward and asked him. It could have started a discussion with our problems. The silence made the stress worse, and yet, I didn't know how to start a simple conversation about what I needed. Somehow, we were lost as partners.

I closed my eyes as he held my hand. I longed for him to someday give up his drinking so we could have a secure family life. I still looked at the problem as being him instead of a disease.

Chapter Twenty-Three
Georgio's Steak House

Saturday night came and I dressed up in a red dress with gold jewelry and black high heels. I wanted to look sexy and hoped that Richie would comment on my outfit. I longed for a compliment and wanted to see a warm smile and a glow in his eyes when he looked at me. My self-esteem and confidence disappeared years ago. I was starved for attention and flirtation. I wanted to have my heart race and feel my skin come alive when he touched me.

Where had all those feeling gone? I thought as I took my last look in the mirror after applying my cherry lipstick.

He walked into the living room and looked sharp in his black dress pants and royal blue shirt. His pants fit tightly around his firm buttocks. His curly, black hair had started to thin-out on top, but he was still handsome. His dark, brown eyes melted my heart, and I felt excitement stirring inside of me going out without the girls.

"You look fine," I said patting his hard bottom as I passed by.

He grinned. "You're not bad yourself."

We put the girls in their pajamas before we took them to Anita's. They were thrilled to be with their cousins.

When we arrived at the restaurant, everyone was sitting at the bar.

"What'll you have?" Richie asked.

"Order me a ginger ale," I replied placing myself on a bar stool. I wasn't a drinker.

I was introduced to the group; they all seemed friendly and I mixed in easily. It would have been nice to talk privately with the women, but it wasn't the environment for individual conversation. It seemed relaxing and refreshing being out with adults instead of having children hanging on me all day.

By the time we were ready to be seated, Richie was on his second drink.

"Go slow on those, please," I whispered as we went toward the table.

"What are you doing, keeping count?" he asked.

I *was*. My muscles started to tighten up as I watched him down one drink after another. I listened to his every word as he pronounced them. I looked for glassy eyes, and watched to see if he still controlled his balance. I did a full alcoholic study without realizing it.

I noticed the change in behavior of some of the other men in the group. Laughter was filling the room and our conversations became louder. People at the other tables turned and stared at us. Drinks were being ordered and served before the ones in front of them were finished.

After we completed eating, a waitress came over to us. "Richie you have a telephone call from Anita?"

Richie? How did she know his name? Apparently they knew him from his frequent stops after work which I wasn't aware of.

"I hope everything is ok," I stated.

I watched from the table when he picked up the phone near the bar. The conversation was short.

"She's having a problem with Debbie," he said sitting down next to me.

"What kind of problem?" I questioned. "Is she all right?"

"It seems that you forgot to bring her blanket, and she can't get her to sleep without it, she's crying." He gave me a cold look and seemed upset that the night was about to end early.

She never went to sleep without her blanket, holding it by a corner and sucking her thumb. I wanted to kick myself. "How did I forget that?"

"Everything okay Richie?" Mike asked.

"We'll have to leave soon. Our daughter is acting up, she doesn't have her blanket."

"The night's young, she'll survive, crying won't kill her," Mike said snapping his fingers at the waitress to bring him another drink.

Both of us choked down our dessert trying not to seem rushed. It wasn't a good first impression with his new friends.

I could see that Richie was trying to get as many drinks in as he could before we left. I stopped counting.

I tried taking the keys out of his hands when we got to the car. "I'll drive."

"I'm fine. It's only up the street," he said grabbing them back. "Well, that takes care of our big night out. We're the only ones leaving. I don't know why you're not better organized with the kids?"

"You could have remembered, I'm not the only parent, although I feel like it all the time."

"Are you saying that I'm not a good father?" he yelled.

I could see he was getting upset. Once he started to shout at me, I fell silent and held everything in while he drove to his brothers. I got aggravated with myself for not being able to handle his treatment or my fear of speaking up. I was sick of trying to please everyone in my life. It wouldn't take much to get him into a fighting mood, but I wanted him to concentrate on his driving. My silence ended the bickering.

We pulled into Sonny's yard, and he walked ahead of me as though I weren't with him.

"Hi Anita," he said wobbling in with his hands in his back pockets. Someone else would think that he was okay, but I knew better.

Debbie ran up to me. I could tell she had cried for hours from her red eyes and wet cheeks.

"I...I...don't have my...my...blanket, Mommy," she said through sobs.

"I couldn't do a thing for her without that stupid blanket. If you gave me a spare key to your house, I would have gone to get it," Anita said.

"I'm sorry she gave you such a hard time. I can't believe I forgot her blanket."

By now my head was pounding. I could feel a migraine starting from all the tension. I wanted to get home to my comfort zone. When I was home, I wanted to be out, when I was out, I wanted to go home. No matter where I went, there seemed to be problems. Nothing was fun anymore, I felt like a dark, black cloud covered me. The only times that I was myself was when I was with my friends or anywhere without Richie.

I gave Debbie a hug. "Get your dolls, honey, so we can leave."

Lori came walking out of a bedroom into the kitchen light. She rubbed her eyes and started crying.

"Richie, do you think you can take Lori?"

When he walked into the bedroom to get Lori's things, Anita asked softly, "Is something wrong?"

"I'll tell you about it later," I said with tears starting to surface.

Once we got home, Richie showered and jumped into bed. Meanwhile, I changed Lori and calmed both kids before putting them down for the night. Debbie ran for her security blanket and headed for bed. *Bless that girl*, I thought, she rarely fussed. This was the first time she had been upset at Anita's.

I was thankful that Richie passed out. I didn't want to have anything to deal with from him. I lay in bed wide awake. It had been weeks since I had a full night's sleep. I didn't want to think about anything except closing my eyes.

Chapter Twenty-Four
A Night at the Golf Course

The following week, Richie asked me, "How would you like to go to the Dighton Golf Club tonight? It's Friday and Frank is going to be there with his wife, Wendy. She goes there quite often with him."

"You mean to tell me that she finds it fun sitting in a bar all night?" I asked shocked.

"She's with her husband. I want you to see how innocent my nights are when I go there."

"I can't imagine how that would be exciting."

"Why don't you just give it a try? You might be surprised and enjoy yourself."

"I didn't enjoy myself at Georgio's with you."

"This will be different."

"I hate asking Anita on such short notice."

"I'm sure if she can't, she'll let you know."

I called Anita. "We have no plans to go out tonight, that'll be fine."

Before going to the club we dropped the girls off. This time I made sure that Debbie's blanket was packed in her bag.

When we parked in front of the club house, I felt strange being there. I usually rode by it wondering what it was like inside and if any women gathered in this tiny building. It wasn't fancy like most golf club houses, and I wondered what could possibly be entertaining for the wives. They never advertised having large rooms for parties or weddings. There was no landscaping with colorful Rhododendrons or

Azalea plants to dress the building up to give a warm welcome. The driveway was dirt and it created dust which flew in the air, covering the car when we drove in.

"Hi, Richie," Wendy yelled, as she descended on my husband. It had been dark in Georgio's when I last saw her, and I didn't concentrate on her looks. Her hair was long with brown highlights, and her soft feminine features didn't need makeup. A pleasant smile came over her when she greeted us.

She gave Richie a long hug with a peck on his cheek.

"Hi, Alberta, it's nice to see you again." She turned to Frank. "You remember, Alberta?"

"Of course, I do." He was a short, clean-cut looking man in his middle thirties.

"Hi, Frank," I replied.

There were two women sitting at a table. They wore low cut sweaters and short skirts that hid nothing. They flirted openly when they walked over to the men at the pool table. The men acted like teenage boys and giggled like young girls while they studied both women from head to toe with sly looks and knowing laughs. I felt sick just thinking about my husband being in this atmosphere. I wondered if these women hit on him when he was here alone.

"Sit here," Richie said as he led me to a seat at the bar.

"Jack, we'll have some fried shrimp, chicken wings and fried onion rings," he shouted to the bartender. It sounded like a routine order with no hesitation.

I felt like an intruder. No one looked familiar to me, and I wasn't comfortable in the environment. *There must be something wrong with me. I'm never comfortable when we go out together*, I thought, putting a forced smile on my face. I tried to ignore the commotion with the men to the left of me. I was afraid that if they caught me looking at them they would think I was flirting; being in my husband's company didn't make me feel any safer.

"So, how's the television business?" Frank asked.

"It's been busy, which is good," Richie answered slapping Frank on the shoulder before sipping his first beer.

"How did you make out with Beverly's television set?" Wendy asked. "She called me wondering if I heard," she said, leaning closer to him.

"I have a few more days until the parts come in. I'll call her."

"I'm sure Beverly will be looking forward to that call," she answered as she slid off her seat and wrapped an arm around Richie reaching for her drink on the bar. She stared directly at him.

Frank acted like an ornament just hanging around, listening to the two of them either joking or flirting. I wasn't quite sure which it was. All I knew was that they were too chummy for my comfort.

The three of them were talking as if I weren't in the room. I couldn't hear everything that they were discussing. I was annoyed, being left out. Richie kept his back to me as he turned to his left to talk to them.

I was upset with Wendy's remark about Beverly and wondered if it was something I should worry about. I felt omitted from his life while everyone talked about his daily routine. He had stopped conversing with me about his customers some time ago. I was hurt that strangers knew more about his business than I did; it rubbed me the wrong way. I couldn't mix in and started to distance myself.

"Alberta, where do you work?" Wendy asked as she leaned against my husband's shoulder. I started to get the sensation that she might be testing me.

The question made me feel that Richie didn't find it important enough to mention me to his friends. I don't think he even knew himself what I did all day.

"I work at home...all day. I chase children; change diapers, run them to the doctors, clean house, do the grocery shopping, and prepare the meals. Are you jealous yet?" I questioned with a smirk on my face.

Richie had a shocked expression, and said to Wendy, who looked embarrassed, "It's not that hard!"

"Really? Try it for a week, Richie, and let me know," I remarked, defending myself. "I think sitting at a desk all day answering phones or keeping busy at a company with multiple tasks would be much easier."

I continued, "Oh, yes, I almost forgot my second job. I answer the phone for Richie's business, schedule his appointments, and return calls. I radio him in his truck to see where he is and if he's going to deliver a TV set that was probably promised weeks ago. Whew, I'm getting tired just talking about it."

"What do you do, Wendy?" I asked waiting for her to beat my agenda.

"I think my job is lighter. I'm a secretary for the President of Stores Limited in Taunton," she answered. "I'm the one with the easier job, I guess."

She smiled back at Richie, seeming proud of her comeback. He laughed with her. I couldn't help but feel that he was helping to make a fool of me. He joined in her game, and it put a knife in me. He knew what she was doing. Men act so foolish in front of women, not knowing they're being pulled in, or do they?

"By having the easier job, you can save energy for the end of the day so you can spend the time here with Frank while he drinks," I replied. I didn't like her by now and didn't care if she knew it. I felt that I had her number.

I shocked myself at how good I was with throwing remarks back and forth. It's funny how I could stand up to strangers but not to family members.

My remark was ignored as the food was placed in front of us. The conversation switched back to the three of them talking about other people and events that I never heard about from Richie. I reached over to pick a few fried chicken wings off the plate.

The hours dragged, and I couldn't wait to go home. Within that time, three of Richie's buddies came in and joined the group. I was again introduced to strangers. By now, I was the only one sober in the group. They were arguing over stupid things, and the men were trying to hit on Wendy while her husband joked with them. I wondered how she could think that their behavior was a compliment.

I was uneasy by now and had enough of what was supposed to be a fun night out. Listening to screaming babies was starting to sound good to me.

"Richie, it's getting late, and I think we should get home."

"Home—it's only eleven o'clock! What's the matter? Why don't you try mixing in with us?"

I tried to whisper, "Why don't you *include* me? You're all starting to slur your words. Is that supposed to be fun?"

"God, Alberta, you don't know how to socialize," he said shaking his head.

"We're leaving *now*," I insisted. "I have to get up early to take care of the kids. They don't sleep in because I've been out late. Besides, Anita has to get her rest."

I grabbed our coats and handed Richie his.

"Sorry, folks; the lady wants to go home," he said trying to be funny. I knew he was upset that I had again ended his night with his friends.

"Oh come on, Alberta, the nights just beginning," Frank said.

"Not at midnight boys. Nice meeting all of you."

Richie was once again insisting that he was in control to drive to Anita's.

"You're in no condition to be behind a wheel."

"I'm capable of driving, leave me alone."

I gave in, better than a long argument, I figured.

We arrived at his Anita's and woke the girls from their sleep.

Once we all had piled into the car, I prayed we'd get home safely. My eyes watched every thing moving on the street while he drove. I was thankful that we only lived a few miles down the road.

Chapter Twenty-Five
Intoxication

Anita called during the week. "Why don't you and Richie come out to eat with Sonny and me? We're going with my sister, Laurie and her husband Ray, and a few friends to Georgio's for supper." Our small town only had one fancy restaurant.

"I'd have to see if I can get a babysitter. I don't have anyone to watch the girls but you."

"Let me call Sonny's mother," Anita offered. "She's at May's for the week. I can pick her up on our way. We'll only be a few minutes from the house"

"I don't know, Anita. She's never been with the kids."

"How hard will it be? We'll only be a few hours."

"I guess its okay."

When Richie got home, I mentioned the invite to him. "I'll be uncomfortable having your mother here. She's never been in our home or spent time talking to the girls, much less babysitting. Not once has she ever gone out of her way to speak to me at family gatherings. It's like bringing a stranger in here. Lori's only two and may be frightened seeing her."

"My mother will be fine," he said. "Don't be negative before you even go out."

"I'm very uneasy with this." I tried to be excited but my vibes were making me feel something else.

God, maybe I am a negative person. My husband wants to be with me, and I get uptight going out. I'm always waiting for the bomb to fall.

I got the girls fed, washed, and dressed for bed. "Guess who's coming to take care of you tonight—Vo," I said to Debbie, giving her a squeeze (it was the name all the grandkids called her). I didn't want her to be scared if she woke up and saw her grandmother sitting in the living room.

The girls had never spent time with her. She'd usually just smile at them when they played. Hugs and kisses from her were rare. I'd be the one telling them to go and kiss her.

I felt like I was throwing my daughters to a wolf. *Stop this, Alberta. You're too protective of the girls. You're just nervous.* I couldn't shake the fear that it wasn't right leaving them with my mother-in-law.

I had Lori in bed sleeping when Anita and Sonny came into the house with his mother. Debbie was sitting in the living room waiting to see her.

"Hi, Debbie," Vo said bending down to kiss her. It relaxed me somewhat seeing her being sweet to my daughter.

Debbie looked up at her with a combination of curiosity and fright. I was glad that Lori was sleeping.

I must have had the same look, for my mother-in-law faced me and said, "We'll be fine, you go and have fun."

"I have the telephone number on the desk if you need us for any reason," I said praying that she wouldn't.

We got into Sonny's car, and I tried to leave my fears behind. *Maybe this will be the beginning of the kids getting to know their grandmother.*

It was relaxing being out with couples that didn't over drink. In fact, not many drank at all, and Richie held himself to one drink. Anita's sister and a few friends of hers joined us. It was a fun night, I wasn't up tight about my husband drinking and no one got smashed. The group stayed a few hours, and we headed back to the house.

We pulled into the driveway, and I could see that the living room lights were still on. "I can take Mom home," Richie said.

"Are you sure? It's not that far out of our way," Sonny asked.

"I'll be fine."

They waved as they backed out of the driveway and started home. We opened the front door to the living room and saw his mother asleep in the armchair.

I smelled liquor! I was sensitive to the odor.

I couldn't believe what I was seeing. There was an empty bottle of wine on the floor next to her and a cigarette hanging between her finger tips. The floor was covered with a wall-to-wall nylon rug. I panicked thinking that the cigarette could have fallen. My mind ran wild thinking about what *could* have happened if we stayed out any later.

I was hysterical, running over to grab the cigarette out of her hand. It was still lit! I ran to the bathroom and threw it in the toilet.

I came back and yelled at Richie, "My God, the house could have burned down with our kids in it!"

He tried waking her, and she didn't move a muscle. How she kept the cigarette in her fingers was a miracle.

Suddenly, I looked up and Debbie was standing in the doorway of her bedroom with her arm around Lori, in my hysteria, I hadn't noticed them. Lori stood there with both her legs in one pajama pant leg. Debbie was four and protective of her two-year-old sister as she stood next to her.

"I changed her," Debbie said with such pride in her eyes. "She was wet and crying. Vo was sleeping."

"Yes, she was." My eyes filled with tears knowing they were safe.

Lori looked so tiny standing next to her sister. She had the biggest grin on her face, as if Debbie did the greatest thing for her. I will never forget that sight.

Richie continued shaking his mother by both her shoulders with no results. "Mom, wake up. Do you hear me? Wake up!"

"I'm calling Anita," he said running to the phone.

They had just arrived at home.

"Sonny, Mom's here, and she's out like a light...drunk. What should we do?"

He heard Sonny talking to Anita in the background. "We'll be right over."

I readjusted Lori's pajama bottoms.

"Debbie, what a big girl you were helping your sister," I said kissing her. I hugged them both longer and tighter than normal thinking we could have lost them.

"I called Vo, Mommy, but she wouldn't wake up. Lori was crying."

"Yes, Mommy knows. That's okay. Daddy will take Vo home, she's tired."

I put them both into bed and covered them up. It wouldn't have been good for them to see their grandmother being carried out of the house.

It was only minutes before his family arrived. One look at his mother and Anita knew from her past drinking experiences that this was serious.

"My God, I think she's in an alcoholic coma," Anita said.

"I'll call an ambulance," I said running to the phone.

"NO!" Richie yelled. "There's no need, she'll be fine.

"If you don't want her to go, you and Sonny take the responsibility if something happens to your mother. I want nothing to do with this, because if she's dead in the morning, it'll be your fault," Anita snapped. "Don't blame me."

They finally agreed to take her to Charlton Memorial Hospital in Fall River.

"I'll call you when we know her condition," Anita said.

About an hour and a half had gone by when the phone rang, it was Anita. "The doctor is pumping her stomach. They're planning to admit her overnight. Another half hour and she might not have made it; they're taking this very seriously."

"Thanks, Anita." She always handled the family crises. "How are the boys?"

"They sat in the car and wouldn't come in."

"What?"

"They were embarrassed. I had to go into the Emergency Room and tell them that she was drunk and that I didn't know how to handle her. They gave me a wheelchair, and I took it out to the car, your husband put her in the chair. The situation was awkward because I had to go in alone with her."

"I can't believe they didn't go in!" I replied.

Anita continued, "Then the questions flew at me; how was I related; any family around and I told them her sons were outside. The doctor said, 'We can't let her go home because she could throw up and choke on it. We'll have to keep her till morning.' So, I left her there. She was still out."

"I'm sorry that you had to handle another situation yourself.

"It's okay. I'll talk to you tomorrow."

When Richie returned, I asked him, "Where did she find the bottle of wine?"

"She must have discovered it in the corner hutch."

We received liquor as Christmas gifts each year. Richie never drank at home. She had to search real hard to find the bottle.

"Your mother will *never* baby-sit for us again as long as I live," I snapped under my breath.

Anita called the next day. "I went to see Vo."

"How was she?"

"She's still drunk and made no sense talking."

"Can you imagine the alcohol staying in her system all this time?" I said. "I get sick thinking what could have happened last night. Thanks for your help, Anita."

My mother-in-law didn't come to our home again after that incident, and we never asked her to baby-sit. I thanked God that she and our daughters were safe, but there was the potential for disaster. The near catastrophe snapped Richie out of his heavy drinking and coming home wanting to fight. He stopped now and then at the golf club but was home at a decent hour. It was an awful way for the family to benefit from someone overdrinking.

Chapter Twenty-Six
Heidi

A year passed and Richie and I thought it was time to search for a puppy. We both loved animals and we knew the girls would love one. His favorite pet had been a baby pig when he was eight-years old; it followed him every morning to the bus stop. Until it became big, it had become a pet for all the kids waiting to go to school.

I called a woman who put an ad in the paper after her German Shepherd delivered a litter. All the pups had their shots and were ready to be given new homes.

"Richie, I'm not too sure how their temperament would be with children," I said with caution.

"What can it hurt to just go and look, they're part Lab and that's a gentle breed."

"Please, Mommy, let's go. Please, please, please," Debbie said looking up with pleading eyes.

"Ok, but if I don't like them, I want no crying. We can keep looking," I said firmly.

Her house was only a few miles away. The girls pushed by us to be the first ones standing on the steps in front of the wooden door. The woman opened it with a big smile.

"Hi, I'm Alberta Lopes. I just called about the puppies."

"Come right in."

She led us into her kitchen where there were four fluffy-haired puppies running in every direction. They all had the same black and brown markings. Two were jumping on each other and nipping at each other's ears. One ran and slid across the floor when we came upon it too quickly and scared it. The puppy hit the cabinet door with a bang, almost knocking itself out.

The largest one was lapping milk out of a bowl with its two front paws in the middle of it. Once he finished, he waddled away with a big stomach and his paws left milk marks on the kitchen floor where he walked.

The girls went crazy trying to catch them. Lori fought to hold one until its weight was too heavy for her tiny hands. She didn't have much strength, being only three-years old.

"Lori, be careful, honey. You'll hurt it if he falls," Richie said as he tried to help her balance the puppy in her arms.

I looked harder into a corner and there lay another puppy. It was so quiet resting its chin on the floor. Only its deep, onyx eyes moved as it looked up at me. It looked completely bored with the activities from its siblings. I could see that it was the runt of the litter. It was the only one that had white markings on its paws and face.

The girls were playing with the other puppies when one grabbed onto the bottom of Lori's pant leg. It growled and shook its head wildly as it tugged with a death grip on them. She started to slide with the puppy on the floor.

"Oh, Daddy, look at this one," Debbie said as she bent over it. The puppy leaped upward and its head hit her under her chin, stunning her for a second. We were tripping over them as they ran under our feet. All of them wanted our attention so we'd play with them.

I bent down to pat the puppy that was taking everything in while it separated itself from the pack. It stayed still as I ran my hand down the soft fur on its back.

"Is this a male or female?" I asked the owner.

"It's a female. She's the runt of the litter."

"I can see that," I answered.

"Mommy, I want this one," Debbie groaned as she tried lifting it. The puppy was like butter in her hands. She couldn't hold it for very long as it pushed its legs against her chest and leaped onto the floor with a thump.

The woman spoke again to me. "She's a very quiet pup, but she does have moments when she joins right in with the rest of them."

Lori was crying as she held her choice. "I want this one."

"We can't take two, Lori," Richie answered. "What do you think?" he whispered leaning over to me.

I gently picked the runt up in my arms, and she licked my face. That was it; the smell of the puppy hit me. I loved it. It had the same effect as a new born baby's powdered body.

"We're going to take this one," I said smiling without looking at anyone or waiting for a vote.

Richie knew that I wasn't going to change my mind.

Driving home, the puppy lay quietly, as it stretched out its body on the laps of both the girls in the backseat.

"What do you want to name her?" Richie asked looking back at the girls.

"Let's name her Heidi," Debbie said.

"Yeah," Lori agreed as she hugged it.

"It's fine with me. What do you say, Mom?" Richie said looking at me.

"I think it's a great name."

That's how we brought Heidi into our family. She stayed in our lives for thirteen years and kept her gentle ways. She was a great pick and never snapped when the girls jumped on her.

Debbie sat nightly on the floor with Heidi watching television. She'd hold her blanket and suck her thumb. There she would lie, flicking the tip of Heidi's ear with her finger. The ears never stood-up straight and ended up drooping down because of it.

When Heidi was a year, she sat under the front hedges outside to stay in the shade on hot sunny days. It was rare that she ever left our yard except to follow the kids to their friends up the street. She ran to greet Richie each time he drove into the yard.

She became a great companion to me when I was alone, and there were many times I was. Heidi was a devoted friend and loved all of us. Our days were full of activity with her, and she became a member of our family.

Lori loved Heidi, but she was most content when she was tucked in bed with her eight dolls all around her. Sometimes it would be hard to find her among them. We bought the girls a children's 365 day storybook. It was the high-point of their night when they picked out their favorite story to be read.

Chapter Twenty-Seven
Financial Problems

Slowly, Richie's drinking picked up again and so did our arguments. He soon forgot about his mother's intoxication in our home. He'd arrive home after supper, and I could smell the liquor as soon as he walked through the door. I was back waiting to see if he came home sober or drunk. I decided one evening to go visit Vic and May, I thought since they were family, they'd be able to help us.

I directed my question to Vic since he had been through a drinking problem. "I need to share a serious problem with you. Our marriage is rocky, and I don't know how to stop it. Richie stays out almost every night drinking. I'm worried about him. Can you talk to him, Vic?"

May cut in and started using every excuse for his actions. She didn't want to face the reality of her brother's drinking. Vic, on the other hand, felt differently.

"May, how can any man expect to have a marriage if he's out every night drinking?" Vic replied.

"Well, I heard that you're out a lot, Alberta." She stated.

"I am?"

"Well, I heard that you go to the gym a lot with Anita."

"Yes, I joined a health club with Anita and your sister, Lena, in North Dartmouth and we go one night a week. I have to beg your brother to baby-sit in order to go, I do need an outlet." I was surprised hearing her remark.

"It doesn't matter who's doing what," Vic snapped back. "I've been through that life. You can't have a marriage staying out in a bar after work."

I loved Vic because he was so honest and fair. The three of us discussed the situation and promises flew around the living room about how they would talk to him. If they did, I never knew about it.

I felt alone and trapped, unless I was with Cindy. Because her life was in as much turmoil as mine with Ernie staying out, she understood my situation, and she always gave me support when I needed it. No matter what the two of us did, our husbands continued to drink and stay out late. Cindy's situation became worse when gossip started getting back to her that Ernie was seeing someone. I feared the same was true with Richie.

I knew it wouldn't take long for this to happen to me because he was making himself susceptible to it. I wasn't ignorant about the women who were hanging around the bars looking for company and ready to latch onto the first available man They'd jump onto a man when he started with the "My wife doesn't understand me" story, that is, if they admitted to having a wife. These women wouldn't care if the complaints were true or not, their aim was to find a man who would entertain them. If he had money to spend on them, all the better; they had hit the jackpot!

Richie had been invited on a weekend fishing trip with a friend who owned a boat. I welcomed his absence and agreed so selfishly I'd have a weekend to be able to breathe. It was wonderful not looking at the clock, holding off supper, and spending time with the girls without stress.

On Monday, I was washing clothes when I felt something in his pants pocket. I stood there with a motel key in my hand. I was sick.

I went into the shop and confronted him. He used the excuse that it belonged to one of the guys on the trip and he had asked him to drop it off. He acted as though I was completely stupid. He was right, but my stupidity was in staying with him. My world fell to pieces. That would have been enough for any couple to break up. I wanted to leave, but felt I was unable to. Fear for the girls not having their father around; fear of being on my own; fear of having to explain to family and friends after hiding our troubles for so long. Being unable to make a decision to leave him, immobilized me.

I had no knowledge at the time that it took years for an alcoholic's bad behavior to come out. The changes happened slowly, and I overlooked them until our lives started to become unmanageable. When Richie told me years ago about his family's history with drinking, I should have tried to get professional help. The signs were there that he was following the same path. I just never pieced it together, as unbelievable as it may sound.

His drinking was getting worse, and the business started to fall behind. He had an answering service, but he wasn't returning the calls. Around 6:00 p.m., I began taking all the messages from the service. The *return call* slips piled up.

Customers were upset: "Where's my television set? I gave it to your husband weeks ago, he said it needed a tube, how long does that take? I haven't heard a word from him. If it's ready, I'll pick it up."

Now, strangers were putting stress on me. It didn't take long to run out of excuses for his customers. People who wanted repairs got tired of waiting for service and took their business elsewhere. I thought about how good his business could have been if he had been serious about it. He let his reputation turn sour, and his word was worth nothing to his clients. There was a time that he was so loved by everyone, but now I saw that admiration change dramatically.

"Richie, what are you doing to your business? Mr. Johnson called, and you told him his set would be ready last week. He'll be calling back soon."

"Don't worry, Alberta, I'll have it ready. I don't know why you're so concerned? It's my business."

"It's *my* business," I snapped, "because *I'm* the one taking the calls and trying to find answers for these people. You don't bother looking at your messages to see who needs a call back. Even your answering service is getting upset because your customers are taking it out on them." I grabbed the pad with the messages. "Look at the calls I've taken in just two days from people who wanted your service."

"I'll get to them," he replied, but I knew he wouldn't.

"By the time you do, they'll have gone to someone else. Don't get a bad name, Richie, for yourself or the business. No one will want your services. It doesn't take long for word of mouth to shut your company down."

"I'm waiting for parts to come in. I can't do anything without them."

"That's fine. *Call* the customer and *tell* them. All they want is a call back."

"There's a lot to do, and I'm only one person running this company."

"I've told you long ago to hire one man or a high school student and see how it works out. You may have a different attitude working with someone who could take the load off you."

"You make it sound easy."

"You have to start somewhere."

"We can't afford to pay someone."

"We can't afford for you to lose the business. I'll tell you what. Tomorrow I'll call your cousin, Josephine, and see if she'll teach me the bookkeeping for the business. Since she does this every day, she'll know which spreadsheets we would need to get set up. This way everything will be logged in, and you won't have to worry about that part of it. When tax time comes, the books will be in order and ready for us to give to the accountant. What do you say? It should take a lot of pressure off you."

"That would help me."

The next day, I called Josephine. She agreed to help me and even got me a ledger, since I didn't know which one was needed. I arranged for her to come by the following morning at 10 o'clock to help me.

I was thrilled to be doing something so important for Richie. Josephine was on time and spent a few hours explaining things to me, but she actually set the books up.

"I'm going to fill in the titles at the top of the books, and they'll explain themselves. All you have to do is enter the receipts every day so you won't get mixed up. I'll break down the parts, gas slips, deposits and all." She sped right along setting up the system; having been a bookkeeper for so many years, she knew all the particulars of a spreadsheet.

It looked simple. She labeled every detail for me. "This is great, Josephine."

"Let me know if you have any trouble, I'll walk you through it."

I was so excited helping with the business and learning bookkeeping. My mind was going to be working again and doing something useful. I started thinking this might have been why he had been drinking so much, the stress of doing the repairs and having to do his own books could have put him under a lot of pressure.

I had him put all the receipts into a box at the end of the day. I couldn't wait to get time to myself to dig into the books. I made the deposit slips out so he could make the trip to the bank. I gave him an allowance that would give him money during the week for expenses, but nothing extra so it wouldn't be easy for him to buy drinks after work.

Weeks passed, and he pushed himself back into work, but he continued to be out nights drinking.

"I'm going to call and cancel the answering service," he said.

"Why?"

"I don't need it.

"That'll leave me answering the phone." I blew! My head started to spin thinking of something else put on me.

The phone rang off the hook. Not knowing if it was family or not, I'd have to answer it.

Money was disappearing from our account. I'd put money on the dining room table to be deposited and discover some missing.

"Richie, I had a deposit of $400 this morning and $200 is missing."

"Oh, I needed some money."

"How can I balance the books or get ahead if you take it before it even gets into the bank?"

"Just deduct it. Can't you figure that out?"

"When I give you a bank slip, I expect you to make the deposit that's posted. I give you money every day. Where did the $200 go?"

"Do I have to explain every penny to you? How do I know? Things come up when I'm out."

After months of frustration, I gave up keeping the books. I started taking some cash left on the table and deposited $600 in the bank over eight months without telling him, proving how easily we could save if he gave us a chance.

I never told him, and he never looked at the bank statements. He was more concerned with the cash on hand. I thought this would be a way to get a cushion for the future. When we really needed it, I'd surprise him.

We traded our Chevrolet Impala in for a used green Volkswagen two door sedan with a standard shift. It was cheaper to run and I loved it, and so did the kids, it was like driving a toy.

A few weeks later, Debbie came down with a fever and chills. I tried aspirin and bed rest but she wasn't getting better. I called the doctor's office and was lucky to get an appointment that afternoon. It turned out to be the flu which was going around and the doctor gave me an antibiotic for her.

A month later a bill for one hundred dollars came in from the doctor's office with a notice stating that Blue Cross Blue Shield had refused to pay the bill. I called the insurance company and was upset to learn that the policy had been cancelled. I insisted that there had to be a mistake. Somehow, they must have mixed us up with another policy holder, but the girl said that they hadn't received a payment in eight months.

"Why didn't you send me any notices?" I said angrily.

"Our records show that there were three notices sent to you. Do you need the dates? I can send you the copies."

Richie was in charge of paying the bills. I had to wait till he got home to get answers.

"No, that won't be necessary. What can I do to reinstate the policy?

"You'd have to fill out the entry forms again, Mrs. Lopes."

"Let me get back to you after I check with my husband," I said trying not to take it out on the poor girl.

I was worried about how we would be able to pay such a high doctor's bill. I couldn't believe he would ignore paying our health insurance. It didn't make sense.

I was a surprised when he came home for supper. I waited till the kitchen was clean and the girls were happily playing in the other room.

"Richie, I got a bill today for Debbie's doctor's appointment last month. I called Blue Cross Blue Shield, and they said we were cancelled. Do you know why?"

"I was going to pay it but we didn't have enough cash in the account to make the monthly payments," he explained.

"Since when did we have a problem paying a bill?"

"I had other ones to take care of at the time."

"You don't let important coverage like this lapse. Why didn't you talk to me about it? This isn't like you. Now what do we do?"

"Just request another form."

"Do you realize what I have to go through? We have to put a good five-hundred dollars out just to get on the plan again. How do we pay that plus the monthly payments?"

"I can't deal with this now," he said, becoming angry.

"I shouldn't be dealing with this in the first place," I said. "We have two small children. They get sick and have accidents. That's not including what could happen to us. All we need is for one of us to end up in the hospital. We'd never be able to pay it."

"Well, I have to go down and take a television set out of the truck."

And off he went, leaving me standing with the bill in my hand. From then on, I became more aware of statements coming in the mail and opened them. A few weeks later, a statement came showing our life insurance policy had elapsed.

"Richie, our life insurance policy stopped."

"I couldn't make the payments. It's not really that important anyway. We're young. Why do we need it?"

"I'm taking over the finances."

"Fine with me," he said with relief. "That's less I have to worry about."

Assuming this responsibility didn't help us any. He collected the money from the customers, but I never saw it. Everything seemed to be collapsing around me.

As much as I tried, I couldn't make any headway, and after a week of frustration, I confronted him. "I'm making an appointment with a counselor to talk about your drinking."

"You're what?" he asked in disbelief.

"You heard me."

"Who are you calling?"

"I have no idea. Guess I'll be pulling names out of a hat." I was too embarrassed to ask anyone if they knew of someone to call. I didn't want anyone to know.

"I don't have a problem," he insisted.

"Would you go halfway with me and talk to someone."

To my amazement, he said, "I don't like it, but yes, I'll go."

I went through the names in the telephone book and picked a "Mr. Ralph Cummings." The appointment was made for the next week on a Monday morning at ten o'clock. I held my breath hoping Richie would keep the appointment.

He gave me no argument and went to the meeting. Mr. Cummings seemed to have no personality, but at least he welcomed us with a warm smile. I felt uncomfortable in his office. He was all business. I wondered how important our problems were going to be to him. I looked around and saw a few framed graduation degrees hung on the wall.

"So, Mrs. Lopes, why are you here?"

"I believe my husband has a drinking problem."

"What makes you think that?"

"Because he stays out drinking every night and we're constantly fighting about it."

"Well, I have a drink every night before dinner. It doesn't make me an alcoholic."

"I told you I didn't have a problem," Richie said with delight.

Oh, my Lord, of all the counselors listed in the telephone book, and I pick this man! He can't be serious? There's no way he's going to understand the situation.

"Does your drinking cause a problem at home, Mr. Cummings?" I asked.

"Of course not!" he said surprised at my questioning him.

"Well—my husband's does."

"Tell me about your life, Mrs. Lopes."

"Excuse me?"

"Your family life, tell me about your parents."

"Why?"

"Let me hear about your relationship with them."

I was taken aback; I didn't need another person in authority digging into my weaknesses. The next hour was spent with him analyzing all my siblings and my mother. He described her as the "queen bee" and all of us kids as the "worker bees" who had to protect her.

"Well, Mrs. Lopes, I believe we should meet again and discuss this further."

"What did all this questioning have to do with my husband's drinking?"

"I don't think he has a problem. I think you have issues to be dealt with about family. My secretary can make an appointment."

I walked out furious! Richie was content. "I told you I had no problem."

"If you think I'm keeping this appointment, you're nuts," I said steaming. "He calls himself a counselor? We came here for help with your drinking, and he turns on me. He drinks, so he thinks you're fine? He never once asked us *one* question about your family's history with drinking."

That was the end of getting Richie back to a counselor. In his mind, he had a stamp of approval on his forehead about drinking. Out of all the wonderful doctors and counselors out there, I picked one that shouldn't even be practicing. It took weeks for me to get over the incident. He didn't have to tell me about my insecurities. I already knew them.

Chapter Twenty-Eight
The Monkey Trees

I had been so wrapped up in Richie's actions that I became blind to the serious changes in my own mental state. The stress caused me to have migraine headaches for days. I was unhappy all the time. My laughter became non-existent. When I felt shaky, I wanted to visit friends so I wouldn't be alone. After staying for an hour, I wanted to run back home to hide. I didn't know how to deal with the confusion.

I didn't want to tell my family about Richie's drinking and our horrible life. My parents and siblings still didn't know our world was falling apart and had been doing so for years. I didn't want others to see that side of him. My father was a very intelligent man, but it didn't occur to me that he could have been a tremendous help to both of us. For years I kept them in the dark about what we were all going through in our home.

I didn't know how to make demands on my husband without leaving him. He wasn't a kid, and I couldn't keep him locked up in his room. I wasn't living. I existed in a sick emotional and physical condition that was deteriorating my ability to think rationally.

I believed in marriages being forever and took my vows seriously. The words "for better or worse," stayed in my mind. *Nothing runs smooth so this must be our hard time.* I just didn't know how to stop this nightmare. I believed that if I were old enough to get married, then I should be old enough to handle my problems.

I tried changing my thoughts and attitude when Richie came home. First, I'd talk patiently and lovingly to him. I tried to control this bottled up anger inside me. That method didn't work, and my sweetness didn't bring him home. It just gave him a nice atmosphere to walk into after drinking all evening.

I wasn't a screamer, but holding in my hurt, anger, and frustration became difficult. The rage was deep within me, and I was trying to control it in front of the girls. I felt like I was being pulled in every direction.

I didn't know how to express my emotions or defend myself. I was intimidated by an alcoholic husband. Whenever he yelled or disagreed with me, I went into a shell. I'd sit back with no reaction or input. I thought that if he saw my hurt, he'd get himself together and stop drinking. After all, he loved me, didn't he?

I finally tried ignoring the whole situation and not bring the subject up to him. I waited to see what he was going to do each day in order to know how I was going to react. I made no decisions or plans for myself until I could figure out what direction he was taking. I felt guilty wanting a life of my own other than being a wife and mother. One day, I realized that there was no Alberta anymore.

My emotions were up and down every day. There were days where I was so on edge that my body trembled and my hands shook. My heart raced and pounded in my chest to the point where I gasped for breath. My hands were constantly sweaty and clammy. Panic consumed me during the day causing me to feel weak and faint.

One Saturday afternoon, I called Cindy in desperation during a panic attack.

"Hello?"

"Cindy, it's Alberta," I said, hyperventilating.

"What's wrong? You sound awful."

"I think I'm having a breakdown. My insides are racing, and I can't calm down."

"Alberta, get the kids and go for a walk. Don't drive anywhere feeling like this. Get out of the house to get your mind off things. If you come back and feel the same, call and I'll come down. Right now I have to go over to my mother-in-law's house next door, but I won't be long, maybe an hour."

"Ok." It felt good to hear her voice and know that she understood.

I tried to figure out where to take the kids in our neighborhood. Nothing was around except houses. Suddenly, I remembered the "monkey trees." They were located down the street in an old cemetery. The trees were only six feet tall with branches so low that they leaned almost to the ground. I had stumbled across them one day taking a short cut back home after visiting a friend up the street. The first time the kids climbed the trees, they gave them that name.

I took a deep breath, not wanting the girls to see what was happening to me.

"Kids, we're going on a picnic to the monkey trees."

"We are?" The excitement spread. Their friends, Diane and Donna, had been playing with the girls.

"Can we come too, Mrs. Lopes?" Diane asked.

"Of course you can," I said with a smile bending down facing them. "Let me get things ready. You kids go wash your hands and don't make a mess."

I tried to get them to do something away from me so I could pull myself together.

What to make? I should have gone shopping days ago. There was no sandwich meat. *Calm down, Alberta!* I talked to myself to stay relaxed.

There was at least a loaf of bread. Peanut butter and jelly sandwiches! What could be easier? I slapped sandwiches together, grabbed Twinkies for dessert, and threw paper cups into a large grocery bag along with a large bottle of Coke from the refrigerator and napkins.

My mind couldn't think of anything else to take. "Ready kids?" I asked.

Four kids became jumping jacks coming around the corner from the bathroom.

"All washed up, Mom," Debbie yelled. She stopped fast and the others ran into her.

"Slow down," I said in a loud voice. Their confusion was only adding to my nervous state.

It dawned on me that Effie had to be called. "Wait, I have to let your mother know that I'm taking you," I said to Donna and Diane.

I dialed their home number. "Hi, Effie, I'm taking the girls with me to the monkey trees so if you need us, you'll know where we are. We'll be about an hour." The neighborhood was well aware of the trees.

"That's great. Thanks for letting me know."

I made Debbie hold the hands of the younger ones while I tried to juggle the large bag. I gave Donna the blanket to carry.

"Stay close to the side of the road, cars will be coming up the street."

It was only three houses down the street before we took the left onto a dirt path which led to a field where the trees were. I relaxed once the kids weren't in the street and could run ahead of me without being watched. I couldn't get my heart to stop racing so I could breathe normally. The weight of the articles in my hands only put more strain on my breathing as I tried to balance the packages.

By the time I reached the area, the four kids were already climbing the trees. The leaves had small buds and I assumed that they were some sort of fruit trees.

I placed the blanket down and took deep breaths. *Please, God, help me relax*, I pleaded. I may have looked composed on the outside, but inside my body was going faster than a freight train. I prayed that no one would come and ask me to leave. I had no idea who owned the property.

"When you get hungry, let me know, I have sandwiches for you."

They climbed, jumped, yelled, and laughed. I watched them with eyes of an adult, awed by the wonder of children. It's amazing how they find names so easily for things, like the monkey trees. How innocent and trusting they are in their world of no constant worry and dependency on parents to protect them.

Lori and Diane were thrilled, being able to reach the lower branches and swing by themselves. They were five-years old; Donna and Debbie were nine and ten.

In twenty minutes, they all scrambled over to the blanket ready to eat their lunch and treats. There wasn't a moment that I didn't enjoy being with them. I couldn't believe doing something as simple as this with them took away my anxiety.

They finished eating and ran back to the challenge of conquering the climb to the top of the trees. A few of them had fingers sticky with peanut butter. They didn't want to wait for me to wipe them clean. The younger ones were happy collecting silly things found on the ground. They ran over to me with colored stones and wildflowers with weeds in-between. We put them in the empty sandwich bags to take back.

Before I realized it, my body had slowed down, and I had enjoyed eating out in the fresh air. The kids entertained me and helped me forget my problems. I had no worries for the moment.

We stayed an hour and a half before I packed up to head for home. I didn't feel like the same nervous wreck that had left home.

Once I placed everything on the counter in the kitchen, I called Cindy. The kids disappeared into their playroom. It was set-up with a miniature stove, sink, fake food, utensils, pots and pans and a table with benches that opened up for storing their toys. The girls played and ate in the room almost everyday.

"Thanks for your advice, Cindy, it took awhile, but my panic passed."

"You're under a lot of stress. It's hard to handle. I'm going through the same thing. It's awful when you don't think you're going to make it."

"I feel so much better, and I wanted you to know how I was doing."

"Call me tomorrow and let me know how the night went."

"I will. Thanks again."

Chapter Twenty-Nine
Getting On Tranquilizers

Richie's drinking began to change his moods and personality. He started coming home wanting to fight and would follow me through the house saying things hoping to upset me. I knew he was looking for an argument when he did this. I wanted to scream at him, but because of my fear of scaring the girls, I kept quiet.

Every day my anger and bitterness was held back so we could live the best we could as a family. I felt that my husband and daughters were doing their own thing, and I was separated from them. We were still going along as if nothing was happening, when in actuality, our family was falling apart. I started to hate myself for feeling sorry for my husband and having no backbone to make demands. What was I going to do and where would I go if we split? I had no job.

My body became a breeding ground of hate, resentment, lies, tears, delusion and the paralyzing feeling of suffocation. The kids held on to any moment that Richie gave them. There would be weeks with him coming home on time, and we'd be fine, but I couldn't relax. I was always guessing—in what condition?

I decided one day to phone my gynecologist about my nerves. "Hi, this is Alberta Lopes and I'd like to speak with Dr. Wood."

"May I ask what it's about?" the receptionist asked.

"I'm having a hard time sleeping. I have a lot of anxiety lately, and I was wondering if he could prescribe something for me."

"I'll have him call you. Could you give me your telephone number?"

I hung up feeling like she knew that I was lying to get drugs. I needed something to keep my body calm.

A few hours passed and the doctor called. "Is this Alberta?"

"Hi, Dr. Wood."

"What's your problem?" He sounded put out by his cold tone.

"I've been under a lot of stress lately, not sleeping and my husband and I are having some marital problems."

"I will prescribe 0.25mg of Xanax but I recommend that you try to solve the problem. That's better than using medication."

"I'm in the process of trying to do that."

"I'll call it in for you. I'm switching you over to Elaine for an appointment in three months. I won't prescribe this medicine without checkups."

I made the appointment and didn't care if they were every week as long as I got the pills.

That was the beginning of my years being on tranquilizers. They were a miracle pill. When I woke up shaky with the feeling that my body was running down the street, I took one. In the beginning they left me sleepy. Within a week, I'd be going about my housework after taking one without realizing that I had calmed down. I never abused them. Sometimes I'd go days or weeks without one. They were a godsend. I carried them in my purse so they would be available when I'd feel nervous.

Our lives kept falling deeper into a downward spiral. Richie's drinking was at the stage of being out-of-control. My days were spent thinking about where he was, if he was coming home, if he was drinking, and wondered if he would upset the girls. By three in the afternoon, my stomach was in my throat.

Slowly, my one hundred and twenty pounds eventually jumped another twenty-five pounds. Instead of losing weight from stress, I was gaining it. I was eating anything in sight whether I was hungry or not. I felt the extra weight as I did my everyday chores.

Effie and I joined Weight Watchers. I started to think that maybe I wasn't attractive to Richie anymore. I was letting myself go. It took me seven months, but the weight came off gradually. I had gotten myself down to 118 pounds and my clothes slipped over my once oversized hips. I could wear anything clingy and it looked great. I joined Gloria Steven's health club in Taunton and faithfully went three times a week after the girls got on the school bus.

Everyone noticed but Richie, the one person who I wanted to wrap his arms around me and have his eyes light-up. Not once did he ever mention my new appearance. I was hurt and felt less attractive. My confidence started to dwindle down to nothing.

My patience was buried deep inside me. I snapped at the girls and was never happy. My positive outlook on life disappeared. When it reached eight o'clock at night and he wasn't home, I knew that he would be staggering in the door.

I thought maybe it was something that I was doing wrong. I tried keeping the house spotless. I went as far as picking lint off the rugs with my fingers. Cindy came over one day and saw me on my hands and knees, wetting my finger tips and rubbing them along the end of the rug against the wall trying to get the dirt out that the vacuum cleaner didn't reach.

"Alberta, what in God's name are you doing? Have you flipped?"

I sat on the floor and broke out in tears. "I don't know, maybe I'm losing my mind. I'm trying so hard to keep up with the house. Richie probably thinks it isn't clean enough."

"You have two active, healthy kids. A house isn't going to be spotless. That doesn't make you a bad mom or wife. Your house is far from being dirty or messy. It's not a reason for a husband to stay out and drink. It's an excuse."

"I don't know how long I can go on like this."

Cindy and I became inseparable and developed a tight relationship. Like mine, her nerves were shattered from trying to handle her problems with Ernie. We gave each other support with our ups and downs. Everyone around us seemed to have it all, but not us. My world kept crumbling.

Chapter Thirty
Police Officer Brings Him Home

One night, I was up watching a late movie that had caught my interest. Richie was still out. The lights were off, when suddenly, the door bell rang. My first reaction was that it was bad news, since it was midnight. I was scared to open the door. I pushed the curtains back from the window and saw Richie with a police officer. I recognized the officer as his buddy, Eddie Pierce,

"Hi, Eddie," I said surprised.

"Hi, Alberta, I'm hand delivering Richie to you. He was all over the road so I stopped him. His van is down on the highway, but I've tagged it so the department will know whose it is."

Richie pushed against me as he staggered into the living room.

I got angry. "Why didn't you arrest him?"

"Oh, we all have a bad night."

Yes, but he has one too often, and you know it. Maybe he needs to wake up behind bars so he can take a cold look at himself and where he's heading."

"I couldn't do that to him."

"Eddie, you would have been more of a friend taking him in than bringing him home. He isn't going to learn a thing from this. He can kill someone on the road."

"Is he getting help?"

"He doesn't think he has a problem."

"I don't know what to do to help, Alberta."

"I do. Don't bring him home the next time. If he were a stranger, you would handcuff him and take him into the station without thinking twice about it."

"I'm sorry. I thought I was helping him."

"You're not. Please don't do this again."

"I'll remember that. You have a good night."

I now feared being alone with him; he was so confused and drunk. First he went to the bathroom to heave his guts up then crawled into bed. Each room he traveled through left the same sour smell of liquor. I was thankful that he passed out in our bed and I slept on the couch. There was no desire to sleep next to him.

I woke up early and confronted him.

"We have got to talk."

"I have television sets to deliver."

"I don't care what you have to do."

"Lord, do we have to go through this again?"

"You're the one causing this, not me."

"I don't want to fight."

"We're not going to. I have one question to ask you. Do you ever intend to get professional help?"

"I don't need it."

"Oh, so you think nothing of a police officer bringing you home drunk?"

"It's no big deal. Eddie was worried about me. He did me a favor."

"Richie, look at me. If you tell me that you have no plans, whatsoever, of getting help, we're separating."

"You can't be serious? And you think you're going to kick me out of *my* house and cause me to lose *my* kids?"

"Lose your kids? Have you noticed them? When are you with them?"

"I'm so busy that I don't have the time to be with them as much as I'd like."

"My God, you're killing yourself. You're doing everything that you swore you'd never do. You're blind to the fact that you're going down the same path as your mother and sister. If you want help, I'll stand behind you. If not, I can't do this anymore."

"When I get home tonight, we'll talk about it."

"No, Richie, I want an answer now while you're sober. Tonight you'll never remember this conversation and I can't handle another night waiting for you to make a grand entrance. The kids and I live in fear."

"Like I would hurt any of you?"

"You already are hurting us. It doesn't have to be physically. If we separate, you'll be the one leaving. I'm not uprooting the girls."

"I'm not going to let you take the kids from me."

"Make up your mind to what you want. I don't care anymore." I walked away leaving him standing there.

Time passed, nothing changed, and I didn't follow through with my threat.

We continued down the road of more broken promises, and my living in a dream world thinking that it was all going to straighten out. My threats went in one ear and out the other. Why should he take me seriously? I wasn't following through. I was still waiting to see what *he* was going to do.

Instead of him seeing that there was hope for all of us, he avoided getting the help. The nights of being able to calm him when he came in angry came to a stop. One night, I was sleeping when he came in after one o'clock, and he stormed into our bedroom tearing the covers off me. I woke up startled.

"Get up and make my supper!"

"Stop this. You're going to scare the kids."

"They'll go back to sleep. Don't use them as an excuse," he snapped looking angry as a bull.

I got out of bed and went into the kitchen. He followed, screaming at me. I could feel the built-up anger deep within me. At the moment, I craved a man's strength so that I could beat the hell out of him. My insides shook from wanting to physically knock him down. He was brave when I was weak. Sober he wouldn't think of laying a hand on me. It wouldn't be in his nature.

It wasn't long before there was a knock on the front door. I couldn't imagine who it was at this hour of the morning. I threw my robe on and opened the front door. Richie staggered behind me.

Two police officers were standing in the doorway.

"Mrs. Lopes, I'm Officer Thompson and this is Officer Gomes. Is everything all right? We received a call that there was loud yelling at this address." I didn't recognize the two reserve officers.

"No, it isn't all right, officer. My husband is drunk, and I want him out."

"Mr. Lopes, I think you should come with us," Officer Gomes stated as he stepped toward Richie.

"There's no need for me to leave, I'm fine."

"I don't think so. You can't stand up, let alone walk," Officer Thompson answered.

Officer Gomes came up to me and softly stated, "This can turn into a dangerous situation, Mrs. Lopes, calls like this get people hurt and killed when someone is in this state."

"That's what I'm afraid of."

"Are you going to be pressing charges?"

"Hey, wait a minute," Richie yelled as he tripped over the foot stool. "She's not going to press charges."

"We can remove him and make sure that he doesn't come back tonight," Officer Gomes replied.

"I want him removed. I'll get a restraining order tomorrow."

"You'll have to go to court for that."

"That's no problem."

"Mr. Lopes, get your things together."

"I can't believe this. Are you arresting me?" He was shocked.

"Not this time, but we are removing you. You're in no condition to drive. If we can't take you somewhere, we'll have to take you in overnight. I advise you to find a place to stay for awhile."

"You can take me to Frank Mederios house. They'll take me in."

Richie looked at me as he passed by. "I can't believe you're doing this to me and the kids."

"This has nothing to do with the kids," I said. I didn't need a guilt trip.

The officers followed him out the front door. I really didn't believe that the girls were sleeping. The poor things were probably shaking under their covers. I was sick thinking of what we were putting them through.

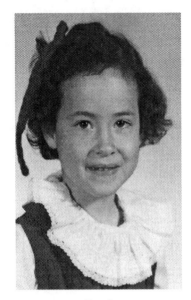

Lori

Debbie

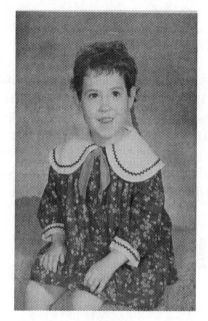

Lori

Left-Debbie & Lori

Chapter Thirty-One
First Restraining Order

The next morning I went to the courthouse in Taunton and filed for a restraining order. I couldn't believe that this serious step was being taken. I was told the papers would be faxed to the Dighton Police Department and they would serve Richie. The man informed me that my husband had the right to go to his business in the house because it was where he made his living.

"Are you serious? He'll come upstairs? That won't keep him away." I said in disbelief. I was in total fear.

"It'll state these rules when we serve him his papers."

"And when will that be? I need protection now. Tonight he'll be drinking and will most likely come to the house."

"We'll have someone served him this afternoon. As for him coming to the house, notify the police in your town and have them keep an eye on your house."

I drove home in tears from having reached this point. I was relieved not seeing his truck parked in the driveway when I got home. By then, I was a wreck.

As soon as I got in the door, I called Anita and told her what was going on.

"Come here with the kids and stay," she said. Anita didn't know every detail about us, but she was aware of Richie's drinking.

"I can't let him know I'm scared. If I do, he'll have the upper hand and be in control of me."

"I think you should call your parents about this."

"I'm not going to have them worried about me when they live an hour away."

"How do you think they'll feel when they hear about this, or even worse, if you get hurt? I think your dad would be hurt and upset at you for not telling him all this time. He would have a right to be mad."

"Maybe Richie will get help, and they won't need to know."

"You have to deal with this as it is. Don't live on hope. You have to make decisions on today."

"I'll think about it. I don't know what to do. Even doing this makes me feel guilty." I started to lose my confidence in going to court.

"Alberta, you have two choices; you either keep living like this or leave."

"I can't live like this. The kids and I are messed up."

"Then follow through with the restraining order."

I thought about what Anita said about calling my parents and still held back from doing it.

Richie didn't come to work at the shop. All day I tried to analyze what his plan was going to be when he sobered up. That's all I ever did. My mind was exhausted thinking about his moves 24/7. My day was on hold waiting for him to drive into the yard.

At four-thirty in the afternoon, the phone rang. It was Officer Gomes.

"Mrs. Lopes, your husband was served the restraining order an hour ago."

"Where was he?"

"He's at Mr. Mederios' home."

185

"Does he realize that he can't come back home to stay?"

"Yes, he does. He has the authority to work in his shop."

"Yes, but you can't imagine the fear I'll be under."

"Call if you need us."

"That sounds all well and good, Officer Gomes, but if he comes here drunk and is abusing me, do you actually think he'll let me get to the phone and call you?"

"We can't be there watching him."

"Now, I can fully understand how families aren't protected even with restraining orders if someone is in a blackout. No wonder people get killed."

"I don't think your husband will hurt you."

"How do you know that?" I was angry.

"We know Richie, and he's not that kind of a person."

"Richard Lopes wouldn't harm a fly, but the wild maniac facing me in a blackout, could. It's a miracle that he hasn't yet."

He had no reply and there was dead silence on the other end. "Well, thank you for the information, Officer Gomes."

I didn't want to carry it any further. Although I had a restraining order in my possession, I knew I was completely alone and didn't feel protected. How was I ever going to get to the phone if he pushed his way in?

Richie didn't go to work for a few days. Finally during the middle of the week, he pulled into the yard. I was washing clothes in the garage when he walked into the shop. I could still smell the liquor in the air as he passed by me. He was playing with dynamite, and I was the one waiting for it to explode.

I wasn't sure if he was still staying at his friend's home and didn't ask. I might have thrown him into another woman's arms. I was doing something that wasn't in my heart. After by-passing each other without a word, I went upstairs.

Not long after, he went on a delivery. I swallowed my pride and went to the Welfare office and applied for help. I kept it a secret because I was too embarrassed to let anyone know. They put me in a job program, and I looked through the openings every week. In the meantime, I collected welfare. I prayed I'd find a job soon.

I looked through the unemployment list for over a month until I found a position with the Town of Dighton. The police department was looking for a dispatcher for the morning shift. Most police officers already knew me and about my marriage problems. I feared accepting any kind of work. Here I was thirty-two years old getting my first job. I was petrified! I didn't want to live off the system, so I applied.

Karl Spratt, the chief of police, interviewed me and I was hired for the 8 am-4 pm shift. The girls were attending school. Debbie was in fifth grade, and Lori was in first. Effie offered to watch them for an hour after school, or longer, if I had to work over-time.

The dispatcher's job gave me back the confidence that I had lost so long ago. It felt good to get a pay check and be able to depend on it every week. I made a monthly schedule of the bills that were to be paid. I took Richie to court, and he was ordered to pay $65 a week for the two children. It hardly touched my expenses, but I didn't care. I was determined to make it on my own.

The Volkswagen wasn't big enough any more so I sold it to a teenager. My father offered to sell me his used white Pontiac station wagon. Every two years he traded his car in for a new one. I took out a two-year loan to pay for it. At first, I was hurt that he didn't just give it to me. My parents were comfortable financially, and I selfishly hoped the car would be a *gift*. I didn't realize at the time that he did me a favor. It made me take responsibility for my bills more seriously. It was a proud moment for me when I made the last payment.

The Dighton Police Department was only five minutes away on Route 138. Welfare paid half my pay for a year, and the Town of Dighton picked up the other half.

Janet Simmons was the secretary, and I looked forward every morning to working with her. She was in her forties and had dark, brown hair, a medium build, and stood about five feet, five inches tall. It was easy to talk to her about anything. She had a pleasant personality and always had a positive attitude.

The police department was small with only Janet and me, the chief, and two police officers on each shift. With not many employees, it made it easy for all of us to open up about our personal lives. There was a sliding window that separated Janet's office from mine, and it was closed only when she had to have a private meeting. We became close friends.

I didn't want to advertise my life about being on welfare. I'm sure the department was aware of it. I never offered the information out to anyone, including family.

I had so many problems at home that I prayed I'd be able to fill this dispatcher position and handle emergencies. I wondered if it would put more tension in my life. My job entailed answering every call for the water, highway, fire, ambulance, and police departments. The public frequently came into the station looking for help or directions. For the first time in my adult life, I felt worth something.

Chapter Thirty-Two
Abducting Lori

Richie called a few weeks later. "I'd like to take the girls out for supper. Would that be okay with you?" The court had given him the right to see them.

"They would love it but let me say one thing. If you come here with a drop of liquor on your breath, I'll cancel the night with them."

"Do you think I'm stupid?"

"No, just a drinker."

"See you tomorrow at five."

"I'll have them ready."

Debbie and Lori were excited. I didn't want the relationship with their father to stop. It broke my heart to see them separated. The girls couldn't wait to go. They each picked out dresses they wanted to wear. Lori was six-years old and looked so girlish with a colorful yellow bow in her hair. At ten, Debbie was growing into a young girl and liked to get dressed up. By 4:30 p.m., they were sitting on the couch, waiting patiently.

Five o'clock arrived, and he didn't come. My heart started pounding. I was furious and holding the anger in. I didn't want the girls to see my frustration. They ran to the window each time a car passed the house. I couldn't stand seeing the excitement drain from them.

Oh, please, God, don't let him do this to the kids. I could handle anything thrown at me, but seeing them hurt, my motherly protection kicked in, and I wanted to shelter them.

Another hour passed, and I had to find an excuse. I was boiling inside. "Maybe you girls should get undressed, I don't think Daddy's coming. He may have been tied up at work."

FORGOT? TIED UP AT WORK? I was wild thinking about it. How could he do this to them? Where was his heart?

"He'll be here, Mommy," Lori said sitting by the window.

"I don't think so," Debbie answered heartbroken as she got off the couch. I could see the resentment in her. She was old enough to see the game being played.

After two hours and no phone call, I convinced the girls to get into their pajamas. There are no words to describe the pain in seeing them so disappointed. I made some hotdogs with chips and hot chocolate. I tried to laugh and talk about anything stupid that came into my mind to entertain them. There was no enthusiasm. The three of us spent the night cuddled on the couch watching their favorite shows, but there was no laughter from them.

They had a hard time sleeping because of the stressful hours waiting for him. "Why didn't Daddy come, Mom? Debbie asked.

"It had nothing to do with you two. Maybe he was away on a call."

They had no knowledge of alcoholism and how it changes a person. The girls were constantly on a rollercoaster with him in and out of their lives. Children just want to be loved and have security with their parents.

I couldn't wait for Richie to get to the shop the next morning. Instead, he called. "Hi, I'm sorry about last night. I had to work late."

"Are you serious—WORK? Do you take me for some kind of fool? You had no consideration at all to make a call. Do you realize that the girls sat here for two hours waiting for you? They had their best dresses on and sat here brokenhearted with confusion and disappointment wondering how their father could forget them. How *dare* you treat them like this? I know you were out drinking."

"I'm sorry, Alberta. What can I say?"

"YOU SHOULD HAVE CALLED!" I screamed in the phone. I was angry and continued in a rage. "Don't you *ever* call to take them out again. I'll not sit by and watch you hurt them like last night. You can hurt me all you want, but I won't allow you to treat them like this. They're innocent in all this. They love you and can't understand why you're doing these things to them."

"It hurts me more seeing them than if I stay away," he remarked.

I was shocked to hear him say it. "So, you're going to stay out of their life because it makes *you* uncomfortable? You know what's sad, Richie? You don't even know how much they love you. I keep that love going in them. They're a joy to be around."

"You live with them, I can't."

"That's your choice. You can go for help and come back as the man I fell in love with, not this out-of-control drunk."

"I have to go. I'm sorry for not coming."

"You should be telling them that. I'll let you get back to your more important issues for the day."

We hung up, and I tried to calm down. I shook my head wondering what was going to wake him up.

A month later, I woke up from a dead sleep with a knock on the back door. I looked at the clock; it was 2:00 a.m. I pulled the curtain back and saw Richie at the back door. I opened the inside door.

"What are you doing here?"

"Please, please, Alberta, let me in for awhile. I'm begging you."

His whole body was shaking like a leaf. He was pleading, and I could see the desperation in him. He was so sick. I opened the door and he came in with tears in his eyes.

"I think I'm coming apart."

I put my arms around him.

"Please, let me sleep here. I promise to leave in the morning. I can't go back out there. I want to be in my home."

"Richie, look at me. You have to leave in the morning. Can you handle that?"

"Yes, just let me stay here tonight."

I didn't have the heart to throw him out. He was truly overcome with the shakes. I had too much compassion and love for him to slam the door in his face.

We went to the bedroom and got under the covers. I held him tight until his body stopped quivering.

"We're going to be all right," he said putting his arm around me.

I couldn't help feeling sorry for him. My heart ached looking at him and wondered what the fear was like that he was experiencing. His personal struggle seemed so worthless with family and professionals that could help him through this alcohol abuse.

"Richie, please go for help. I'll come with you."

"Let's just lie here. I haven't felt this much peace in a long time. We'll talk tomorrow." I was relieved that he didn't try to make love, I couldn't handle the emotions.

It was another night that we avoided discussing the drinking issue. The steps toward working for recovery were ignored.

We were up when the girls got out of bed. It was a Saturday morning. They were thrilled to see him.

"Daddy has to go to work. He just came for a visit to see you," I said.

He gave both of them a hug and sat on the couch. "What's going on with school?" he asked them.

Lori ran for her school papers with the stars on it for her drawing. Debbie sat next to him and talked about her grades. Report cards were brought home the week before. He seemed lost for words not having shared in their every day events and didn't know what to say to them.

"Well, guess I'd better get back to work. I've got a lot of television sets to deliver."

"Can I come?" Debbie asked.

"I have too many stops today, honey, maybe another time."

I knew there wouldn't be a next time. They were promises to pacify her. How was she going to understand, after he had taken her so many other times?

I felt like the worst piece of scum sending him off. We didn't take any time to talk privately about what happened to him the night before, how sick he was getting, or what we *could* have done together about this terrible disease. It was just dropped. I should have demanded that we bring his drinking out in the open. Our family continuously went different ways, and I ignored the situation, still expecting it to fix itself.

I watched him get into his truck. He must have felt so alone and lost. This was his family and home. He had to knock on the door to come in or call to see us. Why couldn't that reality be enough for him to say he wanted help? He knew we'd take him back. All he had to do was admit to being sick and needing help.

Months went by, and we didn't hear from him. One Wednesday morning, I went across the street to see Effie and informed her and Bill of our separation. "If you ever see Richie at the house causing a problem, please call the police. I may not have time to get to the phone."

"Alberta, we're the ones who called them last time. With all the yelling, we thought you were in trouble. We were afraid to get involved."

"I'm glad you did. I never would have been able to get to the phone. Please continue to do that for me."

"We'll be happy to help out."

A week later, I had to go for an annual checkup and needed to do some grocery shopping on my way home. Lori didn't go to school that morning because she was sick. I went over and asked Effie if she would watch her. Debbie was in school.

"When Diane gets out of school, she'll be happy to see her here. Don't worry about it."

It was close to two o'clock when I arrived back home. I decided to put the groceries in the house before going over to get Lori. I put the bags on the kitchen counter then crossed the street to Effie's.

"Thanks a lot, Effie, for helping me. I hope she wasn't any problem?"

"Alberta, I'm not sure if I did the right thing. Richie came looking for you and then said that you wanted him to pick Lori up."

"Oh, God. No!" I was in a state of panic.

"I'm sorry. I didn't know."

"Did he say where he was going?"

"No, and I didn't think to ask. I thought he was taking her home. I watched and he didn't go over to your house. I started to get worried."

"I'm going to go back home and see if he calls. Debbie is due home in an hour."

"I'm so sorry."

"It's not your fault. I didn't mention that I had a restraining order."

I ran across the street to the house in a state of horror. Why would he take her and where? I called Cindy.

"Cindy, Richie took off with Lori."

"What? Are you kidding? How did he get her?"

"I left her at Effie's, and he came and got her. I don't know where to look."

"Don't panic. Give him an hour to call you. If you hear from him, call me. I'll come over."

I hung up and paced back and forth in the living room like a caged lion. I decided to put the food away to keep my mind occupied.

Please, God, don't let him take off with her.

In ten minutes the phone rang, and I almost leaped on it.

"Hello?"

"Well, you're finally home." Richie said sounding intoxicated on the other end.

"Where are you?" I was scared knowing that he was drunk and had Lori in his van.

"I'm in a phone booth."

"What phone booth?"

"You'll never know. If I can't have the kids, I'm taking one of them."

I got violently sick. I knew Lori had to be frightened of him in this condition. I heard of men doing this with their kids, but I never thought it would happen to me.

"Please, let's talk about this. Don't frighten her. She has nothing to do with our problems."

"There's nothing to talk about," he said, proud that he had the control now.

"I want to talk to Lori."

"She's fine."

"I want to talk to her, Richie."

"Lori, honey, you want to talk to Mommy?"

Within seconds, I heard, "Hi, Mommy. I want to come home."

She started to cry and my heart sank. She was only six-years old. What was he thinking?

"Daddy will bring you home. Are you having fun?"

I didn't want her to think that there was a need to fear being with her father. I tried to stay calm.

"Richie, there's no reason why we can't sit down and discuss you having time with your daughters."

"You took my family from me."

"I'm sorry." I was now trying to get on the good side of him. "Why don't you come here and we'll talk. Debbie should be home soon."

"I'll call you later."

"No, don't hang up!"

It was too late. He slammed the phone down.

I called Cindy and told her the story. I was hysterical.

She urged me to call the police. "You can't play with something like this, especially having Lori in his company while he's drunk. I'll call them so you can keep the phone lines open."

"You're right." I hung up and didn't know what to do with myself. I knew that he was in no condition to drive and our daughter was with him.

She called me back in a half hour. "The Dighton Police called the State Police."

Oh, this can't be happening, I thought.

"They want you to stay there. I'm at the pay phone down the street. They want you to call me if he comes to the house. They will be around the corner. Let me give you the telephone number here."

I ran trying to get a piece of paper and pen. "Okay, go ahead."

We waited and waited. After an hour, the phone rang.

"Hello?"

"It's me."

"Richie, please come home with Lori. I want to talk."

"Do you mean it?"

"Yes, just come home."

"You're not playing games with me?"

"No, I'm not."

"I'll see you in a while."

197

I notified Cindy. "I'll take care of the rest," she said. She notified the police and sat in her car just beyond my house.

Richie came up the front steps, and I could see that he was drunk. I opened the door.

"Hi, Lori. I see that you've been on a ride with Daddy?"

"I wanted to come home." I could tell she was scared to death.

I wrapped my arms around her and pulled her in the house before he could grab her.

By then the State Police came flying up the steps and grabbed him.

Cindy came into the house and held Lori while I talked to the police. Her tiny body was vibrating from fear. The guilt was choking me, as I thought about what she had gone through

"You're under arrest, Mr. Lopes."

"What for? Taking my own daughter for a ride?"

Another officer came up to me. "Do you have a copy of the restraining order?"

"Yes, I do." I ran to the desk drawer, and pulled the paper out. I handed it to him.

Richie laughed, "It's no good. I've been back home since it was issued."

I knew that he didn't ask to stay that night so he could use it against me, but he was doing it now.

"Is that true?" the officer asked looking at me.

I felt sick and defeated. "He was back for one night."

I should have lied; it was his word against mine, but it didn't enter my mind.

"We can't arrest him for abduction if you broke the order Mrs. Lopes. He had the right to take his daughter but not in this condition."

The officer turned and directed his remarks to Richie. "It wasn't safe for your daughter to be with you, Mr. Lopes. This isn't a game. You're lucky she wasn't hurt."

"I wouldn't hurt my daughter."

"You could in a drunken state," the officer stated firmly.

"Mrs. Lopes, I'd advise you to get legal advice on this incident. Your daughter shouldn't have to go through this."

The officer looked upset with my decision to take Richie in that night and breaking the restraining order. His hands were tied from taking action against him. I knew that he was right, and I felt foolish. Feeling sorry for him in a sick state became a weapon to use against me. He must have been very aware of the limitations to the restraining order for him to have the confidence to take Lori.

"We'll take him to the station for now, but we can't hold him. You should give some serious consideration to what you want to do."

This incident put Lori in a dangerous situation, and she paid for my poor decision to not inform Effie of the retraining order.

The two State Police officers took Richie from the house. I had felt safe and in control of my children with him out. The incident hit me that anything is possible when dealing with someone who has a drinking problem.

Cindy stayed for a few minutes until we had all calmed down.

"Thank you so much for all that you did for us."

"I'm glad I could help you." She kissed Lori and went home.

I entered Lori's bedroom and tried talking to her. My heart broke knowing the fright she must have gone through. Innocently, I was to blame because I didn't protect her. If Richie had been arrested, it might have opened his eyes to how uncontrollable his life had become.

I heard the school bus stop at the corner and saw Debbie getting off. Her hands were full of books. Heidi was tuned into the kid's school schedule and the sound of the buses. She sat patiently on the grass by the edge of the road waiting. Debbie ran toward the house with Heidi doing circles around her in excitement. I was happy she hadn't come home five minutes earlier.

I never mentioned the incident to Debbie. I was repeating the same mistake with the girls by not talking about the problem. I didn't know if it would put fear into her, so I hid the horrible event from her.

The next day, I went back to court to get another restraining order. Richie was served a second time.

Lori's first day of school in our front yard

Chapter Thirty-Three
Another Return Home

I started to go back to church and took the girls every week. I found so much peace being at Mass until one particular Sunday morning. I was sitting in the pew until it was time to receive Holy Communion. The girls were old enough to sit by themselves.

The line of people stopped half way down the aisle. Suddenly, my legs felt weak and shaky. My heart started to pound in my chest and my hands trembled, I needed air.

I grabbed onto a pew for balance. I felt I was going to collapse. What was happening to me? I wanted to go back to my seat, but I was afraid of making a scene getting out of line. Was I having a panic attack?

As the line started to proceed, I thought I'd never get to the priest fast enough. After taking Holy Communion, I went as fast as I could back to my seat. I stayed long enough to say a short prayer and grabbed the girls by the hand. I left before Mass ended, feeling angry at God. Why would He let something like this happen to me when I was trying to hold the family together?

My confidence and security in going to public places completely faded after that episode. Trips anywhere brought on uncontrollable anxiety attacks. My thoughts about where I had to go the next day had me up for hours.

I'd go grocery shopping, and about halfway through the store, I'd be unable to breathe. I'd hold onto the handle of the grocery cart in a death grip. It felt as if the floor was slanted, and I was falling down hill. I held on so tight that my knuckles hurt.

If the line at the registers were moving fast and at a steady pace, I could wait in line. If I stood and waited too long, I felt as if my knees were going to buckle out from under me. There were times that I left a full basket of food in the middle of the store and walked out. I'd get into the car and cry because I needed the groceries, but I couldn't go back inside.

Debbie and her cousin, Gary, were performing in their fifth grade school play, and Anita and I went together to see it. Paula watched Lori. We walked into the auditorium, and Anita strolled up to the stage choosing to go in the third row of seats. We were situated in the middle instead of at the end near the aisle.

I felt an uncontrollable panic attack trying to take over. I needed the option of being able to escape from the crowd, but sitting up front didn't give me that choice. My comfort zone was handled by hiding in the back of a room in a corner. I never wanted to be noticed. The lights were on, and it made me feel trapped and surrounded by the crowd. Suddenly, I couldn't breathe and had to get out of the room.

"Anita, I have to go to the restroom. I'll be right back."

I walked out of the school and stood by the front door leaning against the building breathing in fresh air. Twenty minutes went by, and I was immobilized, unable to return to my seat. I looked through the glass doors and saw Anita and a police officer walking the hallway. I was aware that they were looking for me. It wasn't until the lights in the auditorium went down low that I could go back in and join her.

"Where have you been? Everyone's been looking for you. I thought something happened to you."

"I'm sorry, Anita. It felt hot in here and had to go outside. I got carried away talking to some people." I lied from embarrassment.

It took months for me to realize that my nerves were unraveling. My body was trying to tell me that it couldn't take any more stress. Instead of dealing with it, I kept going along every day, trying to cope with the strain.

Six months passed, and I tried not to be home when Richie came to the house to work. Weeks would go by, and he wouldn't show up. His absence made life more comfortable for me. I couldn't understand how he made enough money to survive.

I thought we were finally going our own way until he broke down and called.

"Alberta, I'm so sorry for the things that I've done. You and the girls don't deserve this. How are they doing?"

"We're fine."

"I'd like to see you tomorrow."

"I'm not sure if I'll be here."

"If you have plans, don't cancel them. I have to stop at the shop anyway."

"Okay, I'll see you if I'm here."

I wanted to believe so badly that he had changed. If only he could be the man I had known. I felt myself starting to melt and wondered if he was really sorry. Maybe having him away from us for those months made him think differently.

The next morning he pulled into the driveway. He walked up the steps to the back door and knocked. It always felt odd knowing he had to do that at his own home.

"Hi, can I come in a minute. His smile touched my heart, but I fought the feeling.

"You're not allowed in."

"I'm not going to fight.

"And I'm not breaking this restraining order."

He put his hand in his shirt pocket and pulled out an envelope. "I want to give this to you. There's two hundred dollars in it."

"What's it for?"

"Anything you might need. Maybe the girls need things for school. Call me if I can help."

I opened the door to take it. "Thank you. I'll put it aside. You don't spend much time working."

"I've caught up with repairs and delivering the sets that I have down cellar."

I wondered where he was living but decided not to ask. I was scared to get close emotionally. There was no reason we couldn't be decent and respectable to each other. It was the first time in months that he was sober and looked wonderful.

"I haven't had a drink in weeks," he said.

"I'm glad for you." I didn't dare show any excitement with the news.

"I'm going to straighten myself out. Maybe we can work things out."

"I can't do that right now, Richie."

"I understand. I'll let you get back to what you were doing. Tell the girls I love them."

"You can call and tell them yourself. I'm sure they'd want to hear it from you."

"I'll call them soon. I have a delivery at ten so I have to get going. You have a good day."

He turned and went down the stairs, and I heard the garage doors open. I walked into the kitchen and started to wash the dishes. The tears were flowing. That's the way we used talk to each other. He had been such a polite, gentle man. Where did he go? I knew the answer: drinking had swallowed him up.

I didn't receive any more money directly from him. A few times, the court summoned me for a hearing because he was behind on child support. It was supposed to be automatically deducted from his paycheck. I was upset because I had to lose a day's pay or take a vacation day to go to court, and I couldn't afford it.

One evening, Debbie asked, "Mom, is Dad ever coming home? I miss him."

I sat her down on the couch and tried to explain the best way I could to a ten-year-old about her fathers' illness. It wasn't easy. Lori was six and too young to bring into the conversation. She never would have understood it. I wanted Debbie to know that her father was sick because of drinking and that's what was causing all this commotion in our lives.

"Your father drinks too much, and it makes him angry, that's why he yells at us. It's hard to believe that he loves you when he gets this way, but he does. I know this may be too hard for you to understand."

"Why doesn't he stop, if that's all he has to do?" Debbie asked.

"Because, he needs to see to a doctor, and he won't go. He thinks he's fine," I said.

I gave her a hug knowing it was a topic that couldn't be explained too deeply. She seemed satisfied and went to play with Lori.

During the following six months, Richie's few calls to the girls stopped altogether. I made plans on weekends without waiting to see if he was going to call or stop by to see them. The girls were constantly disappointed that he never had the desire to spend time with them or take them with him for a few hours. After the last incident with Lori, I was petrified of them being in his company alone.

One day during the week, I heard his van pull into the driveway. He was taking a television set out of the garage. I watched his every move from the kitchen window and studied his strong arms as he lifted the set by himself.

His walk excited me. I tried pushing these feeling away because peace had returned to my life, and I didn't need the yelling and fighting. That didn't erase the desire to have him in my life, as sick as it may seem. He was my husband and the father of my girls. I loved him and couldn't shut him out of our lives.

Friday came and Debbie wanted to sleep over at her friend's house. Their friends took turns staying at our home. I loved having the kids over and listening to their laughter. I volunteered often as a chaperone for school trips. My time was filled with the kid's events.

An hour later, Effie called and invited Lori to stay over.

"Diane has been asking me all day."

"Are you sure, Effie?"

"I don't mind. We have nothing planned. Maybe you should get out yourself."

"That sounds good."

I jumped in the car and looked forward to visiting Cindy without the girls. She looked surprised opening her backdoor and seeing me standing on her doorstep at seven o'clock at night with no kids.

"I've got a night to myself and thought I'd stop by."

"Glad you came over. Come on in. How's everything going?" she asked.

We sat down with a cup of tea at her kitchen table. Her three kids were playing outside, and Ernie wasn't home. It felt good to be out alone.

"I'm so mixed-up, Cindy. It's nice being home with no fear or fighting, and yet, I miss him. Sounds sick, huh?"

"Not really."

"How's Ernie doing?"

"The same. We fight and makeup. For the moment, it's fine. That's how I live—for the moment. Right now, I've got butterflies wondering where he is at this hour. He should have been home two hours ago."

"I can't imagine living a normal life without all this tension. I envy women that have husbands who actually want to be home and do things with their families," I said. "I watch Bill and Effie every day having this kind of family life."

"I guess we have to deal with what has been handed to us, Alberta."

We talked about our problems with our husbands. Both of us were fighting with every ounce of strength to save our marriages. If we didn't swallow our pride, we'd both be divorced.

When I finished my tea and got up to leave, Cindy asked. "Why don't you stay longer? It's nice to have you here."

"Thanks, Cindy, but I'm going to take advantage of being alone. It doesn't happen very often. I'm going home to take a hot bath and crawl in bed with a good book, unless something good is on television."

"I don't blame you. I'm glad you came over."

"Me too, I needed this."

I drove home feeling relaxed, having had a night to myself. I gathered my nightgown and robe and turned on the hot water and took a long bath. Every pore opened up, and my body felt stress-free.

After twenty minutes, I toweled off and dressed for bed. My favorite shows were on, so I locked the house up and went to the bedroom in the back of the house. Except for the light on my nightstand, the house was in complete darkness.

It was good to stretch out and fall onto the soft pillow. The cool, night air was coming through the open bedroom window. I pulled the blanket over my shoulders to feel cozy. I kept the television on while I dozed off and on. I used it nightly to keep from feeling alone.

About ten o'clock, there was a knock on the door. I grabbed my robe and turned the front porch light on. It was Richie. He hadn't been coming to the house.

I opened the inside door, but kept the outside storm door latched. The screen was up for the summer so I didn't need to open it.

"It's kind of late. What are you doing here?"

I watched his every move for wobbling and secretly sniffed the surrounding air for the scent of liquor. I couldn't break the routine. I didn't find any sign of it.

"I'm sorry, but I was riding by and wanted to see you."

"Don't do this, Richie."

"I can't stand not being with you. It's so painful not coming home at night. I miss all of you. Please, let me in. I promise I won't push to stay."

I could see he was sober. It had been a long time since I had seen him this way.

"I can't." I answered in a frail voice, feeling myself weakening.

"Ten minutes. Just let me sit in the living room with you."

I could feel all the desires surfacing.

I broke down and opened the latch. "Just ten minutes, and then you have to leave."

"I promise."

He came in and sat in the corner of the couch while I continued standing. "God, it feels so good just to be able to sit in my own home. Are the girls in bed?"

I hesitated to answer. I didn't want him to know that we were alone. I knew by this time that I wasn't going to be strong. He looked so good, and when his cologne hit me, my knees began to shake. He looked the same as when I met him; my body started to come alive.

I stared at him without a reply. He looked up and came over to me putting his hands on my arms gently.

"I've missed you."

After not being touched for so long, his hand on my arm stirred emotions that had long been concealed. My feelings came alive and rushed over me. I knew it was wrong, but by then I didn't care. I craved his attention. Too much time had gone by without us making love and my desires went rampant.

He put is arm around my waist and pulled me up against him. I felt like jelly, and didn't fight him. His lips were on mine with soft kisses. I melted into his body as I pressed myself against him. The longing for him surfaced in a big way.

He looked deep into my eyes and I knew there was no stopping. We both started for the bedroom. He untied the belt around my robe, and it fell to the floor. I could feel the passion take over my body and soul. I couldn't think of anything but his touch.

We lay in the bed and held each other. The warmth of his body drove me insane. I couldn't remember the last time he was clear-headed so that we could give each other pleasure. It was wonderful. I didn't want to think about anything but this moment. We made love and talked for hours.

"I want to come home. I can make it different, and we can all be happy. I've changed. Let me prove it."

It felt completely right. I was back in his arms and he showed more love than I ever dreamed he could. My trust was back. He was so tender and showed so much feeling. As usual, we didn't talk about his drinking. He was sincere and I truly felt that the separation made him do a complete turn-a-round. We were going to be happy.

"I believe you this time, Richie."

"I've changed. You'll see." He kissed me, and we made love again. Instead of using common sense, I let my heart take over my emotions. Everything I wanted was being offered to me. For the first time, I slept in peace, with my husband next to me.

I woke up hearing the banging of pots and pans in the kitchen. I'm always up at the crack of dawn, but I had slept like a log. I lay there for a few moments, smiling. He came in and put a steaming, hot cup of coffee on the nightstand. He bent down and gave me a kiss. We acted like newlyweds.

After getting dressed, Debbie arrived home first from her friends. She spotted her father as soon as she entered the front door. She ran to him.

"Hi, Dad!" Her eyes lit up.

"I've missed you," he said giving her a huge hug.

About the same time, Lori came in with her bag of clothes, and Diane trailing.

"Daddy...!" She ran over and kissed him.

"Are you staying?" Debbie asked with hope in her eyes.

"Yes, I am. What do you think about that?"

Lori looked at Diane and giggled.

We became a family again, Richie didn't drink and he was home every night. We worked around the house together and after a few months I felt that I'd made the right decision. The girls loved it when we went to see my parents. The in-ground pool was the main focus all weekend, and sometimes, we'd take our nephews and niece, Gilly, Paula and Gary. My brothers, Bill and Joe, still lived with my parents, as did Leona and Bob. If Albert and his wife, Maria, came with their sons, Danny and David, it was more special. Dad and Mom never complained and welcomed every one of us.

We'd take our children to Nantasket beach to swim or after supper, place a blanket on the sand after the crowds left and let them collect shrimp or crabs that got caught between rocks during the changing of the tide. Maria and I would fill a pail with periwinkles that we collected off the rocks.

All the kids loved the hours spent on the rides at the amusement park. When the kids got older, they loved walking down the steep hill of Beacon Road to the main drag and going to the candy store. Handing them a few dollars each, made them happy filling their brown paper bags up with all variety of hard and soft candies. They'd come through the door smiling knowing they had to let the candy last all weekend.

Since the birth of our daughters, our best times as a family were spent in Hull, whether it was for a day or a weekend. Richie was himself again, and I could feel life flowing back into all of us. It was enjoyable spending time with him. He sat and laughed with everyone and gave the girls the attention they craved. I laughed and bounced around doing my housework. My mind stopped thinking 24/7, and I didn't suffer from migraines. My pills stayed in the bottle. Everyone seemed to be in harmony.

Making suppers was a joy. We sat every night at the table together and talked about our day's events. Months had passed; the horrific years seemed like a bad dream.

Anita & Lori

Chapter Thirty-Four
Boating Years

Richie always loved fishing and decided to buy a boat. He saw a used eighteen foot semi-cabin cruiser for sale at the boatyard in Somerset. It was an exciting time for us. Gilly, Gary and my niece, Paula, pitched in to help us get the boat in shape. They loved being with us, and I'd take them for the whole weekend. It turned into a fun project for all of us. The boat contained sleeping quarters but no bathroom on board. It was the only disadvantage.

The boys helped their uncle with the heavy scraping and sanding. It was hard work and took a good two months to complete the outside painting. I made curtains for the windows and did the cleaning inside the boat to get it thoroughly spotless. The girls puttered inside helping with the window cleaning or dusting.

Our big moment arrived when we were off for a day of sun, swimming, boating, and fishing. We took the boat to the Fall River Mariner to be placed in the water. Richie didn't want to pay the fee to keep it docked so he invested in a boat trailer.

I put the food, snacks, and cold drinks together. Being by the water all day would build up everyone's appetite and there'd be no end to eating.

We never got out of the bay. There wasn't a time that the engine didn't have some kind of problem. Richie didn't chance going out into open water. I felt so sorry for him because he wanted to take all of us deep sea fishing.

The boat was constantly being repaired, there was no doubt: he had bought a "lemon." We made the best of it and fished off the boat in the bay or stayed on shore and fished. The kids loved diving off the boat to swim. No one came home disappointed. The kids didn't mind that we never went out into the open ocean. It was fun just staying in the bay and being together. They'd take turns bringing their cousins or Cindy's daughter, Jeri.

I'd often come home with a migraine headache because of the wind blowing in my face, and my eyes hurt from the reflection of the sun on the water. The constant rocking of the boat only added to the headaches. After spending the whole day out in the water, I'd suffer for it. I kept a hat on and wore sun glasses to help protect my eyes from the brightness, but I'd develop a headache just from the heat.

My family and relatives were migraine sufferers. I had developed them off and on since my early teens. It was normal to spend three days in bed with my head pounding. Most of the time, I would be behind closed doors, away from noise. There I'd lie with a wet, ice-cold cloth on my forehead and over my eyes. I'd press the palm of my hands against each temple and try to keep pressure on them. I was aware of what would bring them on and sun was a big factor.

If the boat engine refused to start, we didn't make it a wasted day. We'd take the kids to the shoreline with their pails and walk on the rocks looking for periwinkles. Lori would often come close to falling on her face trying to catch a crab or tiny shrimp stuck between the rocks. We all loved the ocean and our favorite times as a family were spent there.

Boating was one of many things that we did with our nephews and niece. In the winter, I'd take them sledding or ice skating. They'd come to our house during a snow storm and build a huge snowman or a snow fort. Because our front yard slopped, water settled to form a big skating rink for the kids.

Gary and Jeri went with us on a trip to Punxsutawney, Pennsylvania, to visit my sister, Leona and her husband Bob. We rented a camper, and I made all the meals beforehand including desserts. They owned a farm, and the kids loved it.

There were cows, chickens, ducks, pigs, sheep, and a loud rooster that was determined to wake me up at 5:00 a.m. every morning, going under our camper to crow. I threatened my sister, telling her it would be our dinner some night.

It was a great time together; we hated to see our vacation end after only a week, I didn't know how long it would be before I saw my sister again.

Paula may have been six years older than the girls, but she loved spending time with them. She brought her friends to the house and the living room became a dance hall once the record player was started. Debbie and Lori looked up to Paula. The gatherings were a great time in our lives. Richie came home nights and calmness filled the house at bedtime. I knew he stopped for a drink some nights because I could detect the smell, but I didn't want to start any arguments and continued to ignore it. We were happy again and that's all that mattered.

A few years went by, and Paula moved to Florida when she was eighteen-years old. She moved in with a girlfriend named Toni. Anita made plans to take Gilly and Gary, along with Debbie, to visit Paula for two weeks. Sonny had to work and was staying home. Debbie was invited to go and was twelve-years old by now. Anita invited Richie and me to join her, but we didn't have enough money. Lori was eight-years old, and it would have been difficult for Anita to watch her. She was devastated when she found out they had plans to go to Disney World and she wouldn't be tagging along.

My parents came to visit one Sunday. Dad overheard Debbie, all excited, talking about going to Disney World with her aunt.

My father looked over at me and asked, "How come the rest of you aren't going? You should be taking Lori."

"We don't have the money for that, Dad. Anita's paying for Debbie." I was embarrassed letting him know that we didn't have money for a vacation, nor did Richie show any interest in going.

I went into the kitchen to make coffee, and he followed me. "I'll give you five-hundred dollars to put toward the trip for all of you to go."

"I can't take that from you," I said, shocked.

"How do you think the others in the family have been going on trips?"

"I just gathered they had the money. Why would I think differently?" I hadn't realized till then that he financed the trips my siblings took through the years.

Within a week, I received a check from Dad in the mail. I couldn't wait to tell Richie.

"Isn't this great? We can all go!"

I'd never been to Florida and had dreamed of going so often. I was as excited as the girls.

"I don't think I'll be able to take the time off. You go and enjoy yourself."

"I want us to go together. It'll mean the world to the girls. We have enough money."

"I can't leave the business that long, and besides, it doesn't interest me," he answered.

"It doesn't interest you to be with your family? We'd probably never be able to afford going on our own."

Nothing budged him. I started to worry about him having time on his hands with us being gone. Would he turn back to drinking? The good years never stopped my fear thinking about it.

I wasn't going to say no to such a great gift. Lori was ecstatic knowing that she was going to Disney World. I was just as energized having something so special to look forward to with the family. The money would only be enough for Lori and me to stay a week.

We landed in Fort Lauderdale, and it was like another world, seeing my first Palm trees. Lori ran around trying to collect fast-legged lizards running on the sidewalks or climbing up trees. She'd grab onto their tails only to see the broken limb in her fingers. The tiny creatures entertained her the whole week. Toni, Paula's roommate, ended up calling Lori "Lizzy" by the time we came home. Lizzy was a name that Toni continued to call her for many years.

Ft. Lauderdale fascinated me with its thick crowds and constant, busy activities. The memories of our time there would last forever. It was a week of fun, laughter, eating ice cream, going to places where and when we wanted. Our worries were forgotten.

Anita and I got along perfectly. No one fought about where someone else wanted to go. Each evening we ended up at the pool and swam or would just lie in the sun. Disney World was a dream fulfilled. Anita and I acted like kids ourselves. I hadn't felt that much freedom since I was single.

Our week flew by, and I didn't want to return home. Debbie was staying another week with Anita, and Lori flew home with me. I had been mentally relaxed being with the girls. This had been my first vacation without my husband.

Richie picked us up at Logan Airport in Boston. He gave hugs and kisses, acting excited about our return. It had been great having time for me. Lori's eyes sparkled like diamonds as she continuously talked from the back seat about the rides and characters at Disney World. Her conversation was mostly about the lizards.

"You were catching lizards?" Richie asked her.

"Yeah, Daddy. It was so much fun. Their tails kept coming off when I got one."

"That's because they're not supposed to be caught," he remarked.

He drove with a smile while he listened.

"How was your week?" I asked.

"Business as usual, nothing exciting happened."

He half turned looking at Lori sitting in the back seat, "Now Daddy doesn't have to be alone. I missed you, pumpkin."

"Me too, I wish you were with us."

"I had too much to do. I'm glad you all had fun."

As we pulled into the driveway, I felt the anxiety hit me. It had taken time for all of us to get back being a family. From Richie's years of drinking, I waited for the bottom to drop out with him clinging to the bottle again. Once Lori and I had settled in, he came home at night, but he flirted with a drink here and there. I felt he had to stay away from drinking completely. There were no arguments over it, because I held my feelings inside to keep peace in the house. I thought this kept everyone happy.

I didn't like leaving him for a week and giving him an open opportunity by himself when we left for Florida. With us gone he had no reason to rush home and he could spend time with his drinking buddies. He must have taken advantage of his time alone, because he started stopping off at the golf club again. He was continuously giving me a solid reason to live in fright with his return to drinking.

For the next week, I went around doing the routine chores. I missed Debbie, and so did Lori. I envied Anita and the kids sitting in the sun, walking in and out of the gift stores, eating by the pool, swimming and sightseeing.

During my trip, I realized how much I had stopped making my own decisions when Richie and I got back together. I fell into the old pattern of depending on him. It was odd because

I had become independent without him. From being self-sufficient for so long, I couldn't make up my mind if I missed being alone.

I was extremely happy when Debbie returned home; the house was empty without her. She told me that after Paula had spent two weeks with her family, she decided to move back home to North Dighton in a few months.

I realized that it had been healthy for Debbie to get away and do something different; we all needed that break. I wondered how she and Lori felt having their father back home. Did they feel secure that he would be home every night, or did they sit on pins and needles like me? I think none of us escaped the uncertainty. None of us voiced our opinions about the ups and downs in our lives. The events happened; they were over, and we went on with our daily activities.

I started to become jealous when I noticed couples laughing together or holding hands. Richie and I fell in the routine of taking each other for granted. It should have been the opposite after what we had gone through.

He started to go his way, and I went mine. I had my job at the police station, and he had the work in the shop, which seemed to be slowing down. The familiar distance had reappeared.

Slowly, he started to come home later each night. I could hear the kids arguing more and knew they were becoming worried with the same signs starting to reappear with their father. Everyone was up tight, and my patience wore thin. Again, I held my anger so the girls wouldn't be upset.

I wanted to make changes in the house. Things had stayed the same with nothing new to brighten our lives. I decided to start with our bedroom; maybe some nice wallpaper would transform the familiarity. Richie knew how to wallpaper and said he'd teach me instead of hiring someone. I measured, cut, pasted, and layered the walls with the paper. Before I knew it, I was the one doing the work; he was nowhere to be seen.

"Aren't you going to help me?" I asked once.

"You seem to be doing a great job," he answered joking.

Without realizing it, I was looking for an excuse to release my bottled-up anger about his stopping to have a few drinks at night. He was home early, but I knew the pattern.

"What else is different in my life?" I said slapping the paste on the wallpaper with such force that it splattered on the floor.

"What do you mean by that remark?" Richie asked.

"What do you do at home?"

"I don't have time to do the little things around here," he stated, aggravated.

I hated making a big deal out of doing the wallpapering, but I was left to do another thing around the house alone. It seemed we did nothing together. I stopped knowing how to just sit down calmly and talk. My silence never stopped him from staying out. His life seemed to start when he was out with friends. Maybe if I had shut my mouth, there wouldn't have been a quarrel.

"If you came home at a decent time like other husbands, you would."

"I'm home at night."

"Yes, after you've stopped for a drink."

"Here we go again. I'm home, aren't I?"

"Richie, you can't play with drinking. You've got to stop completely."

He walked out of the room and went down to his workshop. That made my resentment worse, and I didn't know how to control it. After an hour of wallpapering, I took out my frustration by cleaning the room spotless. I had a bomb sitting in my gut ready to explode from the terror of our lives possibly being turned upside down again.

He came back up to the living room, and I told him about a customer that needed an answer that evening about his television set.

"I'll call him in the morning."

"No, I'll be the one taking the call without an answer for him. I'd like you to call him back, please. He's expecting a callback today."

My voice was loud. I had lost control in trying to discuss anything rationally. The girls were in school so nothing was going to keep me calm.

"Alberta, keep your voice down. Do you want the whole neighborhood to hear you?" He wasn't used to seeing me in a wild state.

I looked out the window and noticed Bill and Effie sitting on their front steps enjoying the summer warmth. I flipped out. I walked straight to the open window. "You think this is yelling? HOW'S THIS?" I felt my insides open up. My mind was saying, *Stop this, you're out of control*! But I couldn't. All the disappointments, broken promises, and false hopes that faced me day in and day out made me lose it. This small flirting with drinking at night made me think we were heading for disaster. I needed to end it.

"What's the matter with you? They can hear you across the street. Get away from the window." He tried to pull me from it.

My loud voice accelerated into screams. "Everyone in the neighborhood already knows that you're out drinking every night. What else is new?" I couldn't calm down.

"I'm going downstairs," he said storming out of the living room. It was his private hideaway. Why not? I was out-of-control not knowing how to deal with his constant excuses for drinking.

I looked across the street and Effie's family had disappeared into their house. *God, who and what have I become?* I was ashamed of myself for the scene I put on for my neighbors.

I went into the kitchen and leaned on the sink. Our garage was under the kitchen, and the window was high above the driveway. I saw Effie walk to her mailbox by the street. She opened it and sifted through her mail. Before turning back, she stopped and looked up at the sky. It was a beautiful, clear day in the eighties without a cloud anywhere. She smiled and turned to go up the front steps.

I watched her and the tears poured out of me. *When was the last time I felt that way about life?* I felt like my sun had faded and that no sunshine was ever going to be around me. *Will I ever feel like that again?"* I wondered.

Her garage door was open, and I saw Bill putting his plumbing tools away. I wondered what it must be like for Effie and the kids to have him home every night. They never yelled, and they did so many things as a family.

About a half hour before the school bus arrived, Richie said he had a delivery to make and would be home later. By now, I knew it was just talk. I had no faith in what he said or did. I was sure our spat helped him find an excuse to go out and drink.

I struggled to keep my marriage together for the girls. If I didn't have them, I would have walked out years ago.

It wasn't long before Debbie and Lori stopped asking where their father was at night. His empty seat at the supper table was disregarded.

(Boating Years) Left Back – Jeri, Debbie & Lori

Back row-Alberta – Middle row left – Lori, Anita, Gary, Debbie, Paula in front (in Florida) Below: Left-Toni & Anita

Chapter Thirty-Five
Reaching Out for Help

I spent another night by myself and going to bed alone. After being lied to so often, I no longer bothered calling Richie's hangouts to see if he was going to be late. *Why do I keep taking this man back? Let him drink himself to death, I don't care anymore.* It was midnight, and I knew this late hour meant heavy drinking.

My serenity never lasted long. I was back to nighttime becoming a waiting game, being on edge and bracing myself for the sound of the ladders clanking on his truck when he drove into the driveway.

I heard the front door open and close. He entered the bedroom and became a raging bull. His calm personality was gone, and he was now looking for a fight. He ripped the covers off me and got on the bed. Placing one knee on top of my chest, he swung the other leg on the side of me.

With his hands around my throat, he yelled, "I'm going to kill you!"

I couldn't believe this was my husband. The air was being shut off from my throat. I was horrified! He weighed too much for me to push him off. My thoughts ran to the girls finding me dead.

I looked up and saw the Crucifix above our bed. I pleaded out loud as my breath disappeared, "Jesus, Mary and Joseph, help me!"

Instantly, he took his hands off my throat, I gasped for air.

"What are you nuts?" he said with a shocked expression.

I was choking from the pressure he had applied to my vocal cords, and I couldn't talk.

Suddenly, he just turned, fell on his side of the bed, and passed out.

After that night, I wanted to make him disappear from my life. One part of me started to pray that he'd be killed in an accident so I wouldn't have to make the decision to leave him. His death would solve my problem.

Another part of me asked God to forgive me for thinking such a terrible thing. I wanted the kind of life we were leading to stop, but I didn't know how to do it. I didn't realize that I kept our nightmare going by putting up with this abuse.

I heard his heavy breathing and couldn't relax lying in bed after such an ordeal. Within an hour, a panic attack overwhelmed me. I sat up and tried to calm myself. I had the frightening feeling that I was separating from my body. I got out of bed and went into the corner of my bedroom. I sat down on the rug, curled up in a ball, and pushed my knees into my chest. I stayed immobilized in the pitch black room.

Oh my God, I'm coming apart. That moment was the first realization that I was on the verge of a breakdown. I stayed frozen in that position for hours. By then, I knew that I had been pushing my body beyond its limit.

Have I waited too long? Am I going to get control of myself?

Fearing there was no hope of returning back to reality, I got up and went into the bathroom to take a tranquilizer. I returned and got under the covers, but my whole body shook uncontrollably. I was scared to death one pill wouldn't work and fought my desire to take more. Before long, I passed out.

Waking the next morning, I couldn't concentrate and my legs were like jelly. I fought to breathe normally. My hands and insides were trembling. My heart was racing so fast in my chest that I felt dizzy.

After I forced myself to get the girls off to school, I went into the bedroom and woke Richie. I shook him on the shoulder. "Richie, wake up,"

"What time is it?"

"It's close to eight-thirty. Get up!"

"What's the matter?"

There was no strength in me to talk above a whisper, I was completely weak. I truly believe that I had had a breakdown.

I sat on the edge of the bed because my legs couldn't hold me up. "I can't do this anymore. You could have killed me last night."

"What are you talking about?"

"Do you remember what you did to me?"

He looked at me and answered honestly, "I don't remember a thing."

"That's because you're now having blackouts from drinking."

I sat quietly for a moment because it was a strain to talk. I didn't tell him about my sitting in the corner. I didn't feel close enough emotionally to share it with him. He wouldn't have understood.

"I'm going to the Alcoholics Anonymous center in Taunton today and ask for help. I'd like you to come with me."

"AA? What are you going to do, blab our private business all over the place?"

"I'm not holding a thing back with them, I'm coming apart. You have no desire to stop drinking."

"I don't have a problem. I can stop anytime. I really don't want you to go, Alberta. We can handle this."

"No, we can't. It's too much for us. We need professional help."

"I'll be very upset if you go."

"Then be upset because I'm going. I'm on the verge of a breakdown." I still couldn't share what happened to me during the night.

"Let's not be melodramatic about this."

He looked at me like I was insane. I didn't want to open up emotionally to him. Because I had lost all the trust I had in him, I thought of him as my enemy.

"So, you won't come with me?" I asked one more time.

"No, and that's final."

"Well, I'm not ashamed to ask for help."

I got up from the bed and walked at a snail's pace into kitchen, as if I were walking in slow motion and not aware of my surroundings. I washed the dishes left in the sink from the kid's breakfast just to keep moving. I had to be doing something to keep up with my body that was racing at high speed. There were five hours before the bus would bring the girls home.

I drove into the parking lot of the Alcoholics Anonymous Center. I didn't doubt for one minute that I needed to be there. The receptionist was very friendly and put me right at ease.

"Hi, my name is Alberta Lopes, and I want to talk to someone. My husband has a drinking problem, and it's at the stage where he's abusive."

It felt like a ton came off my shoulders just by voicing my problem out loud to another person. *God, why did I wait over ten years to reach out?*

"Have a seat, Alberta, and someone will be with you shortly."

It was an old building, located in the downtown business area. It looked like it needed multiple repairs inside and out. It had old fixtures, chipped paint on the walls, and uneven floors.

Fifteen minutes passed before a gentleman came to me and extended his hand.

Hi, Alberta, I'm Ron Mello, come in," he said as he led me to a room in the back.

I settled into a comfortable arm chair in front of his desk.

"I want you to be aware that I'm a recovering alcoholic," Ron stated. "I volunteer my time here helping others who are suffering from alcohol abuse. I'm told that your husband is at the stage of being abusive. Has he been drinking long?"

He's been drinking as long as we've been married and before I knew him."

"How long is that?"

"It's been ten years at least."

"Has his drinking become worse over the years?"

"He's at the point of trying to hurt me."

"Does he remember it the next day or want to talk about it?"

"No, he doesn't remember, and if I don't talk about it, he's thrilled. To be honest, Ron, I've lost interest in talking. In fact, neither of us discuss it."

"Not remembering is a sign that he's having blackouts. Tell me about the stages. Did he drink when you met him?"

Before I knew it, I was spilling my guts out to a stranger and tears were streaming down my face, I was begging for someone to help me so I wouldn't have a complete mental breakdown. I told him about the tranquilizers, how they were the only thing keeping me together, how I couldn't get through the day without them, and how I needed them to help me survive.

A half hour went by with me explaining all the details to Ron from the moment I met Richie to revealing his family history with drinking. Once I got to the part about the girls being surrounded with this unhealthy family life, I broke down.

"I'm supposed to be there to protect them. I'm not a good mother," I said, my shoulders shaking, and my crying with loud, uncontrollable sobs.

"Living this way doesn't mean you're a bad mother, Alberta. You can't control an alcoholic. They have to want to help themselves and develop the desire to stop. If not, they'll lose everything, home, family, and their jobs. I did. It's normal for a high percentage of drinkers to think that there's still no problem after being left out in the street. If they don't get help, they'll die from it."

"What can I do to help us?"

"You have to get selfish and help yourself and the girls."

I told him about my episode of sitting on the floor in the corner of the bedroom.

"That's a strong sign of a mind breaking down. Your body can only take so much stress. Stress is a killer. If something happened to you, what good would you be to your girls? What's more scary is that your husband could get custody of them in his condition. He'd find you unfit. Your daughters would be in a worse environment."

He continued, "If you left the house, he could keep you out. He'd have grounds to divorce you and claim that you walked out leaving him and your daughters. We don't tell couples to leave unless it's life-threatening. We're here to help you as a family."

"I would take my girls with me. I'm so lost that I don't know what to do next."

"My recommendation is for you to go to Al-Anon. Have you heard of it?"

"I've read it's a group of family members who support each other with their problems with the alcoholic."

"These meetings will help you to understand that drinking is an illness," he said. "There is just so much you can do to help your husband. It's a great group of people working together to show you what you can and can't do to help the alcoholic. You'll learn what you're probably doing wrong to make the situation worse. There comes a time when the alcoholic has to swim or sink by himself. You can't *make* him stop. His actions have nothing to do with what you or the girls do. This is his battle."

Ron smiled and placed a pamphlet in my hand. "Here's a booklet with locations and times that Al-Anon meet. If you find you need more counseling, call me. Here's my business card. This is a free service."

Free—what a gift! This way Richie couldn't be on my back about how we couldn't afford the counseling. I couldn't help but think that if I had been aware of AA instead of going to Mr. Cummings' counseling, maybe we would have been on the road to recovery years ago.

I arrived home by lunchtime and found Richie's truck was still parked in the driveway. I wasn't surprised. I'm sure that his curiosity got to him with my trip to AA.

When I got to the kitchen, he was making a sandwich. "Want one? I'll make it."

"Thanks, I can't eat right now."

"So, how did you make out? Am I a drinker?" he said trying to be funny.

"You're at the stages of blackouts. I'd like us to go to counseling together. There's no charge for it."

"I have no problem. What did they tell you to do?"

I was putting up my defense and wouldn't let him get off that easily. "If you want to know how to handle this problem, then you have to come with me. I'm not going to go to meetings and come home to explain what was said so you don't have to go."

"You mean you're going to start going to meetings? Why?"

"...because, we *need* help! I need help. At least, I'm admitting we can't do this alone anymore. It takes more of a person to ask for assistance then to ignore the catastrophes that are happening in our family. I've let too many years go by as it is."

"I told you before that I don't like anyone knowing about our personal affairs."

"When are you going to face the fact that everyone knows you're never home and that you're out drinking? It's a small town. Don't you realize that you're seen at the Golf Club more than usual? Do you honestly think people don't know you're drunk?"

"Well, I wanted to see you before I left for work. I'll see you tonight," he said, walking out of the kitchen.

We were finally talking, and he couldn't handle the truth about himself. I let out a deep sigh and let his dismissive action roll off me. I was on too much of a high after the visit to the center; I didn't feel alone anymore. There were other families out there going through this nightmare, too. Knowing that somehow gave me strength.

234

Chapter Thirty-Six
Al-Anon Meeting

The next afternoon, I pulled out the booklet that Ron gave me. I had a couple of hours before the kids came home from school so I made myself a cup of tea, and sat on the couch to relax.

It was Friday, and I saw a 7:00 p.m. Al-Anon meeting scheduled in Taunton the following Sunday night at the Memorial United Methodist Church. It was only ten minutes from the house, so I planned to attend. I called my niece, Paula, to come over and keep the girls company that evening.

Sunday night came and I looked forward to going to the meeting. When I arrived at the church, I learned that there were three meetings going on at the same time; an AA meeting downstairs, and the Al-Anon and Alateen meetings on the main floor.

I was amazed at how many people filled the foyer. Men and women along with teens paced the building. Everyone was rushing to one or another of the three meetings.

"Hi, Alberta, how are you?" I turned to see a familiar face.

I hadn't seen my girlfriend, Sandy Simmons, since our high school years.

"Sandy!" I gave her a huge hug. "How have you been? Lord, how many years has it been since we've seen each other?"

"It has to be over ten, I'd say. What on earth are you doing here?" she asked me.

"Richie has a drinking problem, and our lives are so upside down. Why are you here?"

"I married John Thibert and he's been fighting the same problem. He's downstairs at the AA meeting, I just came up to use the restroom. I come weekly to support him."

"I thought I'd try Al-Anon. I need something. It's reached the point where his drinking is out-of-control." Knowing Sandy had to understand, I wasn't embarrassed to admit my problem to her.

"Does he want to come to a meeting?"

"He may, I'm not sure."

"Well, John and I are here if you need us. I have to get back to the meeting. The Al-Anon is down the hall. Good luck!"

"Thanks, Sandy, I hope to see you again."

Seeing her gave me comfort. I walked down the hall and followed the Al-Anon arrows. My heart was pounding with anticipation, since I wasn't sure what went on in these meetings.

When I entered the room, a short, blonde woman in a black pantsuit looked my way.

"Hi, you look new to the group."

"Yes, I am."

"Well, my name is Helen."

"Hi, Helen, I'm Alberta Lopes."

"I'm the counselor for the group, and just for your information, we go by first names here. Welcome to our group, and please, find a seat and get comfortable."

There was a mixture of men and women talking while pouring their coffees from a side table with a platter full of mixed assortments of pastry. Once I found a seat in the corner, a few people came over and politely introduced themselves.

Within ten minutes, Helen started the meeting. "Hi, everyone, we have a new person with us. Her name is Alberta."

"Hi, Alberta," they all said at once, causing an echo to bounce off the walls of the large, empty room, which only contained the chairs.

The group looked over at me and I could feel myself blushing. I hated being the center of attention. It had been years since I was in a closed area since my attack at church. I was now trying to fight the familiar, unwanted, sweaty feeling trying to overtake me.

"Would someone like to read page nineteen in the book? Alberta, what about you? After you're done, we'll discuss the subject."

Helen acted excited to get me involved. Two men sitting in the room looked up and smiled at me.

I hated to read in front of people, and I became uncomfortable. I wasn't good with words; I'd hesitate, mispronounce them or babble fast with no emotion.

"I'd rather sit in and listen if it's okay."

"Sure, that's fine. Betty, could you read?"

Betty picked up the book and started to read about the non-drinker trying to control the alcoholic. They were short paragraphs about what actions the family member was doing wrong by reacting to their loved one's drinking behavior. The group was asked to have a discussion about it.

"Can anyone relate to this action?" Helen asked looking around.

A young brunette about twenty-five stood up. "Ralph came home last night, and we fought for an hour over his drinking. I told him if he did it one more time, I was leaving him. Our son Johnny didn't need this."

A man in jeans and work boots cut in. "Jessica, would you really get up and leave him? You're always telling him that when you get mad. Do you think you have the strength to walk out on him? Where would you go?"

"I mean it this time."

Helen spoke up. "Don't make threats that you can't keep. Don't say it and then stay. You have to carry out what you say to an alcoholic. If not, they mentally block you out. Make sure you have plans on where you'd go before you say it. You're helping to do more harm with their drinking when you threaten and don't follow through."

"It would be hard to go to my parents because I never told them about Ralph's drinking," Jessica answered.

"Why not?" An older woman with bright, red hair asked, sounding impatient.

"They would be upset knowing that I was staying with him."

"Your parents might be more supportive than you think," the woman replied.

Helen cut back into the conversation. "The more you do for the alcoholic, the more you cripple them. Hiding the drinking events from family only protects the drinker." She continued, "You're allowing them to go on with their behavior without taking responsibility for their actions by you covering up for them. Why should they stop drinking when you're helping to hide it?"

I listened and finally got the courage to speak up. "It sounds like you're talking about me. I'm doing all of that and probably more."

"Alberta, you've taken the first step, you're here. Listen to what we're saying. If you feel trapped in a situation at home, call one of us. Take telephone numbers. We are here to support each other."

"Hi, my name is Jake," a man with silver-white hair cut in. "The more I stopped covering up for my wife, Janet, the harder it was for her to find an excuse to drink."

"Do you find you cover up for your husband?" Helen asked me.

"I hold it all in because I'm trying not to fight in front of the kids. I want them to still respect and love him. I feel so torn up."

A young girl with a short, boyish hairstyle wearing a pair of faded, gray sweats spoke up. "It's not healthy doing that. You need to vent but not with him,"

"That's easy to say," I said. "What do you do when they're in a blackout and being abusive? I can't just get up and walk out."

"If it's at that point, you need to seriously see about kicking him out for the safety of the kids," Jake said.

"Does your family know about it?" Jennifer questioned.

"No, and I know that they'd be upset that I kept it from them."

"How would you feel, Alberta, if you had a daughter who suffered mentally and physically from a husband's abuse and wasn't telling you?" Helen asked.

"I'd be sick over it."

"They deserve to know what's going on."

"You're right," I said. I hadn't looked at it from my parents' perspective.

Helen looked directly at me, "The more you hide his drinking, the longer this merry-go-round continues. Someone has to get off it to stop the routine events that are happening. We call it the merry-go-round effect because the more you continue not talking about the drinking, hiding it, defending him, or not making any changes, you keep the merry-go-round going. Everyone's actions stay the same and the family ignores the daily upsets."

Helen looked back at the group. "The one thing you all have to remember is that they drink because it's a disease. It's not because of something you've done. The more you argue with them, the better excuse they have to run back out and not come home. You can't reason with anyone who's drunk," Helen said trying to reassure us. "You have to take care of yourself. If you get sick from this stress, you won't be there for your kids. The more you let go, the less guilt you'll have. Your battle is protecting your children."

The meeting was like a shot-in-the-arm for me. I felt a ton of weight come off my shoulders. Knowing that I wasn't alone was a relief in itself. All these years I sat home, a few miles from this church, feeling separated from the world. *There must be thousands suffering from this*, I thought. By now, I had no doubt that Richie was an alcoholic; there's a name for him being so sick.

The meeting lasted an hour, and from it I got the strength to go home and face any problems because of the high I received from the group support. Richie surprised me by not staying out and was at home. Paula had gotten a ride home from a friend.

He came and sat next to me on the couch. "How did your meeting go?"

"I really enjoyed it. I can't believe how many families are going through this." I tried to let him know that it was a problem all over, not just with us.

"Really?" he said looking mostly amused.

"Would you go to one AA meeting? I'll go with you. I want to understand what you're going through."

"If it would mean that much to you, I'll try one meeting."

Were my prayers going to be answered? Was he ready to get help?

Chapter Thirty-Seven
AA Meeting

Another Sunday night arrived, and Anita watched the girls so that Richie and I could attend an AA meeting.

We should be back in a few hours," I told her. "Here's the telephone number and address in case there's an emergency."

When we pulled into the church, he was stunned by the crowded parking lot.

"Holy cow, look at how many cars are here," he said. "Did you see anyone we know last week?"

"As a matter of fact, I did."

"Who?" I could see his discomfort sensing that he'd be embarrassed if someone knew us.

"Sandy Simmons, her name is Thibert now. We were close friends growing up and spent our teen years together. She lived in my neighborhood, but we haven't seen each other since we were in high school. Her husband, John, is an alcoholic and she comes to the meetings with him."

"I don't know them," he replied.

"Maybe they'll be here tonight, and I can introduce you."

Instead of going to my Al-Anon meeting, I went with Richie to give him support. The AA meeting was held downstairs in a huge room filled with rows of long tables, and it was the largest room in the building. Several of the attendees were smoking and the room as packed with thick, grey smoke; my throat inhaled the visible vapor and my eyes watered. Others were going in different directions to help themselves with coffee and snacks that had been placed on tables against the back wall. The sounds echoed from people walking on the old, wooden floors. I could smell the familiar stale liquor from the ones who had been drinking. It didn't matter, at least they were *here* and not in a bar. They wanted help.

We didn't see any small tables so we sat down at a long one with a few couples. Most everyone mixed in, though some looked lost sitting off by themselves. Speakers got up and introduced themselves as alcoholics with such ease.

"Hi, my name is Ralph, and I'm an alcoholic." He openly admitted having a disease.

He talked about losing everything he had owned, including his family, job, and a home. Constantly moving from one location to another, trying to find places to sleep had become a normal hardship. The story saddened me when I heard that he had once held a high administrative position.

Two women spoke, but from my husband's frequent trips to get coffee, it made me feel he couldn't relate to their lives. Another man got up to speak, and his poor attire made me thing that he was there just to have a place to get warm and get food for the night.

Richie surprised me and stayed the whole time without complaining, but I sensed that he wasn't comfortable being there. I was disappointed that no one spoke about the life-style he was leading. Here I was trying to control the speakers. I wanted him to connect with someone and have the desire to return to the next meeting.

My friend Sandy wasn't there that night, and I had hoped to meet John and introduce him to Richie. I wasn't letting go and having my husband decide what he wanted to do, I was trying to control everything.

When we got out of the meeting and walked to the car, he said what I feared. "You know, I really listened and thought maybe I had a drinking problem. There's no way I'm as bad as those people. Those are real back alley, falling down drunks. My life isn't like that. I have my business, home and family. They've lost all of it."

"You've lost your family time and time again, your business isn't stable, and you've been kicked out of your home in the past. You're not in control of your life, and I don't see any signs of your drinking stopping. Why do you have to wait till you lose everything?" I could feel him slipping away from me.

"Are you serious? Do you honestly believe that my life would become that bad?"

"Everyone starts slowly. Now is the time to try to control it."

"I promised to go, and I did. There isn't a thing wrong with me. I drink no more than my buddies. Their wives aren't up in arms over it, and I can give it up anytime I want. What's wrong with me enjoying a drink now and then?"

"Richie, you can't stop at one drink. You drink until you are drunk out of your mind in blackouts."

"So, I have a few bad nights. I can't believe you almost had me thinking I was an alcoholic."

My heart sank. Even with this serious conversation, he couldn't get honest with himself. Of all the meetings, this one didn't have speakers that he could relate to. The door closed; he wasn't coming to terms with his drinking. I wanted everyone and everything to fix him. The one good thing that came out of his attending that one AA meeting was that he didn't feel as comfortable over-drinking. He was trying to control the amount he drank.

Our lives stayed the same with him coming and going as he pleased. The meeting made him more convinced that our problems weren't that bad. I tried to adjust to the fact that I was going to be alone in this marriage. I continued to go to my Al-Anon meetings, and Sonny and Anita started going with me to the church to attend the AA meetings. We hoped

Richie would see the family support and have the strength to fight this demon. While the three of us attended, Richie, who needed it the most, was out drinking. I'd hear a speaker and wish he was there to hear their testimony.

I called Ron and decided to get private counseling.

"Hi, Ron, it's Alberta Lopes."

"Hi, Alberta, how are you doing?"

"Not good. Richie went to an AA meeting and came out convinced that there was no problem with his drinking. His brother and wife have been attending meetings with me."

"What about Al-Anon meetings, are you going?"

"I've been to a few and plan to continue because they do help me."

"I'm glad to hear that. Right now you have to worry about you. If not, you're not going to have the strength to help your daughters."

"Can I have one-on-one counseling with you?"

"I can see you for awhile. Usually Patricia Casey counsels the non-drinker but she's helping her family with a parent who has cancer. I can see you tomorrow at 10:00 a.m., if that's fine with you."

"It's a good time because my girls will be in school."

"Okay, I'll see you then."

"Thanks, Ron, I'm looking forward to seeing you again."

We met the next day, and Ron talked a lot about what the alcoholic feels and how Richie was in denial.

"It took twenty-years of heavy drinking for me to lose everything, including a loving wife and two beautiful little girls. Until Richie admits to being an alcoholic and has no control over his life, he will not stop his routine."

"Are you saying that there's no way of me helping him if he continues like this?"

"You can't save him. *He* has to save *himself*. You can help by helping yourself. You have to stop defending him and hiding his actions, the more you do that, the more he doesn't have to come to terms with the fact that his life is uncontrollable because of his drinking."

He changed the subject. "Have you called your parents?"

"No, I haven't."

"You're acting like your husband. You have to break the cycle by facing your problems. By you not telling anyone, you're protecting him. Promise me next week you'll call your parents and talk to them.

"Yes, I will, but I feel like I'm going ahead, and he's staying behind."

"He is, but that's his choice. Someone has to stop the family merry-go-round effect of someone drinking. If no changes are made, everyone's life keeps going in the same direction with no results. You have to get off it or no solution will ever be reached. You have to let go and put it in God's hands."

"Helen from Al-Anon mentioned the merry-go-round effect."

"That's a way of describing the fast motions that keep going around and around in an alcoholic family day in and day out without anyone ever trying to stop the routine of drinking. The members keep the ride going by defending the alcoholic so they can hide their conduct. This gives them a reason not to change or give up their destructive behavior. You don't mean to do this, but it makes the situation worse.

"It's so hard when he comes in the door drunk wanting to fight. He's well aware that it upsets and scares all of us, especially Lori. For some reason he always goes into her room to wake her up."

"Do you leave him alone with her?"

"No, and nothing happens. He tries talking to her. "

"You can't allow that."

"I follow him in her room to make sure he comes out and he goes into our bed. He avoids going into Debbie's room."

"Why is that?"

"I'm not sure. Debbie isn't scared of him at all. Maybe it's because she's older. I think he knows that I get angry when he wakes Lori up when there's no need for it."

"He knows you won't fight back because you don't want to frighten the girls. This gives him control."

"It's now to a point where he is violent. How much more do I take?"

"If violence is coming into play, then I would advise you to get him out of the house. The safety of the three of you is more important. He'll find a place to lay his body down."

"I don't see any light. I try love, getting angry or giving him the silent treatment, but nothing brings him home. My nerves are shot, and I'm always jumpy."

"Talk to your doctor about that. You need to get your rest and to stay calm."

"I've already told you that I'm on tranquilizers."

"Keep going to your meetings. Find someone you are comfortable with and get their telephone number. If you're in the area, drop in at the center. You may relate to someone here."

"Thanks, I will."

"I'll see you next Thursday at the same time."

"I appreciate you seeing me. I'll see you then."

The first thing I did the next morning was call my parents. They were absolutely astounded. They never saw us fight or detected any tension between us, and the girls seemed stable to them. They loved Richie and were heartbroken to learn of his drinking.

In time, I got to meet other people at the center. I was jealous of the men who talked about how they gave up drinking. Why couldn't Richie stop? I listened to their stories and realized how their lives were still upside down even without the drinking. Marriages were held together at a high level of stress with the temperaments of both partners always on edge. Couples still fought, the non-drinker watched every move to see if their mate was still drinking in secret, or each accused the other of cheating. Putting their lives back together wasn't easy. The alcoholic attended AA meetings every night trying to stay sober.

The social life was hard for the drinker because liquor was usually present at parties. It was difficult for them because the temptation was there. The alcoholic was always just an arm's length away from taking that first drink. Friends were ignorant to the dangers of the disease and continued to offer them drinks with the usual nudge. "Oh come on, one drink won't hurt you!'" not knowing they were addicted, because they don't admit to having a problem or inform people their alcoholics.

Alcoholics who saved their marriages sat and told me that the relationships were never the same. No matter how much they struggled to change, their partner wasn't there to help them. With years of fighting, having had no intimacy or shared events, caused them to lose interest in each other.

They were emotionally drained. Too much had happened through the years.

I could relate to what they were saying because I was used to Richie being out so often that I started to do what I wanted, when I wanted. I didn't think of involving him or asking because he was never around for us.

My resentment started to pile up inside me when he came in late. He might not have been drunk, but he was opening the doors again to the restlessness at home. Skipping supper without a call was now a normal thing for him; I was supposed to *assume* that he wasn't coming home when he didn't phone. When he was home, I'd wish that he weren't, and then I'd complain if he wasn't. I stopped everything to entertain him. He began to infringe on my free time and what I wanted to do. I couldn't plan an evening with friends because he either wouldn't come home or would come in drunk. My personality changed to being more independent. I was starting to be more relaxed with him out of the house. I didn't know what I wanted any more; my feelings were twisted and rung out.

Chapter Thirty-Eight
Physical Abuse Stage

Debbie had her friends sleep over a lot on weekends, but now I began to notice that she wasn't having as many sleepovers. I also noticed the kids didn't visit her that often. She was spending a lot of time in her bedroom and seemed withdrawn.

I went into her room one night after I washed the supper dishes. "Debbie, is everything all right with you?"

"Yes. Why?"

"You seem quiet lately. How come Donna or Jeri haven't been coming over?"

"I've had things to do, Mom."

"It's not like you not to be running around with your friends. It's Saturday, why don't you invite them over tonight?"

"What time is Dad coming home?"

"Is that what this is all about, your father?"

"What if he comes in late and he's drunk? Why can't he be like my friend's fathers? They're home every single night, and they don't drink, either."

"I wish he was like that too, honey. You have every right to feel this way when our nights turn into a waiting game on how and when he comes home."

"I'd rather go to their house, and then I won't see it."

I hugged her, holding back tears. Her early years were being spent thinking about parent problems instead of enjoying her life to the fullest.

She was thirteen-years old and ready to enter her first year at the Dighton Rehoboth High School in the fall. Lori was nine and in fifth grade at the Dighton Elementary School.

My children had been sleeping at their friends' homes to avoid hearing the conflict between their mother and father. I allowed it, thinking that they wouldn't be home if he came in drunk. I felt relieved with them out of the house in case it happened. I pushed my kids out instead of keeping them home and handling the problem with Richie. It took years before I started to notice that the closeness I had with my girls had started to drift. They were getting older and bonded closer relationships with friends.

The next afternoon, Debbie got an invitation to sleep over at Jeri's, and Diane called Lori over to stay at her house for the night. I didn't want them to wait up for their father, so as always, I let them go.

Richie wasn't home, and I decided to write a letter to my girlfriend. I enjoyed the peace of not having to worry about anyone except myself. It got close to eleven, and my eyes became heavy. I was too tired to wait up for the news on television, and much to my surprise, I heard Richie's van pull in. I was relieved and thought, *Thank God, it's only eleven o'clock so he can't be too drunk.*

I heard him come in and walk into the kitchen, only to go out again. My curiosity got to me so I went into the kitchen without turning any lights on in the house, and I looked down in the driveway. The light was on inside his van, and I saw him sitting in the driver's seat putting a tall Vodka bottle to his mouth. I stood in disbelief as I watched him drink half of it in one gulp then he pulled out of the yard. I had no idea where he went.

I went back to bed, but sleep was the last thing on my mind. Now, I feared him coming back home. In half an hour, the van pulled back into the yard. The sound of the key opening the door made my heart pound. I lay still, not moving a muscle, hoping for him to ignore me. That wish quickly faded.

"Hey, wake up," he said, shaking my shoulder vigorously. I could smell the liquor. "Why aren't the kids in bed?"

"They're sleeping over at friends." I hated to tell him we were alone, but I knew he would have searched their rooms.

"Good. Get up I want to talk."

"What's the matter?" I was talking calmly, but I was both afraid and angry.

"Just get up," he said walking into the living room.

I wanted to push him against the wall and knock him out. Instead, as always, I figured not arguing would keep him calm. You'd think I would have realized by now that he was *looking* for a fight.

"Why aren't the kids here?"

"What do you mean?"

"Why aren't they home?" he questioned in an angry voice. I suddenly noticed him swaying.

"They have a right to go out. What's wrong with you?" I knew this was another moment that I should walk lightly to pacify him, but I was so angry inside that I could feel myself shaking, wanting to swing at him.

"Where's my supper?"

"I don't make suppers at this hour. You're a big boy. You could have eaten while you were out."

Suddenly, he grabbed my hair and pulled me down to my knees near the armchair.

"What are you doing?" I screamed trying to get my hair out of his fingers.

"I'll teach you." He was so close to my face that I could feel his hot, liquor-soaked breath on me. His eyes were bloodshot, and his stale breath turned my stomach.

"Stop, Richie. You don't know what you're doing," I pleaded. I panicked, realizing that he was in a blackout. There was no reasoning with him. Knowing that the girls were gone gave him the opening to vent his anger with no reason to stop. They weren't home to hear it.

"You don't want to get my supper?" he said wobbling, with a death grip on my hair. It felt like every root came loose from my scalp.

He started to bang my head against the armchair repeatedly. My head felt like it exploded; my stomach churned and I felt nausea well up in my throat. My surroundings became fuzzy. His voice seemed far off, and I was on the verge of passing out. Words couldn't come out of my mouth. I felt like a rag doll being thrown back and forth.

Suddenly, he let go of me and I fell down onto the rug. "Get up!" he yelled.

Instead of waiting for me to lift myself up, he left me there. He turned and went into the bedroom, mumbling, "That'll teach you."

I was stunned and unable to move. The pain shot up into my head, and I couldn't function. I was shocked that he physically hurt me so badly. Years ago, he wouldn't have hurt a fly. My fear rose, knowing that he was now capable of killing me.

I thanked God the girls weren't home. It would have frightened them to death to see his rage, and they would have felt helpless watching the abuse. Knowing I was alone and defenseless, he felt brave attacking me.

I've suffered from ungodly migraines before, but this time I felt like my skull was broken inside my head. I moved very slowly to pull myself up onto the living room lounge chair. It was a miracle that he didn't come back to continue the beating. I wouldn't have had the strength to fight him off. I heard him snoring in the bedroom, so he must have passed out.

My body tried to relax knowing the attack was over. The pain in my head was too excruciating for me to walk into a bedroom to get a pillow to rest my head on. I tried to control the tears, for they only added to the pain in my head; I felt it would burst. I needed some aspirin, but I couldn't get up from the chair.

I sat awake until the morning sun came through the large living room bay window. It shone on my face and made my head throb. I felt blinded by it.

"Hey, how come you slept out here?" Richie asked walking over to me. It was 8:00 a.m. and he obviously didn't remember anything that happened during the night.

"I have to go to the hospital," I said in a soft, weak voice. I was in no condition to drive.

"Hospital, you sick?" he asked.

"I think I've got a concussion."

"Did you fall or something?"

"It hurts too much to talk." I couldn't lift my head to even look up at him or speak above a whisper. "Last night, you came home drunk and kept hitting my head into the armchair."

"I did?" He hesitated for a few minutes like he was thinking. "We don't have to go to the hospital, you rest, and I'll hold off on calls today and help out."

"I really think I need to be seen by a doctor, there's severe pain when I move."

"Let me move you to the couch where you will be more comfortable."

I got up and moved with baby steps holding my skull together with my two hands.

"Rest and I'll get you a pillow," he said looking worried.

He came back with a bed pillow, lifted my head gently, and placed the pillow under it.

He was worried all right. If I went to the hospital, he would have been arrested if I pressed charges. Even with his abuse, I hated to do that to him. I wanted to stop this nightmare without drastic measures. I was becoming sicker than he was by not ending the violence that could kill me, but I couldn't ignore it much longer; it was now very serious. I didn't have the strength to get up and walk over to the phone to call Ron.

It was 11:00 a.m. when the girls came through the door. They took one look at me and became concerned.

"Mom, what's wrong?" Debbie asked.

"Let your mother rest. She's not feeling too good today," Richie jumped in. "She has one of her migraines."

I couldn't believe how fast alcoholics come up with answers. He knew I wouldn't correct him in front of them. If they knew what he had done, they would never again feel comfortable leaving me home alone with him.

He stayed home all day and couldn't do enough for me. No matter what he cooked, I couldn't eat. I was so nauseated that just the thought of food upset me.

I had no choice but to get up from the couch to use the bathroom. Every step made my head feel like it was going to explode. I couldn't open my eyes more than halfway. The light in the room was too agonizing for me. This pain was ten times worse than any migraine I ever had, and I had some awful ones.

It took me three days before I could get myself off the chair without pain. I knew deep down that I had a concussion. I started hating myself more and more for putting up with his abuse. Still, I couldn't make the decision to leave.

I must have been insane and weaker than I thought. I was innocently being an abusive mother, letting our children witness all the fights. I was thankful that they could get out of the house and stay with friends.

Years ago, I never would have pictured him turning violent. He wasn't a happy drunk and became a Dr. Jekyll and Mr. Hyde, two entirely different personalities.

His drinking now caused him to go into drunken rages. He looked for excuses, not only to verbally, but also physically abuse me as well. He would imply that the house was not clean enough, the kids were not up waiting for him, supper was not sitting on the table, or I didn't pay enough attention to him. He was always unhappy or angry. Nothing I did pleased him. We weren't together long enough when he wasn't drinking to have a healthy relationship.

I saw him change before my eyes from a man with a great sense of humor, and a hard worker, into a complete stranger. Years ago, he swore never to drink like his mother or sister, yet he was on that same road without seeing it, and I did nothing about it. I ignored all the advice from Al-Anon and Ron.

He lost the drive to accomplish the things he talked about when we first married. Now all that faced me at night was a sick man who was killing himself. Every morning he smelled of liquor when he went to work. I was embarrassed for him knowing he couldn't hide it from his clients. He lost customers and work dwindled. Richie was no longer a proud man.

We were all on an emotional rollercoaster. Day after day, I waited to see if he would come home drunk or sober, and the familiar sounds of him staggering in the house continued.

He followed the routine of going into Lori's bedroom, waking her up.

"Hi, Lori, Daddy's home."

"Hi, Daddy." Lori answered half asleep.

I got out of bed and followed him every time. "Leave her alone. Stop waking her up, you're going to scare her. What's wrong with you?" I'd whisper as I pulled on his shirt.

"I just wanted to say hi to her."

"Richie, go into your own bed."

I think he knew this upset me and did it every night when he was drinking.

About a month later, he came in well after midnight, smashed. I heard him bang against the hall wall as he stumbled. Suddenly, the sheets were pulled off me in one swing. Then with a strong grip, he grabbed the right sleeve to my nightgown in an attempt to lift me.

"Wake up!" he shouted, as he pulled me to the edge of the bed.

I talked calmly through my teeth as a rage built up inside me. It was so strong that I shook. I didn't want to wake the girls, but it couldn't be avoided. I got out of bed and walked into the living room with my back to him. He followed behind me.

Without looking at him, I headed for the couch in front of the large bay window. "I'm going to sleep here tonight, you go to bed."

I didn't look at him as I started to lie down. I felt nauseated from holding back my anger. I wanted him to disappear out of my sight and life.

He came toward me. "I'm going to throw you through the picture window."

As he tried to lift me, everything inside me erupted. All the years of pent-up hate surfaced. I went wild fighting back like an animal.

Something in me snapped. I hit him full force with my closed fist right between his mouth and nose. I put every ounce of strength I had into the swing. I tried to block out the pain in my hand from the connection with his face.

"You fucking son of a bitch, you bastard!" I yelled as loud as I could. My fists pounded into his face again and again. I didn't care if he came back and knocked my teeth out. I kept repeating vulgar, filthy swear words that I'd never used in my life. "You will *never* lay another hand on me as long as I live; *never, never, never.* DO YOU HEAR ME?"

My screams came from deep within me. I wanted to beat him into the ground. The more I hurt him, the more satisfaction it gave me.

He kept stumbling backwards, desperately trying to get away from me. Being drunk, he had no control and moved unsteadily. I continued to pound him. His eyes bulged in fear as he fell backwards. I kept swearing, as I attacked him.

"What's the matter with you? Are you going crazy?" he said in absolute horror. He was terrified of me. His arms were up trying to protect his face.

By now Debbie had left her bed and walked into the living room. Upset, she cried out, "Dad, what are you doing to Mom?"

Richie couldn't understand how I got the courage to attack him. I never fought back before now. I went at him like a madwoman. From that moment, he lost control of me and the situation. He wasn't seeing me as a weak, frightened wife anymore.

He went over to Debbie. "Dad's okay, you go back to bed."

She walked past him and wrapped her arms around me. I was sick and tired of what he was doing to me and our daughters. I was disgusted with myself for allowing the girls to live this way. Debbie was trying to protect me. She was becoming an adult, looking to stop the fighting.

I watched him become weak and wondered why I waited so many years to stand up to him? *Is this all that it took to end this nightmare?* A punch in the face was probably too much, but it would have saved us all from living these years of hell.

I realized at that moment that the abuse went on because I allowed it. There's a time to make demands on someone and to refuse to live in any way which is unhealthy. The first time it happened was when I should have kicked him out until he got help, not fourteen years later. My children needed me to give them a safe life, and I didn't. Instead of protecting Richie, I should have been protecting my children. I used every excuse to stay; I was Catholic or my children needed him. I didn't want anyone to know about his drinking, yet everyone did.

He walked into the bedroom looking defeated and tried wiping the blood from his lip and nose. I got Debbie back to bed and stayed until she was calm. Then I went back to the couch and lay down. My skin crawled at the thought of getting into bed with him. I couldn't stop shaking after the ordeal. The tears rolled down my face as my heart raced in my chest from losing control. I never had happiness or security in our marriage. Why was I holding onto something that was never going to be?

Why was he so blind to what he had become? Didn't he have any guilt about how he was treating us?

Chapter Thirty-Nine
Leaving Home

The next morning, the girls went off to school, and I made myself a cup of coffee. I tried to relax after recalling last night. How could Richie and I have become such maniacs? Neither of us ever raised our voices or argued when we dated. He had every sign of being a gentle man. His drinking was tearing all of us apart. Our children were living in complete fear and insecurity every day.

I heard him in the bathroom washing up. I sat at the kitchen table and waited to see if he'd have a cup of coffee with me. I wanted to talk about how our marriage was on a path of destruction. Instead, he walked right by me without even looking in my direction to acknowledge me, and went out the back door.

I was just as much in the wrong by not confronting him in a quiet tone to discuss the situation. There was too much pride in me to beg him to talk about our marriage and save it. I wanted him to become humble and admit that he needed help with his drinking. I needed to see that he was sorry for his violent behavior.

I sat numb for an hour after he left the house until the phone rang.

"Hello?"

"Hi." It was my mother.

It was rare that my parents ever called me.

"I thought I'd call and see how you're all doing?"

"Not too good, Mom, Richie's still drinking. I've got to find the strength to do something about this situation."

"What about counseling?"

"We've been that route."

I didn't dare tell her about last night. She would have committed me to a state hospital for the insane, knowing I was still staying in this abusive marriage. Dad probably would have driven down and sat us both down to handle a problem that I couldn't. I didn't offer any details.

"Dad and I talked last night, and we would like to have you and the girls move in with us."

"Thanks, but I can't."

"Just listen for a moment. You can just separate and see if things can be worked out. The girls can go to school here and make new friends. They're young and will be able to bounce back easily."

"This is an important time in their life, Mom. I think they need to be in their own home and close to their friends. Moving away and going to a new school, would devastate them. They'd hate me. I don't want them to suffer from a decision that Richie and I made. Besides, I'd feel it, too. All my friends are here, and I like my job. It's only two minutes down the street."

She was quiet for a moment, so I continued. "You know what you can do for me? Leave the door open. Let me know that you're both there for me and that I can come home, if that step really needs to be taken."

I wondered if she was relieved. Mom loved family around her, and the girls and I would have filled her life with daily activity. It would have been so easy to run home and have my parents put me under their wings and take the burden off me.

"Okay, promise you'll call us from time to time. We worry about you."

"I will, give my love to Dad."

I hung up and cried my heart out knowing I couldn't hold my marriage together or help Richie. I knew that if I stayed any longer, the girls would grow up thinking they would have to put up with the same treatment from a man. I needed to show them that there were choices. I knew deep down that God doesn't want anyone to be abused by another human being. Maybe it was too late and they had already been damaged emotionally from this ungodly life.

Richie never laid a hand on me again. His drinking didn't stop but I was now in control with no fear. He didn't come home late and started to eat supper with us. We were together, but we stopped communicating. There were no smiles, warm touches, hugs, kisses, or the desire to talk about anything. Our need to reach out and make love evaporated. We displayed polite actions in front of the girls.

I needed to make a decision to leave the house. The last fight had been over the edge, and I wanted to get out of his reach. I didn't want to wait for another night with him coming in drunk. I could depend on my job and a weekly paycheck. My problems would be solved one step at a time.

He came home the next Thursday night sober and in a rare talkative mood. "I've got a chance to get into a golf tournament this weekend. I'd be playing Saturday and Sunday. Do you mind?"

I knew then his reason for breaking the ice; it was something for him. By now, I didn't care what he did. It opened the door for me to act on my decision to move out.

"I don't think it would interfere with anything," I replied with no change in expression.

"I'll be leaving Saturday around seven in the morning and coming back around eight at night."

"That's fine. I'll make my own plans."

Friday morning, I called Cindy. She had apartments that she rented.

"Cindy, do you have any apartments open?"

"I have two. Who's interested?"

"I am."

"You're giving up your home? Alberta, are you sure you want to leave the house to Richie? You may lose all chances of getting it back. He'll have grounds to keep it if you leave."

"His business is here, and he'll always be able to reach me. I remember what Anita said to me a while back, 'You either stay living like this or do something about it.' I can't continue to live like this, and at the same time, I'm sick inside about taking this step. I'm not sure if it's the right choice."

"Only you can make this decision. If you need a place, I can give you one right on the main highway. It's awfully small, but it's semi-furnished. It has only one bedroom, a bathroom, and a tiny kitchen that can't fit the kitchen table so it's out in the living room. There's a pull-out couch that converts into a double bed in the same room. It's a second floor apartment."

"That's perfect. He can't get to us. Being furnished makes it easier. How much will you charge me?"

We agreed on a price that was in my budget range. "I'll take it."

"How are you going to get the furniture out of the house?"

"…With your help, of course."

"What? Are you serious?" she asked.

"Are you free tomorrow and Sunday?"

"Nothing like short notice," she said laughing.

"Here's my plan. He leaves Saturday morning at 7:00 a.m. to go to a golf tournament, the same on Sunday. Friday during the day, I'll pack our clothes, bedding and food and take them over to the apartment Saturday morning. Sunday I'll fold down Debbie's bed and bureau. That's all I'll need. The girls can sleep together."

"Are you sure?"

"I'll call you after 8:00 a.m. to get moving.

When Richie left for his deliveries on Friday morning, I boxed all the things that he wouldn't notice missing, like clothes from the kids' drawers and mine; he never looked in them. I emptied the important things out of the kitchen that I would need. I packed all the small things and took them to the apartment. The girls were at school, and I could get it all done before they came home. I decided to wait to tell them Sunday after their father left.

Saturday morning, he left for golfing and had a few drinks before coming home, but he acted fine. I knew he needed to control the drinking in order to play again on Sunday. We talked for about and hour and he went straight to bed to get some rest. Nothing seemed out of the ordinary to him. I packed a few more things before going to bed. I developed a knot in my stomach. I was still questioning my actions. If he came in drunk, I would have felt justified to walk out with our kids. As it was, I couldn't help feeling guilty.

When he left Sunday, I sat the girls down on the sectional and told them about my plans to move. They were very upset and began crying.

"Why do we have to leave our house? I don't want to go," Debbie yelled.

"I don't either," Lori said, crying along with her sister.

I put my arms around them. "I know this is hard on you. I can't live here any more with your father coming home

263

drunk. It's not good for any of us when he and I fight. One of us may get hurt. If we leave, he may stop drinking. It doesn't mean we will never come back home, and you're only four miles from your friends. They can come over to the apartment. You'll be three houses away from Jeri, Debbie."

"Why doesn't Dad leave?" she asked.

"He has his business here, and it would just be easier than us waiting every day to see if he's been drinking. I don't want all this fighting anymore.

"Who will take care of him, Mom?" Lori asked.

"Your father will be fine. He's a grown man and can take care of himself."

"I still don't want to go," Debbie said, sounding heartbroken.

"I know you don't and that's what's making this decision so difficult. I love you two and I know this is hard for you. I don't want to go either, but you have to trust me; it's the right thing to do for now. Cindy is coming in an hour to help us take your bed and bureau, Debbie. I want you kids to go and get anything special you want to take."

"Can we take Heidi?" Lori asked as she put her arms around the dog's neck and kissed her.

"We can't take any animals, honey. The apartments too small and it's on a highway. We don't want her to get hit by a car. Besides, she'll keep Dad company and be here when we come back home."

My eyes filled, and I prayed to God that I was doing the right thing. I knew this wasn't going to be easy. I started to take the big items apart. Cindy came and helped me move Debbie's double bed and two dressers; there was no reason for me to take ours with the double sofa-bed in the apartment.

The only way we could transport the furniture was on top of my car. It was almost comical. Eddie Pierce was the officer on duty directing traffic at the corner of Route 138 and Middle Street, a block from where I was moving. We had to go right by him every time we brought more items from the house. He gave me an odd look each of the five trips it took to move everything.

I was proud of myself, and thought the move went easier than I expected. I tried pushing my guilt aside. The girls were not excited with the apartment. They were still hurt and couldn't understand why I was making this move.

I had one more trip back to the house and the girls insisted on coming back with me. They didn't want to stay with Cindy and the kids. I collected the items at the house and was about to leave, when Richie pulled into the yard. My heart was in my throat seeing him walk up the front yard. It was 1:00 p.m. and he wasn't supposed to be back until 7:00 p.m.

He walked in the door and Lori wrapped her arms around him. She clung to him crying. Debbie stood by her bedroom door weeping. I was absolutely sick inside. Now, it seemed wrong. I lost all confidence in what I was doing.

"What's wrong? Why are the girls crying?" He looked scared.

"There's something I have to tell you."

The girls were crushed. I don't think they knew what was more painful; leaving him or their home, perhaps both.

"Richie, I have an apartment, and we're moving out."

"You're what?"

"I can't do this anymore. I'm sorry."

"When did you decide this?" he said, traumatized sitting down in the armchair.

Lori jumped on his lap. *God, how am I going to leave?* I looked at him and knew I still loved him. I was fighting to keep my own emotions in tack, for my daughters didn't need to see me crying.

"I've been thinking about it for a long time."

"You're not taking the girls!"

I knew that something had to be done fast or nobody would be able to leave, including me.

"Yes, I am. Okay, girls, say goodbye to your father."

Debbie screamed, "I'm not leaving."

Lori was now sobbing her heart out, with a death grip on her father's neck. "I don't want to leave either."

I physically, but gently, pulled Lori away from him. Taking her hand, I opened the door. "Debbie, I'm not asking again, we're leaving.

What am I doing to my children? There was so much raw emotion that I felt weak in the knees walking to the car in the driveway.

Richie made me feel worse by yelling out the door, "You're rotten, breaking this family up."

It took me hours to calm Lori and Debbie and settle into the apartment. I tried to make them feel like it was going to be fun sleeping together in one bed. They didn't like knowing that I was going to be sleeping on the sofa bed.

The Dighton Elementary School abutted our new backyard so they could walk to it. They had school the next day. I knew everything was happening to them too fast, there was no time for them to adjust. My jobsite was less than a mile down the street, and I could leave later than usual if they were upset.

I decided to drive them over to the school the next morning. The entrance was only three houses down from us. They got out of the car, and I sensed the distress in them; my guilt was drowning me.

I drove to work and worried the whole day. I refused to move to my parents for fear of uprooting them, and now, their lives were torn apart. One moment they are happy and secure, and the next, they're out of their house and in an apartment, completely separated from their father. I questioned myself, but knew that I couldn't change my mind.

It took a couple of days for Richie to find out where we were staying. At night he'd pound on the door downstairs. He'd yell outside. I knew he was drunk. I felt safe knowing I didn't have to answer it. The day before, I introduced myself to the tenants on the first floor and told them not to open the door for him.

We were only two houses from Cindy, so the girls became even closer to her children. Her daughter, Jeri, and her two sons, Bruce and Darryl, were all close in age.

Lori was quiet and had a hard time adjusting to the move, until I decided to take one of Cindy's kittens. I wasn't looking forward to cleaning up after an animal in an apartment, but she needed something to love.

Lori picked an all grey male and the kitten took her mind off the situation. She fell in love with it and named him Dusty. We kept it in the house because it was so scared to go out. Lori was afraid that it wouldn't come back or would get killed on the highway. It was the only thing giving her comfort. Every day she rushed into the bedroom to find it sleeping on their bed. She couldn't wait to see the cat since it was so playful.

Lori spent every free moment with the kitten and didn't seem upset any longer with the move. Debbie, on the other hand, held her emotions in, and I couldn't find out how she felt about all this. None of us talked about this move.

One afternoon, I made a terrible mistake in thinking Dusty was old enough to discover the outside world. I put him outdoors, or so I thought, until I went downstairs to call him a few hours later. I opened the door to discover him between the inside door and the storm door. He was frightened to death of the outside and clawed my arms, when I picked him up, trying to jump out of them and get upstairs.

A few months later, I tried it again. Within an hour, I went out to find him. He was nowhere to be seen. I panicked calling and calling without any sign of the cat. I felt guilty and was horrified thinking Lori would never forgive me, and she didn't. Every day Lori was outside calling Dusty, but he never came. Each time, she came in crying. The strain of living in the apartment was worse without her pet.

Six months passed, and I was questioning myself about the decision to take the girls out of their home. I started to miss it myself. *God, did I do the right thing?* None of us seemed happy. It was like being on a bad vacation and waiting to return home. The only good thing was we all slept at night without waiting to hear Richie's truck pull in. After a few weeks, he stopped coming to the apartment door. He probably realized that I was determined not to breakdown and open it. He never tried coming by when he was sober either.

It was so hard going to work knowing how brokenhearted the girls were about living in the apartment. Richie now controlled the house with Heidi, with whom they had played with daily. Debbie missed lying down with her to watch television. I tried to tell myself that the girls were better off out of the house with no fights, yet, they were a mess mentally because of the separation.

The stress really built up with Lori, and one morning, she refused to go to school. I was sweating bullets, knowing I couldn't call the police department at the last minute for a replacement. I was due at work in a half hour. Replacing a dispatcher wasn't easy. It took hours to get someone for the day shift.

"Mom, if Lori's not coming, I have to go," Debbie stated.

I kissed her goodbye. "I'll take her today," I said as Debbie opened the door to go down the stairs. It was her last year at the grammar school.

Lori sat in the rocking chair in her heavy winter jacket. She refused to move.

"Lori, you have to go to school, honey. Mommy can't call in sick."

"I'm not going," she screamed and started to cry. She hadn't given me a problem until that day.

I could feel the emotions building up in me; my nerves were on edge, and my patience disappeared. I tried to pick her up, but she was dead weight, as she wrapped her tiny fingers onto the spindles of the chair like glue.

I kept looking at the clock noticing that I had little time to get to work. There was no reasoning with her. By now, my own bottled-up resentment and frustration was ready to burst.

My anger turned to Richie. Here I was left to deal with everyone's confused gut reactions. I was trying to keep my daughters stable while there wasn't any time or way to deal with my own hurts and fears.

"Lori, we have to go, please!"

"NO! I'm not going." By now she was sobbing and determined not to get out of the rocker.

I wanted to put my arms around her and just spend the day with her. That's what she needed; she was hurting. If it were another kind of job, I would have called in sick. I was torn between being a mother who should have been comforting her daughter and having a job to get to. It took all my strength to pry her enclosed fingers off the chair. I carried her down the steep, narrow stairway to the door. I couldn't let her go or she'd be gone.

Once I got her into the front passenger seat of the car, she started to open the door screaming, "I'm going to jump out of the car." She was nine-years old and frightened.

I grabbed onto her coat and could feel her trying to pull out of the sleeves.

God, help me with her, I begged.

Thankfully, there were only three houses to reach the entrance to the school. I pulled into the long driveway of the school and parked in front of the doors. The principal was nearby, and saw Lori jump in the back of the station wagon. He realized I was having a problem. The other children were already off the buses and settled in their classrooms.

"Do you need some help?" he asked looking into the driver's window.

Now, I was in tears. "Yes, she's having a hard time today, and I can't stay home."

He went into the back seat of the car, and gently carried her out. My heart broke seeing her so scared, and I was forcing her to go to school.

"She's not mentally in the right frame of mind to attend," I said with my voice breaking up.

"We won't force her into the classroom. I'll have someone talk to her."

I broke down, my body was shaking. I admitted to the school principal that we needed help. I told him about my separation. My nerves were hanging by a thread. I followed him into his office, while he scheduled an appointment for me and Lori during the week.

"After a few sessions together, I think we should talk to Lori in private."

"I understand, and that's fine," I said. I then rushed to work arriving a few minutes late.

This was one time that I should have taken Lori's cries more seriously. I worried about Debbie who showed no emotion. That evening I sat with the girls on the couch wrapping my arms around them.

"I know this is hard on you two. Lori, I'm sorry I couldn't stay home with you today. How did your day go?"

"Mrs. Peters let me color and read instead of going to class today."

"Debbie, are you okay? You never talk to me."

"I can see our apartment from my classroom, and I'm always looking to see if dad's truck is over here."

I didn't realize how much our being away from home was taking out of them. They were in the same emotional situation at home. If I could turn the clock back, I would have taken the time every single night to talk about our feelings, hurts, and fears. This responsibility was up to me, I was the parent. Instead, the three of us went about doing our own thing and didn't talk about our feelings again.

It wasn't long before Richie got our telephone number and started calling the girls. When he and I spoke, the conversation was abrupt, but civilized. On a Sunday morning, six months after I left the house, he called and asked to take us out for lunch. I broke down and agreed, not knowing if I was doing it for me or the girls.

He was sober, we loved being with him. That day he was full of laughter and we rode down Cape Cod to spend the day fishing. After going to a seafood place to eat fish and chips, he took us out for an ice cream. Being a family that day was beyond words.

Going home, I could see that the girls were more relaxed after being with him, I was too. I knew in my heart, I wanted to be with him. I looked at a life with him again with no drinking.

We saw him on weekends for about another six months. Finally, one day he called and begged me to come home.

"Richie, there is a lot to sort out before I come home."

The girls overheard me talking to him.

"Please, Mom, let's go home," they pleaded.

It had been over a year of peace without having to live with the fighting and it was wonderful, but I had to put up with the girls being unhappy. I missed my home. Richie deserved time to prove himself after all this time separated. In a month, we returned to our house.

Things went great, and I believed that my leaving made him come to realize what he almost lost. He had never expected me to get up and leave the house. He put himself into his work, and the girls started to have their friends over.

I told my girlfriends and family that I moved back home. I told the news to Janet at work, and she looked at me, dumbfounded.

"How many times are you going to do this?" She shook her head with disappointment and turned back to her desk.

I was embarrassed telling her, but I wanted to try anything that would bring us back as a family. Each time gave me hope that maybe this was the time he would give up drinking. My mistake was not demanding him to get heavy counseling before coming home.

We made plans with Sonny and Anita to rent a place on the water in Marion for two weeks in the summer. The kids were excited. Richie planned to join us after work each week night and on the weekends. It was only a half hour drive from home. Our time together with the two families was wonderful. We cooked on the beach and the kids lived in the water. The cousins played, enjoying time together, and the parents had the privacy to talk. Richie and I never mentioned our past problems. Our conversations were always about local events, or how Sonny or Richie's business was doing.

After our vacation ended and we settled back at home, Richie and I still couldn't connect intimately or emotionally. I didn't know how to get close to him. Everything with us felt artificial. It was like being roommates. With our years of fighting and breaking up, we continued to go our own ways, not seeing the old patterns of our lives happening again. I put myself into the girls and my friends. He built up his friendships outside the home, and the girls clung to their friends. None of us turned to each other.

We were role playing; I became both the father and mother, Richie was the breadwinner, and the girls tried to live a normal life with parents who weren't stable. When I think back on our situation then, I realize how insecure and scared the girls had to be with their lives. There was no way they could control anything. My mental state depended on how Richie acted toward me, and the girls went along depending on how their parents acted together. We were all on the merry-go-round that Ron and Helen spoke about so long ago.

It didn't take long for Richie to pick up where he left off, stopping for a drink now and then. Each night the girls and I were back on the rollercoaster. He got upset easily and complained about the overload with his work. He seemed restless at home, and he became even more distant with me. Our goodbye hugs and kisses started to fade. We ignored the fact that we needed time together without the girls to build any kind of relationship. We truly didn't know each other. I never knew the real Richie without drinking. Slowly we drifted in different directions.

The clock became my main focus again, and I resumed taking my pills. My patience was hanging on the edge. My mind was back to racing, and I had no energy. Laughing and having fun disappeared.

Richie came home at a decent hour, but he knew by my looks that I was disappointed in his decision to have that drink.

"Don't go getting all upset over me having a few drinks. It's nine o'clock, I'm home, and I'm not drunk."

"You're starting all over again. You want to sink, you do it alone. I'm tired of watching you kill yourself."

I sat next to him and put my hand on his. For the first time, I spoke in a quiet tone with deep love that was trying to burst out of me. With all the years of abuse, my emotions felt like I surrendered to the impossible.

"We can't get through your drinking. I don't know if I even want this marriage anymore. Promises after promises are broken, and we turn right around again starting this life of confusion. My God, Richie, we have never had a year with peace in our family. I've lost all faith in you. Our daughters are mentally broken from your actions. I helped put them through this pain by allowing you to stay here with us. They love you, and you keep hurting them. This disease is too powerful for me to fight. It's up to you to put your life together without drinking."

"What if we go to counseling?"

"You make the appointment for *you,* not us."

I got up and walked away. It was the first time I let go and put his drinking problem in his hands.

Chapter Forty
Richie's Return to Counseling

For weeks Richie confronted me about counseling. "I'd like us to go to counseling together."

"I'm not interested. I honestly don't have it in me any more."

"I don't want our marriage to end, please, give me a chance."

"I think we've both had enough. My mental state can't handle the ups and downs. Do it for yourself. I'm trying to deal with life by going back to Al-Anon."

There were no more happy times for us. I didn't want to get back on the rollercoaster. We left it that way until a week later when Ron called me.

"Hi, Alberta, it's Ron."

"Hi, how are you?"

"Good. I got a call from your husband about a week ago."

I replied in a nonchalant way, "Really?"

"I've seen him a few times and I think he may want to take this further. What if you come to counseling with him?"

"I don't know if I have the desire for it anymore, Ron. I'm tired of him drinking when I think things are fine. I'm worn out."

"It's the first time he's making the move."

I felt resentment. "So now that *he* wants help, I'm supposed to bend again?"

"I don't want you to do anything you don't want to, but if you want to try it, I'll set it up in two days. He wants you to attend."

I sat in silence and became angry. I always felt guilty saying no to anything. I was constantly trying to please other people.

"Give yourself a few sessions and see how you feel," Ron suggested. "You're not committed. It's really up to him to take the steps to get better."

"I'll come in, but I'm not happy about it."

"The meeting will be at 11:30 a.m. on Friday."

I hung up and felt like a rug that had been stepped on for the thousandth time. I prepared myself to come out of this feeling like a fool again. Richie never mentioned going to any meetings with Ron. I waited for him to come home after a delivery.

"I didn't realize that you were going to counseling. Why didn't you say something?"

"I wanted to make sure that I was comfortable with it. You were right. I have to want it for me first. I have some deliveries on Friday so can we just meet there instead of me coming all the way home again?"

"I see no problem with it."

I went to the AA center on Friday and saw Richie sitting in the waiting room.

"Hi, I'm glad you came," he said holding my hand. "I was afraid I'd be late because of my deliveries."

I couldn't put a smile on my face. Every part of my body didn't want to be there. I felt like my life was on hold while he tried to straighten his out. I was getting tired of the baggage in our relationship.

Ron came out of his office with a big smile, "It's nice to see you both, come in."

"I'd like you to meet Patricia Casey," he said turning to the woman already in the room. "Patricia, this is Richie and Alberta."

She looked to be in her early forties with dark, brown hair. Her attire was casual wearing jeans with a white button-down blouse.

I tried to smile when she said hello, but all I wanted to do was run out.

Ron took over the meeting. "We've been talking about a plan for your counseling. I'm a recovered alcoholic, and Patricia is a non-drinker. I'd like to set a reasonable time limit on counseling before we go in depth with it."

Patricia looked directly at me. "Alberta, I'd like to counsel you for a few weeks while Ron talks with Richie. After that time, we'll put the two of you together to see how you feel about what we've covered with the drinking process. Does that sound all right with the both of you?"

I felt drained and waited for Richie to speak. "That's fine with me," he said. I just nodded my head yes like a robot.

We started our sessions. For the next two weeks, I met with Patricia and felt choked as she talked about my letting go of the problem and letting Richie take responsibility for his actions. The heavy burden was too much for me. I couldn't live a normal life with him while he drank. The truth was that by then I really didn't care. I was too petrified to build up my hopes that he was serious about this counseling. *Was he going for me or himself?*

The weeks flew by, and we met again, together with Ron and Patricia. "We counseled you separately to get a feel on how the drinking problem was affecting the family. Our next level is counseling you both together for two months. Are you willing to do that?"

My heart said yes, but my head said no.

"That's a long time," Richie replied.

"It took you years to get to this point, and it'll take awhile to get better," Ron said. "Alcoholism is not curable. You have to learn how to stay sober. Why do you continue to go out with your buddies? Don't you see that you can't handle the drinking by now?"

He gave no answer.

"Let me put it to you this way, Richie. If you don't want to get hit by the train, you have to stop playing on the tracks. Each time you go into a bar, you're back where you started. You can't pick up that first drink, because you can't handle it. You can be away from it for months or years, and that first drink hits you like you never stopped. It takes a good year for liquor to get out of your system."

Richie continued to just sit, showing no emotion. I was hanging onto hope since he came home every night without drinking, or at least I didn't think he was during these months.

"Why don't we start the next meeting on Monday," Patricia stated.

I tried to give Richie the last benefit of the doubt that he meant it this time. I didn't feel secure with him avoiding the questions. By his actions in the office, I felt that he was wearing blinders and only saw the negative things that were going to affect him by giving up drinking. His own personal desire to continue these actions was only destroying his family. I couldn't shake the feeling that he was going to the counseling to please me and not to cure himself.

After the two months of counseling, I still hung onto hope. He heard enough to have no doubt that he was an alcoholic and that his condition was hereditary. We covered his mother's and sister's drinking with our last session.

We sat in the hall and waited to be called into Ron's office. The final meeting arrived and the questions and answers flew among the four of us. After an hour, Ron decided to learn what we felt with the meetings.

"Richie, have you come to a decision with your drinking?"

"Yes. I honestly don't think I have a problem. My buddies drink just as much as I do. Their marriages aren't falling apart."

My heart sank.

"After spending three months with us, you still feel the same?" Ron asked. "You don't see that you're an alcoholic."

Again, he didn't answer.

Patricia looked at me. "How do you feel, Alberta? Do you want to continue counseling?"

I felt numb and angry for having believed all these months that there was a chance with his recovery in counseling. "I have no desire or strength whatsoever left in me. If he can't see what this disease is doing to him and his family, then I have to move on."

"Alberta, we can still counsel you," Ron continued.

"Thanks, but I've heard enough. I came because he had me thinking he saw the light. I'll continue a while longer with the Al-Anon meetings."

We got up and left the office, and what feelings I had died. It was as if I had turned off a light switch and put up a protective wall. I didn't even feel anger. What a loss. Richie couldn't see the path he was heading down because he didn't believe he was an alcoholic with a disease that was controlling his whole life. At that moment, I disconnected from him completely. We went our separate ways; he went to work, and I went home to make supper for the girls.

Chapter Forty-One
Breakdown at Al-Anon

I was coming up on my fourth year attending Al-Anon meetings. Sonny, Anita, and I had stopped going to the AA meetings. There were no reasons to go on trying to help Richie. We had gone through so many breakups that I lost count of them.

Each week someone at my Al-Anon meeting talked about how his or her loved one stopped drinking. I could see that a few people were holding their marriages together and were becoming emotionally drained, and others, like me, didn't want to hold on any longer. They watched the drinker's every move or had lost all trust. They feared their mates would fall off the wagon and go right back to drinking. They waited every night holding their breath, something that I had done for the past twelve years.

The following Sunday, I pushed myself to go to another Al-Anon meeting at the church. Sandy walked into the hall at the same time. We talked before she went downstairs to the AA meeting with John.

I walked to my meeting down the hall. Five men were present and crowded between eight women. I sat, but I felt no real desire to be there that night.

Helen started the meeting when we were all settled. "Who would like to read Chapter nine? Alberta, would you start?"

I looked at her in fright. I hated reading and had explained that to her numerous times. I still couldn't shake the fear of being the center of attention and possibly making a mistake reading after all these years. *Why did she call on me*? My heart started to race, and my face felt beet red. I didn't know what to say. I had been refusing to read and felt immature about it. Everyone was looking at me, waiting for an answer.

I picked up the book and turned to the page. My hands shook, and my mind wasn't concentrating on anything that I read out loud. I felt eyes on me, and my hands got clammy. I started to feel faint like my air was being cut off—I needed to get out. I stopped in the middle of a sentence, jumped out of my seat, and started toward the door.

I turned and screamed at everyone sitting there. "I've had enough of these stupid, worthless meetings. God damn it, I'm mentally exhausted coming here while my husband is out drinking every night. And don't tell me to live my life while he comes in and out of it leaving a trail of heartbreak."

Foul words came out of me, my brain tried to tell me to stop. This wasn't me. I had always been a lady but somehow that person got buried years ago. I was an angry, uncontrollable maniac at this moment. I slammed the door and could hear Helen's feet on the floor as she ran, following me down the hallway.

"Alberta, wait!" She was out of breath trying to catch up to me.

I stormed down the corridor. Other counselors left their meetings to see what the ruckus was all about. Many joined in the chase, wanting to console me. My ranting was heard downstairs in the AA meeting. People were coming from every direction to see what was wrong with me.

Helen caught up to me, "Alberta, I'm sorry. I forgot that you didn't want to be called on to read. Come back in."

By then I was too embarrassed to face the group and never wanted to go through an Al-Anon door again. I had lost control of my life.

Nothing could stop my uncontrollable, furious actions. The tears rolled down my face, and my pride went out the window. I looked at the group that surrounded me and cried, "I can't do this anymore! Nothing is changing."

I screamed like a wild woman. "I don't care if I ever come back to this damn place again! I'm sick of coming here. I'm tired of being told how to separate myself from him and go on with my life. We're not supposed to live separate lives. I can't do this....DO YOU HEAR ME?"

The commotion and yelling were so earsplitting that others were trying to calm me down. They made me feel worse, smothered.

Sandy came running up the stairs and broke through the crowd to get to me. She grabbed me by the shoulders. "Alberta, what's the matter?"

I was beyond hysterical. "I'm fucking tired of all this. NO MORE! Four years is enough for me," I screamed as I pushed past the group around me.

I couldn't breathe. I felt like I was being programmed to make Richie's life comfortable. I knew they were wonderful people but I had to make a decision with my own life. I wasn't living, and my girls were emotional messes.

"Let's sit down and talk," Sandy said, trying to hold my hands. I was like a bear by then. No one was my friend at this point. I didn't want any advice; I didn't want any answers, and I didn't want to hear anyone's voice.

"Let—go of me. I want out of this fucking place," I yelled, pulling my hands away from her. The more I swore, the better I felt. "You have a husband who comes to the meetings. You're working it out together. He *wants* to help himself. You have something to fight for, Sandy—I don't," I yelled back at her.

By now I was sobbing so hard that I shook all over. People filled the hallway and stared at me. I felt like a freak. I shoved and pushed past everyone to get to the door. I had to break loose, or I'd completely lose it. I was drained of any hope. My body and mind were too tired. I had been put through a wringer far too long.

Once I opened the door, I breathed in all the air that my lungs could take. I ran to the car to be by myself. I prayed no one was following me. I couldn't handle another person in my space.

My hands shook as I put the keys into the ignition. I cried my heart out, knowing I lost the battle. I was faced with a decision about still loving Richie. How could I love and hate him at the same time? I was about to lose me if I didn't stay away from him. I couldn't live with him and wondered how I was going to live without him.

I had never stood on my own two feet. I went from my parents' protection to a marriage in which I couldn't make any decisions. I faced supporting a home and two daughters alone. How was I going to do it? I still felt helpless about making a decision to get him out of my life.

It was an effort driving and concentrating on the road. I wanted to go somewhere to be alone and cry till I was dry. The only thing that kept me together all these years was Lori and Debbie. They needed me, but I had let them down. I dragged them through the mud with me and hid the pain that I was going through. We all acted as though our daily abusive lives were normal.

I pulled into the Memorial Park across the street from the church and let it all out. I sat there throwing questions at myself. *What have I done to my life? Why did I leave Danny? Why did I continue with Richie after seeing his drinking from day one? How could I have been so stupid and blind? Why have I allowed this problem to continue for years without making demands? I've become a doormat. My God, I have no life of my own. My girls have lived their whole life with unstable parents. How are they going to live their adult life after being subjected to all this? Look at what I've done to them. Please, God, let me end this kind of life. I don't believe in divorce, but I was coming apart. I can't give anymore. I'm living my life for him and there's nothing left for me. All I'm doing is giving, giving, and giving without any getting.*

My mind was racing with fourteen years of events that were a disaster. *What happened to my dream of loving and being loved, having children who were going to be happy? What happened to the dream of Richie going places? My days have always started and ended with living in fear. God, I don't even want to go home. If the girls weren't there, I wouldn't. Too many are depending on me, I can't breathe!*

"What about *my* life?" I screamed out loud. I sat there for an hour trying to put my broken heart back together.

Feeling nothing, I drove off slowly, emotionally drained. All my anger and hurt came out of me. I pulled into the yard and sat there feeling physically and mentally dead. There was no desire to open the car door and get out. If I got hit by a truck at that point, it would have been a blessing. How could I wish for such a horrible thing?

I had married for better or worse but this stress was unbearable. I couldn't bring myself to finalize it by divorce. My mind was tired from trying to solve problems every waking moment. I walked into the house feeling drugged and got ready for bed. Even sleep did not come easy.

The next day, I went by myself for a ride to the river at the end of Main Street. The girls were in school. I sat for a half hour looking out at the water and watched the seagulls flying around the shoreline. Peace came over me.

All you have to do is drive the car in fast. Lock the doors.

My mind raced until I heard a car pull up next to me.

"Hey, what are you doing in my neighborhood? Come over to the house for coffee." It was Cindy.

I never told her or anyone about my thoughts at that moment. Would I have done it? I don't know, but I had to be sick to even think about it. The kids would have been left alone and been worse off than they were already. Just in time, my Guardian Angel appeared through Cindy.

After that episode, I knew that I had to make a decision. If we went on this way, I would end up in a mental institution, or worse. I couldn't go on with this turmoil in my life any longer.

Chapter Forty-Two

A Call from the IRS

One night, about a week later, after Richie had been drinking and came in late, I knew it was time to confront him. I waited until morning. When he got up, I demanded that we sit at the kitchen table and talk.

"This isn't going to work, and I have no more in me to give. My understanding and patience is gone. I want you to leave on your own, without any fighting, so I don't have to call the police. Let's just end this nightmare. You go and do your thing without having to defend your drinking."

He moved out with no hassles. The business equipment stayed downstairs, but he didn't use it because he took a job working for someone else in the Swansea area. He never came to see the girls which tore my heart out.

I had to protect myself from being sued by Richie's customers who wanted their television sets that were left to be repaired. He evidently felt no guilt walking away and leaving me with the headache. He never cleaned the cellar or took the television sets that were left sitting in the shop. I put an ad in a few newspapers requesting customers to call or come to pick up their sets.

It was one of the most embarrassing times for me. People were wild, seeing parts missing from their sets. He took parts from one set to put into another. No one knew if any were in working condition or not. Even if some of the customers wanted to take him to court, they had no address at which to reach him; he had left no forwarding address.

I had no intention whatsoever of divorcing him. I was Catholic and didn't believe in it, but two years after we separated, an unexpected phone call changed my mind in a hurry.

"Hello?"

"Mrs. Lopes?"

"Yes, can I help you?"

"This is Mr. John Phillips from the IRS."

"From where?"

"I'm from the IRS, Mrs. Lopes, and I'm calling about a balance of $8,200 owed in back taxes."

"A balance is due? You mean my husband hasn't paid our taxes?" I was lost for words.

"No, he hasn't, and unless it's paid, there'll to be a lien put on your house."

"A lien, what do you mean?"

"It means that if you ever go to sell your home, you'll have to pay the government this balance before you can take your profit."

"But we're separated, Mr. Phillips."

"That doesn't matter; you're still a married couple. It'll be dropped if you pay the full balance owed.

"You mean to tell me that if he continues to ignore our taxes, I'll be the one responsible for this?"

"That's right."

"That doesn't seem fair."

"We can't look at things emotionally, Mrs. Lopes. We can meet and work out a payment plan."

"So, I can make payments and he can still refuse to pay future taxes?

"Yes, he can."

"I don't see how someone can walk away and stick the other one with this? Can I get back to you on this, Mr. Phillips?" I knew complaining to him wasn't going to change the situation, whether it was fair or not.

I took all the information down and hung up. I sat in complete shock. A lien on our house! Richie hadn't been paying our taxes for the past four years. Where was my mind? How could that have gotten by me? Filing taxes at the end of the year was always handled by him, and it hadn't once entered my mind if they were being paid after we separated.

I had enough on my plate, and now I had the IRS on my back. My anger at the moment built up to a boiling point. How am I going to deal with this? Richie and I hadn't talked to each other for over two years.

I sat for hours wondering how I was going to pay off this debt. It was going to be my responsibility to pay it every year. How could I afford all of this? I had no choice but to find a way to get in touch with him.

I called Anita to see if Richie gave his phone number to her and Sonny. "Let me see if I have it in my address book." I waited a few minutes. "I do have it. Got a pencil?"

"Yes, go ahead." I wrote it down.

"Is everything okay? It's not like you to call him."

"I have some financial problems with the house that I need to talk to him about. Thanks for your help, Anita."

I hated the fact that I had to phone him. Letting him know I needed help wounded my pride.

"Hello?"

"Richie, it's Alberta."

"Hi, how are you?"

"Not too good."

I told him about the phone call from Mr. Phillips. There was complete silence.

"You're not going to avoid talking about this, it's not something that we can push aside any longer. You've got me in a mess." I tried acting sweet; I didn't want to upset him, or he'd hang up and avoid all my calls. I continued, "You haven't been paying the taxes and, obviously, have no intention of doing so in the future. I shouldn't have to do this on my own.

"Well then, we'll just have to sell the house."

"Sell the house! I'm not going to have the girls lose their home on top of everything else they've been through."

"Well, I don't have any money, and unless you can pay the taxes, there's no choice, you'll have to sell."

"And where do you think I can get that kind of money?"

"That's your problem." Then he said, "I want $10,000 for my share."

"Richie, we paid $16,500 for the house. Your share would only be $8,250."

"Well, I want $10,000."

I was furious inside. "I'll talk to you later after I figure this out."

I had no choice, but to lower my pride and call my father for help. It was the first time I ever turned to him for money.

"Hi, Dad, it's Alberta."

"Hi, honey, how are you?"

"Dad, I'm in a tough spot right now." I explained my whole conversation with Mr. Phillips to him.

"What I'd like to do is borrow $10,000. I promise, every week I will send you something. I know it's asking a lot because it will take me forever to pay it off."

He was silent for a moment. My father was a good business man. After all, he had run a military unit and had been the President and CEO of Pyrotector, Inc.

"I'll tell you what. I want to meet with the IRS at Attorney Pimentel's office in Taunton with Richie present. Call Doris Correia at his office and schedule it."

Doris was a close friend of my parents. She had been Dad's secretary when he worked at Anderson Aircraft in North Dighton.

"I'll give the IRS a check for the amount that you both owe and a check from the balance to Richie. There's one catch. He'll have to agree to sign the house over to you. I won't do this unless he agrees. He's to have no part in the house in any way."

"I'll talk to him and call you back, Dad, thanks."

I hung up and was embarrassed beyond words. Who would ever think I'd have to call my parents to help me pay my taxes?

I dialed Richie back and told him about my call to my father and what he'd do to help us both.

"I'd only be getting $1,800!"

"My dad is putting out $10,000 so you're coming out with more than your share." I continued trying to keep my voice calm. "What else do you want? There's one more thing. He won't give us the money unless you sign the house over to me."

"What?"

"You have no intention of working out this marriage, and you haven't been here for over two years, so be fair and give our kids a home. I'll take care of the future bills but don't stick me with taxes that you ignored. We're both lucky that my father is taking care of this. He shouldn't have to do this in the first place. They're not his bills."

"Okay, let me know when the meeting is."

"If you don't show, Richie, you're not getting the balance. Do you understand? I'm firm on this."

"Okay—okay!" He snapped and hung up.

I picked up the phone and called my dad. I phoned the attorney's office, and Doris made the arrangements with the IRS and scheduled a date.

"Doris, I would like to start divorce procedures."

"I'm sorry to hear that."

"I don't want one, but I will be stuck with future taxes which he won't pay. If that's going to happen, I might as well be completely on my own."

"I'll tell Attorney Pimentel."

I phoned my father and Richie and gave them the time and date of the appointment.

On the day of the meeting, I arrived at the attorney's office; Richie was sitting with the IRS representative and my parents when I walked in. I listened to the legal talk between the lawyer and the IRS man. I tried my best to concentrate, but I didn't understand the legal words being used. I was thankful that my father had the knowledge to protect my legal rights with the actions being taken.

Richie sat there motionless without saying one word. Dad handed a certified check over to the IRS man. The attorney then had Richie sign official papers for the house to be fully released to my name. The bank title was already there. He signed his name, and Dad handed him a check for $1,800.

Then the part that almost broke my heart came next. The lawyer also served my husband with the divorce papers. He wasn't aware that I had filed. As sick as it may sound, I still prayed that maybe we would get back as a family.

There wasn't much said between any of us. Legal papers were thrown at us to sign. It was so degrading when I saw my father pay a bill so outrageous. I knew that he must have also covered the charges for the lawyer.

Dad walked over and shook Richie's hand. It was a sad scene. My parents saw only the good side of him and witnessed the love and closeness that we all had when we went to visit them. There were no visible signs that we weren't getting along. They were dismayed when they heard about our problems.

A few days later, Richie called, he sounded very upset. "I was told by someone that I didn't have to agree to those terms with the lawyer and lose my house. I could have demanded $8,000 for my share before signing it over to you."

"My father did us both a favor. You should be happy he paid a bill that was *our* problem, not his. You can start your life over without owing anything. I have to take care of the future taxes. Don't feel as though you were cheated."

I hung up, relieved that he hadn't spoken to anyone before the appointment. If he had retained a lawyer before the meeting, things would have dragged on and I would have been in a horrible financial situation. Though I knew neither of us could afford an attorney.

The next day I called the bank to take his name off the mortgage insurance policy on the house. I didn't want his name on anything to do with me.

"Mrs. Lopes, I wouldn't advise you to take his name off. If something happens to him, the house would be paid off. It's only $3.50 a month. His name on this insurance policy has nothing to do with his name on the house, that's been removed."

I was stubborn and wouldn't listen to good advice. "I want it off."

"Well, I can't go against you're wishes, but I still don't think it's a wise move, Mrs. Lopes."

I was sent the papers and signed off having Richie on the insurance. He now had nothing to do with the house.

In the meantime, I needed to find ways to bring more money into the house. My dispatcher's job wasn't enough. A friend told me that a telephone directory company moved into town and was looking for proof readers. I signed up for the job. It was just up the street from the police station. My job was to match the names and addresses in the telephone book against a master list which they provided. I picked up a batch of one-hundred telephone pages at a time and corrected the names and addresses. The work was easy, but time consuming. Chief Spratt gave me permission to work on it when it was quiet at the station. Some weeks I made over $100 dollars. I'd take home what I couldn't finish at work. The amount of pay depended on how fast I completed a batch. I got good at finding the mistakes in the phone book,

I still needed more income and talked things over with the girls. Debbie was sixteen-years old and mature enough to watch Lori, who was twelve. I went to work three nights a week as a waitress at Friendly's in Raynham. Occasionally, I offered to work on a Saturday. I was now balancing three jobs that were exhausting, but I met the monthly bills and also the unexpected ones that always seemed to come up.

Lori & Richie

Debbie & Richie

Chapter Forty-Three
The Divorce

Twice, Richie failed to appear for our scheduled divorce court dates. The judge passed it over and scheduled a third.

"Your Honor, it's not fair. I'm losing vacation time from work, and he's allowed to ignore the court date."

The judge didn't reply to me. I was furious. No wonder people disregard court orders; there are no repercussions, they can get away with it. I could understand why child support wasn't carried through. It took years for children to get the money due to them, if they ever got it.

Richie was no different. He was so far behind in child support payments that I was summoned to show up at his hearings. I'd be angry about missing work and felt that it should have been between him and the court. To me, the whole system was screwed up; protecting the criminal and allowing them to avoid their responsibilities of support for their children.

He showed up on the third scheduled date. We both leaned against opposite walls in the corridor of Taunton Probate Court, staring up at the ceiling or looking elsewhere. We avoided each other as if we had the plague.

What happened to us? What are we doing here?

He was wearing a dark navy suit with a crisp, white shirt. His two-toned navy-blue tie with white designs matched nicely. I felt I looked presentable in my professional gray suit. I chose a black and gray pin-striped blouse and black high heels. We dressed as though it was a special day, but it wasn't. The world that we once shared was about to come to an end.

I wanted to go over and wrap my arms around him and say, "Let's get out of here." Instead, I continued to ignore him and the actions we were taking. Were we supposed to be enemies or friends? I never experienced divorce before, and this horrible day confused and upset me.

I looked around and saw that there were close to seventy people, all looking lost. They were walking around searching for their attorneys, being called into the courtroom, or standing against the same wall looking defeated.

My heart felt crushed as I held back tears. My knees felt weak, but there were no chairs for anyone to sit on while we waited for our lawyers. Everyone had serious expressions on their faces as they followed behind their attorneys. I felt like I was in a production line.

Finally my lawyer came and led me into an empty room. Richie came in and sat opposite me with his attorney. The room consisted of only one long table, there were other chairs spread haphazardly around the room. The old building had high ceilings and our movements echoed when we walked across the uneven floors or when the conversation started. The loud noise within the empty room contributed to the cold atmosphere. There was no warmth in the room. The two attorneys talked as if they had two minutes to solve our problems. My soon-to-be ex-husband and I continued to avoid eye contact. I tried to get a fast glimpse of his expression only to see him with a blank stare as the two lawyers continued to speak to each other.

I didn't meet with my lawyer before this gathering. I had no idea if he was going to fight for what I needed. Richie was in the same boat. The lawyers were deciding our lives.

The next thing I knew, we were ushered out of the enormous room and asked to sit in the courtroom. My stomach was in knots knowing that our private life was going to be open to strangers sitting in the same room. I felt I was sitting in a stadium, waiting to be put on display. Panic began to rise in me; I wanted to stop the legal procedures.

The attorneys continued to hurry in and out of the rooms. Many whispered in their clients' ear while others stood with the client's married partners. It was a battlefield. Who was going to get what? Who was going to be punished?

I watched and realized that the only winners would be the lawyers. They had nothing to lose. To them, we were all numbers on a check, whether they won or lost the case. It didn't matter if someone could afford their services or not.

The two lawyers went up to the judge, leaving Richie and me sitting alone. They leaned in to talk to the judge, sitting on the bench; though, to me it seemed more like he was sitting on his throne. The judge looked over his glasses at us. We couldn't hear a word they were saying. I sat there thinking they must have already spoken together about our case. Everything seemed planned out. I wondered if they scheduled lunch together after their cases were finished.

I sat motionless, not knowing what I was or was not entitled to. I sensed Richie felt the same way, since he wasn't saying anything. I believed I had exhausted every avenue to save the marriage. What choice did I have?

The attorneys' backs were to us. The judge continued to look at us without smiling. He finally gave his ruling. Not much to decide. The house was mine, and Richie would continue the child support. There wasn't anything to fight over. I felt helpless. I had placed my whole future in the attorney's hands.

October 30, 1979, it was over. Seventeen years of hanging onto a hopeless marriage that couldn't be saved because of his drinking. We joined the ranks of families divorced due to alcohol abuse. There was no other reason as far as I knew. Richie and I were frozen in place. I couldn't shake the desire to hug him. Again, I pushed these feelings aside. Even at that second, I wondered if we could work it out. I didn't want to put my hand on the hot stove; I'd been burned too often already.

We walked out of the courtroom and exited together. There we both stood next to each other for a few minutes on the top step of the courthouse.

"Do you want to go for coffee?" he asked.

I looked at him and thought, *we're divorced, and he wants to go for coffee! When did he ever ask me something so simple when the kids weren't around?*

"I don't think that's a good idea, Richie."

Was it? I'm not sure. Was I wrong saying no? What would we do after that? How are couples supposed to act once they're divorced?

There were so many questions that I needed answered. I was scared to ask them. Neither of us ever talked when he was sober enough to answer them. Intimacy wasn't something we shared. We loved each other, but I don't think we were really *in love*. If he had been sober through the years, maybe we would have found out.

I truly believed deep in my heart that he had been in love with Judy, and I with Danny. Circumstances and wrong decisions stopped our futures with the right persons. We both missed our opportunities to be with our true love.

We can never turn back the clock. *Was drinking the only demon that killed us? Would he have done the same with Judy? Would I have been happy with Danny? More questions never to be answered.*

I stood there feeling sorry for us both, and especially for our precious daughters. They loved us. I prayed that they wouldn't be screwed-up emotionally because of our years of conflict. That was one of the most important reasons for my divorce. Was the damage already too deep?

I wanted our children to know that they didn't have to live this way with a man. Did I stay too long for them to realize this? None of us needed any more hurt. I had my divorce without really wanting it. My real desire was to have a life with Richie.

I looked up at him. "I truly hope you find what you're looking for, and most importantly, I hope you face your drinking problem. If you don't, you're going to be running all your life in the wrong direction and come out a lonely man."

"And you? What are you looking for?"

"I'm looking for happiness, contentment, peace, laughter and getting to know who Alberta really is. I got lost in all this conflict. I want to wake up and see the girls living a normal healthy life. I want us to be able to make the girls feel safe and loved by both of us."

"I think we can do that."

"I'll never talk bad about you to them, I haven't yet. They're old enough to make their own decisions about their feelings for you. Keep in close contact with them, they need you more than you realize. You have to keep the doors open with them."

"Do you think that you'll marry again?" he asked.

"I don't know. I need to learn what went wrong with us and find out what I want. If someone special comes my way, then I'll deal with that when the times comes. I don't think the girls need to see another man with me right now."

I felt so sorry for him. He looked lost. It didn't feel right ending our marriage. My eyes filled. He was such a wonderful man with big plans for us and the girls. He hated his mother's drinking, yet he was sick with the same disease. His problem was in not facing it. All our dreams flew away in a few hours of being in a courtroom that we both dreaded.

There wasn't a day without turmoil and stress living with an alcoholic. A small part of my heart still hoped that the divorce would wake him up. What was it that AA says? "They have to reach rock bottom." Was this it? What could be lower? Here stood another man who lost a family who loved him. We hated the disease, not him.

I never had the chance to truly get to know who Richie really was; he was never sober long enough for me to find out. Both of us were cheated of having fun together and loving Debbie and Lori the way they should have been.

I wanted him to be happy and enjoy life. I knew that he was a good man who got screwed up by a terrible disease; he was a sick man.

I hated to walk down the courthouse steps. It was the most heart-wrenching feeling when I left him behind. I reached the bottom of the steps and looked up. He stood there, all alone, staring at me. There was no wave or smile. I turned and walked toward my car to go home.

Richie continued to work in the television shop in Swansea. I tried to avoid going into his repair shop in the cellar, unless I had to get something out of the room. It was too painful. His equipment was scattered on the workbenches, and a few television sets sat on the floor that people didn't claim. Not seeing or hearing him working in the shop, or laughing at his favorite television shows, felt the same as losing him due to death.

He wouldn't accept the divorce and us not being a family. He continued to call when he was drunk. I'd hang up when he used foul language, which was often when he drank. There was no reasoning with him. He followed me in his van every chance that he could. One night the girls and I were driving to Anita's for supper when I saw his truck behind me.

"Mom, Dad's behind us!" Debbie screamed with fright.

"I know. Don't turn around and look at him."

He rode my bumper and honked the horn driving all over the road. I did something insane. I went faster and refused to pull over. We had another four miles to go to reach Anita's.

I was going so fast that it felt like the tires were off the road. God had to be with me, because I could have crashed into a tree and killed all of us. I was scared to death and wasn't thinking clearly. We traveled away from the populated neighborhood and came into a section of total darkness with no houses or street lights. I was more afraid of being pulled over by him.

I finally made it to Anita and Sonny's driveway, and as soon as I stopped, the kids ran out of the car screaming, with me following. In seconds, he pulled beside me and followed us into the house.

Anita was in the kitchen and Sonny, hearing the commotion, came running out of the bathroom in his boxer shorts. "What in God's name are you doing, Richie?

He leaned against the sink to balance himself.

"I wanted to talk to her."

"Leave them alone. You're scaring your own kids. Look at you. You're a mess. You're drunk," Sonny yelled at him. Everyone saw Richie's problem but him.

"Sit down and eat with us." Anita went to the stove and opened the oven. She placed the food in front of Richie. I knew she was trying to get a decent meal into him.

He didn't put up a fight; he sat and dug right into the meal. I noticed that he had developed a large stomach, like a beer belly. I knew that it wasn't from eating too much. The rest of him was in proportion. He still had a nice build for a man forty-four years old.

"Everyone come and eat." Anita said as she grabbed plates out of the cabinet for the rest of us.

I sat across from him and wondered how a handsome man with so much ambition could have nothing in his life. He had so much knowledge in the field of electronics and threw it all away.

Sonny came back out in his pajamas and smiled at the girls. "Hungry?"

They smiled and said, "Yes." They were both uptight seeing their father in this condition.

I knew Anita wanted Richie to eat so he'd sober up before he got behind the wheel.

Nothing else was said to him about his drinking. We all laughed while we discussed events going on around us. We acted like a normal family eating together, but we weren't; nothing was normal with us.

When I was ready to go home, I worried about him following me. "Girls, we better get home. You have school tomorrow."

Richie started to get up. "Why don't you spend time with us?" Anita said to him. "We haven't seen you in awhile." I knew she was trying to keep him there until we got home.

Driving home, I realized how stupid I had been, racing to get away from him. I was lucky I didn't have an accident. My body shook with fright thinking about it.

Months went by with the same harassing calls or him showing up drunk on my doorstep and my having to call the police to get him to leave. I refused to give in to his behavior. Once I said something and stuck by it, he began to see that I wasn't going to break down and give in to his threats.

The phone calls gradually stopped. The worst heartbreak was the fact that he still avoided calling the girls. He never had any longing to visit them, and they missed him terribly. I went on with my new life, working at three jobs, which didn't leave much time to dwell on all that was happening. I was thankful for that.

Finally, with him staying away, I found calmness in my life. There had been happy times in our life together, in-between our madness, and they were missed. I just couldn't tolerate the numerous fights and abuse; they outweighed the good times. The only time I heard anything about him was through Anita. One day she told me that he was staying with her and Sonny.

I went over to see Anita one morning, when I knew Richie would be at work. We started to talk about him and what he was doing.

"Richie is very sick, Alberta."

"What do you mean?"

"His stomach is getting huge, and his skin and eyes are yellow. I think his liver is getting damaged from his drinking."

"That would be awful, Anita. You really think he's that bad?" Why should I have doubted it?

"Yes, I do." She looked worried. "He sleeps all day and hardly ever eats."

After a few weeks staying with them, Richie walked out of their home with no advance warning. They learned later that he had a girlfriend. I never knew why he had gone to live with Anita and Sonny for that time, unless he wasn't serious over this girl.

Winter settled in with our usual and frequent heavy snowstorms, and I didn't travel much except to go to work. Richie and I never contacted each other, and I gradually stopped asking about him.

Chapter Forty-Four
A Visit Home

June arrived, and I needed a break from the months of being closed in during the winter and trying to keep up with three jobs. I phoned my parents and asked to visit them for the weekend. They were thrilled, and so were Debbie and Lori. We had made many trips to Hull with Richie, but he wouldn't be with us this time. Those shared weekends had been special times for us all. It would be the first time since my divorce that I was going to visit them. Years had gone by with me pretending that my life was secure and happy while I was in a potential breakdown.

I had the girls excused from school on Friday. I wanted to make it a long weekend. The hour ride to Hull through the back roads was relaxing; I tried to avoid the thick traffic on the expressway. I stopped at Kings Castle in Whitman so that the girls could have a ride on the paddleboats on the pond in front of the amusement park before continuing on our trip. They looked forward to spending a half hour at the location every time we drove to my parents. Our ritual would continue on our way home when we stopped for ice cream at Peaceful Meadows Dairy Farm in Whitman.

I smelled the familiar salt air as I reached Nantasket Road in Hull. I opened all the windows as we drove. We could see the white-capped waves hitting the beach. I took Dad's favorite back road along the shoreline. The seagull's cackling calls sounded overhead, and a few of them were fighting over the leftover food dropped on the beach by people during the day.

How did I walk away from all this? Why didn't I try to make a new life here or swallow my pride and make a call to Danny? It seemed so long ago. What's passed couldn't be relived.

The only good thing that came out of our marriage was having Lori and Debbie. How beautiful they are with their distinctly different personalities. How did they keep the humor in their lives when they witnessed their parents fighting for so many years and eventually having only one parent?

Even the station wagon seemed to struggle going up the steep grade of Beacon Road. I parked the car and the girls helped carry our weekend bags to the house. Knowing that the girls were coming for the weekend, Dad finished hosing the outside pool area and had it sparkling clean. Usually I filled the car with their friends, but this was going to be a family weekend.

I went in the front door, and Mom came over to hug us. It took everything in me not to fall on my knees and come apart when she put her arms around me and gave me a soft kiss. A loving touch was something I hadn't had in years. I wanted someone to protect me and take my hurt away; I wanted to be happy again.

Mom prepared cold drinks and brought them to the pool area. It didn't take long for the girls to get into their bathing suits.

"Dad, why don't you join us by the pool?" I asked.

"I have a lot to do," he said smiling at me. Then he hesitated, "I guess it can wait. I'd like to hear how you're doing."

Laughing loudly, the girls jumped off the ladder and teased each other in the pool. It felt good to watch them being so openly happy for a change. They were young girls and growing so fast. Debbie was already in her third year at Dighton-Rehoboth High School, and Lori was in her last year at the Dighton Elementary school.

Mom and Dad sat in the lawn chairs by the pool and listened while I told them about Richie's drinking all through our marriage. I could let a few tears fall because the girls were totally engrossed in swimming and not paying attention to us.

The evening came, and all of us watched Dad with his pet cockatoo. He bought the bird when they first moved to Hull and loved trying to train it. When he took it out of the cage, it stayed on his finger while he whistled softly at it. Suddenly, it would fly around the room enjoying its freedom before landing on his head. The girls laughed because Dad had no hair on top of his head. The bird's feet had nothing to grab onto and they slid, making the bird do splits.

Dad put the bird back in its cage, and we had supper, after which, the girl's took showers, said goodnight, and then went to their bedroom to watch television. Mom and I talked for awhile then Dad called me from the bathroom. I couldn't imagine what he wanted.

The bathtub was full to the rim with steaming, hot water with fragrant bubbles giving a soft scent to the room. He stood there smiling; he had placed a heated towel on a stool next to the tub, and a hot cup of tea was on the table next to it.

"Take some time for yourself, honey," he said

I hugged him until I thought I'd break his ribs. My eyes filled.

"I know," he said and walked out.

I will never forget that moment. One gesture showed more love than I could have ever imagined. It isn't the words, so much as the actions, that we remember.

I sank into the hot water, and the bubbles rose into my face and hair, but I didn't care. It was love that had wrapped itself around me.

Saturday morning arrived, and Dad was up early. The girls were already digging into the blueberry pancakes that Mom had made them.

"Good morning," I said feeling the warmth of being a family. It was the same love and security that I knew growing up. Why couldn't my poor innocent daughters have had this? I didn't realize how damaged our lives were until I came home to my parents.

"You'd better eat up fast, Alberta. I have somewhere to take you," Dad said.

"Can we come too?" Lori asked.

"No, this is special for your mom." He winked at the both of them.

"Wow, a surprise just for me!" I said, teasing the girls.

An hour later, Dad and I were traveling to Quincy.

"Not going to tell me where you're taking me."

"No."

Our conversation for the next twenty minutes was light. My father and I never shared deep conversations. I was partly to blame because my life, emotions and dreams were never discussed with him. Even after I talked at length about my marriage the day before, Dad didn't say a word about the bad events in my life. I truly thought that was why he wanted to be alone with me.

We came into the city's business area.

"Where are we going?" I asked as he opened my door after parking the car.

"Just follow me."

We came to a tiny building between others with a sign above the entrance that read, "Dr. Lester Brackly Optical Service."

"What am I doing here?" I was puzzled.

"I'm buying you contacts."

"You are!" My mouth dropped open.

"I know how you've hated your glasses since you were a kid."

Another kind act by my father that almost brought me to tears, knowing he remembered such a deep and personal thing that had bothered me all these years. I was in first grade when I got my first pair.

Within the hour, I had an eye exam and was fitted for contacts. For the first time in my life, I walked out into a world with no glasses on my face. No more marks on the side of my nose, no more raindrops to wipe off, no more steam-fogged glasses after opening an oven, and most of all, no more ridicule.

"Now I need makeup to bring out my beautiful eyes," I said. I hugged my father with deep emotion. I hadn't had such kindness in so long that his love tore at my heart.

The peaceful, comforting, secure weekend came to an end. The girls had school Monday morning. It was wonderful falling asleep at night hearing my parents talking in the next bedroom and listening to the girls down the hall talking together. It took away the loneliness.

"Call us if you need anything and come home more often," Mom said, her eyes full of tears. She knew they had to send me off to help myself like Richie had to help himself. They could only help so much and only if I asked for it. How could they understand or fathom how I could still love him after he abused me? Until it happened to me, I didn't understand that kind of love either. No one knows what we will put up with until we experience it.

Chapter Forty-Five

Changes in the Girl's Lives

The years passed as I watched the girls starting to put their lives together; they seemed to have adjusted to their parents' divorce. The activities in Lori's life were no different than any other teens, or so I thought at the time. She was so busy coming and going with her own friends that I didn't pay attention to the deeper problems moving into Lori's life. She was then in her senior year at the Dighton-Rehoboth High School.

Lori's personality attracted friends, and they loved her. She was the life of the party. It was rare that she wasn't laughing or joking around, and she had the most wonderful, infectious laugh. The house came alive with teens on weekends. I loved it.

Three years before, when Debbie was in her senior year, she had developed a mad crush on a boy; his name was Brian Dutra and he was the quarterback for the Dighton-Rehoboth High School football team. She was extremely shy and thought there was no chance with him because he was always surrounded by admiring girls.

It wasn't until she turned sixteen and got a part-time job at Almac's grocery store in Taunton that her chances improved. She discovered that Brian was employed at the same location. Working together made it easier for them to get to know each other. They became friends, and when they weren't working, they spent every moment together.

After a few months, Debbie brought Brian home to meet me. I could see why she was attracted to him. He was a handsome boy, nearly six feet tall, with a nice athletic build and a winning personality.

He had a warm smile, a very polite manner and seemed to adore Debbie. As a mother, I couldn't be happier for my daughter. Brian was very close to his family. After I met them, I could understand how he grew up to be the person he was. He had two brothers; Larry and Craig, and a sister Cheryl. All of them were extremely close to each other. They respected their parents and spent a lot of time with them. Their family life was very important to all of them. Brian's good manners were never an act to impress me. It is a trait that he has kept to this day.

Debbie left Almac's and started helping Anita and Sonny with the bookkeeping for their business, which they ran from their home. Sonny bought a piece of property on Winthrop Street in Taunton and moved the business there; he erected a large sign with the family name, "Lopes Construction Company" printed on it in large bold lettering. The company expanded over time from one truck to twenty or more. Business increased, and so did the pieces of equipment needed to keep pace.

After keeping steady company for five years, Debbie and Brian planned their wedding for August of the following year. Everyone was excited. They made such a wonderful couple; she couldn't have found a more perfect match. He and his family mixed easily into our lives. It was heartwarming to see how the whole family got along so well when they were together.

Lori started seeing Jimmy Westgate, a boy she met through Diane's boyfriend, Joe Arruda. Jimmy entered the same high school as Lori. It was hard getting to know him because he didn't come to the house very often. When he did, he was so shy that I had a problem trying to converse with him. My daughter seemed to be crazy about him, and I hoped that there was more to him than I saw. I didn't care for the fact that he didn't mix in or talk much. He'd be at the house just long enough for Lori to get ready to go out, always seeming anxious to leave; a trait her father had had.

Her life with him was private. I wanted to give her some space in the relationship and didn't want to seem overbearing or ask too many questions. I thought the more he got to know us, the more comfortable he'd be with the family.

It's funny how certain warning signs are in front of us, and we continue to ignore and close our eyes to them. We think the warnings are our imagination and disregard our gut feelings. Brian was so outgoing and open with his life and family that it was hard for me to warm up to Jimmy. I couldn't get rid of the feeling that he was hiding something or didn't want me to know him. I remembered back to how Richie had shown these same traits when I first met him. He held back with opening up to my family, too.

During Lori's senior year, the school principal called me frequently about her not showing up at school or skipping her classes. The first time he called, I was very upset and couldn't wait for her to get home. She was dropped off at home by someone in a dark, blue, beat-up van, with no rear windows, and dents all over the body. I didn't recognize the driver and knew he wasn't one of Lori's regular friends who came to the house. I couldn't make out the others sitting in the back.

As soon as she walked in, I confronted her. "Why didn't you come home on the school bus, Lori?"

"Oh, a group of us got a ride home from a friend."

"Who was the driver?"

"His name is Johnny Silvia. I don't think you know him. He's in my senior class and lives down the street."

"How was school?" I asked.

"Boring!"

"Really? You weren't in school. The principal called me today. Why are you lying?"

312

"…Because I knew you'd be upset."

"Don't you think I should be?"

"Ma, I know that I shouldn't have gone, but someone mentioned going to the Cape for the day. A group of us skipped."

"I don't want to get a call about it again. Nice day or not, you belong in school. This is your last year, and you need to graduate."

"I'm keeping up with my work."

"I don't care. No more skipping. Don't plan on going to any friends tonight. I want you home."

"Why?"

"If you skip school again, Lori, you'll be grounded more than a night."

Her attending school didn't last long, and no amount of grounding could keep her in line. It was at these times when I wished her father were more involved in her life, or at least show her he cared. I knew she felt the abandoned by him.

The situation got worse.

I found out through a friend of mine that Mr. Silvia, a neighbor down the street, was supplying kids with liquor and allowing them to drink at his house. We weren't sure if our daughters were involved. I should have reported him, but I let it slide. Big mistake! Taking action would have been better than doing nothing. It wasn't long before I found out that Lori and her friends were in the group going over to his house.

When Lori came home I asked her pointedly.

"Are you drinking at Mr. Silvia's house, Lori?"

"No, we go over there because his son, Johnny, invites us. He's the one who drove me home in his van. All the kids go over there."

"You're telling me that his father isn't passing out liquor?"

"Some of the kids drink."

"And you're not taking any?"

"Of course not."

"You're only sixteen-years old. I don't want you in that atmosphere. People in the neighborhood are talking about the gang drinking and getting loud."

My demands didn't bother her at all. A week later, I saw her and her friends walking toward his house. I waited until she came home about an hour later.

"I saw you walking toward Mr. Silvia's house. You're grounded for two weeks. I want you home after school."

"Mom, you can't be serious? I swear I didn't drink any liquor. The other kids go, and their mothers aren't mad."

"I don't care about the other kids; I care what you're doing."

She ran to her bedroom and slammed the door.

Nothing I did or said stopped her from lying and continuing to do the same thing again. After two weeks staying home, she sneaked back to the neighbor's house. Another two weeks were added to her being confined to the house, but grounding didn't discourage her. It never scared her into straightening out.

I tried to be both a mother and father to her since Richie wasn't in their lives. It had been years since any of us heard from him. She missed him so much, and I believed that he could have helped her emotionally.

Around 10:00 one evening, I was in my robe watching television, when I heard a knock on the front door. Lori and Debbie had gone to a movie. I opened the door and facing me was Mr. Silvia. Since the screen door hadn't been locked, he opened it and stepped into the living room.

"Hi, Mrs. Lopes. Is Johnny here?"

"Why would he be here, Mr. Silvia?"

Suddenly, I felt fright and the blood rushed to my head. He was swaying, and the smell of liquor hit me. He was so drunk, he almost fell.

"I really wanted to come over and say hi to *you*."

For the first time in my life, I feared being raped. I felt naked standing in front of him in just a robe. I tried to stay calm and not act nervous or afraid.

"Well, I'm really busy, Mr. Silvia. I'm expecting my girlfriend any moment."

He stared at me with a cold smile on his face. I glanced at the telephone, but thought it might trigger a battle if I grabbed it to call the police.

"It was nice of you to stop by anyway. Maybe we can make it another time."

He walked backwards and grabbed the door handle, still smiling at me.

"That would be nice," he replied almost falling once he stepped down on the porch landing.

When he left, I locked both doors. I sat on the couch with my heart racing and my body shook thinking of what could have happened.

I ran to the phone and called the police to come to my house to take a report. I told the officer the whole incident in detail, including the talk going around about Mr. Silvia passing out liquor to minors.

"Mr. Silvia is really harmless. I guess he gets drunk now and then." The officer acted like the whole ordeal was nothing. He was a reserve officer and I didn't recognize him.

"Well, I don't agree with you. I'm going for a restraining order tomorrow to protect myself from him."

"I'll go over there and talk to him."

"I think you should. Why wait for something to happen before taking action."

I was furious after being so frightened, and the officer was ready to blow it off.

The girls returned, and I told Lori about Mr. Silvia.

"To be honest, Mom, I think he likes you."

"I never met the man!"

"He told me how he thought you were attractive."

"Lori, I'm taking a restraining order out on him tomorrow. Don't ever return to his home again."

The next day, I went to court and filed a complaint against him and walked out with a restraining order. It was up to him to explain the papers to his wife. To my knowledge, Lori didn't go back over there.

I couldn't wait for Lori to graduate. I believed that her fast-paced life would come to a halt when she did. She was devilish and wanted fun, but she didn't know how dangerous her kind of fun could be. All her friends, including the boys who came to the house, seemed great. I knew them, and they were all well mannered and fun-loving. They were comfortable, and included me in their joking and conversations.

I loved having them at our place because I knew where Lori was and what they were all up to. Their mothers and I were close, and they seemed to have rules for them. My niece, Paula, came over frequently to join Debbie and Lori. Laughter filled every corner of the house. I couldn't understand how Lori got into so much trouble with her friends, unless she mixed in with another group, other than the ones I met. I couldn't get any information out of Lori.

During this period, Anita told Debbie that Richie moved in with his girlfriend. I hoped she was nice so we could all get along; the kids didn't need to be torn between us. I thought, since it seemed he was getting his life together, he might invite the girls to visit them. All I wanted was for him to stay in his daughters' lives. Hopefully, he would straighten out being with this new woman. My main concern was with the girls having a good relationship with their father.

Chapter Forty-Six
A New Man in My Life

When I was forty-two years old, I met a new man, Al Sequeira. My life changed with this unexpected meeting. We met while I was out searching for a new car, and he happened to work at the dealership that I stopped at in Taunton. He saw me drive into the lot and watched me walk from car to car and look inside each one. He strolled out and introduced himself as the manager.

He looked to be in his early fifties with black, wavy hair and a tint of gray starting around his temples. His beard and mustache were closely trimmed. He was wearing black slacks, a gray sports jacket with a white shirt, and maroon tie. He was a handsome and distinguished looking man.

I was invited to go into the manager's office with him and talk about what kind of car could fill my needs and to see what deals the company could offer me. As he spoke, I found his relaxed manner and easy confidence attractive.

I surprised myself confiding personal information to him, more than I had ever done with a stranger. Before I knew it, he said he would fill out a loan application to see if I'd be approved. I was curious about my credit because I was on my own and was interested in building a good credit rating. This would have been my second major purchase.

Over the next few days, we talked on the phone about the car and information on the loan. Gradually, our conversations became more personal. I never did purchase a car from him, but we became good friends and continued our phone conversations. I lived only ten minutes from the dealership, and he'd stop by on his way home when he got off early. He lived in Rochester, which was about a forty minute ride from the dealership.

At first, I refused his offer to go out because I didn't want to get involved with anyone. Within four months, my life became more relaxed with Al in it. I looked forward to the phone calls. He was a gentleman and made me feel special being in his company. My heart skipped when he looked at me, something I hadn't felt in years.

Our dates on weekends were spent going out to dinner and dancing. I enjoyed hearing a band and letting loose. I became myself again. Al and I never left the dance floor until the band stopped for the evening. Being with him felt wonderful! Our conversation flowed easily, and there was easy laughter between us. I was completely comfortable in his company.

The day came when he invited me for a home cooked dinner at his house. He wanted to treat me. His interest in cooking was a side of him that had been hidden and not talked about on our dates.

I drove to Rochester so that I'd have my car for an easy, fast getaway if I became uncomfortable being there. When I took the exit ramp off the expressway, he was parked under the overpass waiting for me. He wanted to lead me to his home so I wouldn't get lost. Al impressed me, when I least expected it.

When we drove into the driveway, I saw my dream porch. The house was a two-story farmhouse with a porch that wrapped around the front and one side of the home. I discovered during our afternoon conversation that he owned ten acres of property that went through to the street directly behind his house. There was a two-car garage, and beside it, across the backyard were two attached buildings; a small barn and stable which were now used as a workshop and storage shed. His land was completely private and welcoming.

When Al opened the backdoor, his daughter, Carol, who was eighteen, was lying on the porch daybed reading a book, soaking up the sun coming through all the windows that encircled the room. She looked up and smiled at me, but she didn't give up her comfort to greet me.

At first, I was uneasy getting this close to Al. Now, it was more than dating, I was invited to meet his children. His younger son, John, who was sixteen, said hello and rushed out having other plans. Lynne was twenty-six and married, and his other son, Alan, was twenty-nine and living on his own.

Al continued to put the Sunday dinner together for us. I watched him become a chef; he thought there was nothing unusual about a man cooking. In March of 1970, his wife, Jean, died in a head on tractor trailer accident, when she was thirty-seven years old. John was only three-years old at that time, Carol was five, Lynne was thirteen, and Alan was sixteen. He had to learn to cook and take care of four young children. He became both the mother and father while Lynne and Alan had added responsibilities with their siblings.

The aroma of the stuffed pork roast cooking in the oven, whet my appetite. He placed a salad in front of me. The atmosphere in the kitchen was very informal and relaxing. Carol insisted she had eaten earlier, but I knew it was an excuse to give us time alone. We took our time to enjoy the meal longer. I dug right in and helped him clean the kitchen and we laughed as we flirted with each other. A few hours later, he brought out brownies with a scoop of vanilla ice cream along with a hot cup of tea for me while he drank coffee.

I drove home feeling my strength to keep him at bay disappear. Respecting him was easy after seeing another side of him that was so special.

After six months of Al and I visiting each other every weekend, I foolishly thought staying now and then at Al's home was all right, since the girls were old enough to be alone. Debbie and Lori seemed to adore Al, and he felt the same toward them. I had too much faith and believed that Lori would behave and could be trusted. She had been coming home and didn't cause anymore problems.

The overnight trips ended when Effie finally told me that Lori had wild parties at the house. She said she had called the police one night because the noise in the house was very loud and kids were also outside in the yard. Some were doing wheelies with their cars on the street. It was hard to believe that no one informed me about it at work. The police officers on duty during my hours never said a word to me. I didn't notice the 4:00 p.m. to midnight report when I came in at 8:00 a.m. after the weekend. I read the midnight to 8:00 a.m. files, so I would know what was happening prior to my shift. By Monday, the Saturday and Sunday reports were old, and already filed away, so I didn't see them.

There were times when Debbie stayed at her cousin, Sandy's or with Cindy's daughter, Jeri. I didn't realize this or that Lori had been staying alone. I made calls a couple of times during the day to check on the girls. Anita also invited them overnight on Saturdays, but Lori wouldn't go with her sister. Of course not, she had the complete run of the house, and able to have her uncontrolled parties. It was amazing how blindly I went along, not knowing about any of this behavior and assuming that the girls were fine when I checked in with my phone calls. Lori never mentioned Debbie wasn't home.

Signs that should have given me warning were passed over and innocently ignored. I believed everything Lori told me. She was so good at telling lies with a straight face. One Monday morning, I discovered a window screen in the room off the kitchen had been cut.

"I want to know what happened to this screen," I demanded.

"I got locked out, Mom, and cut through it to get into the house," Lori answered.

"Where were your keys?"

"When I was leaving, I pushed the inside lock on the door knob and thought nothing about looking for my keys. Once the kids dropped me off, I realized that they were in my other bag in my bedroom."

"You couldn't tell me about it?"

"I knew you'd be mad."

"Yes, but the screen needs to be fixed."

I noticed some deep gouges in some of my pots and pans and scratches in some Teflon-coated ones. I yelled at the girls for being so careless and informed them of how expensive it was going to be for me to replace the damaged ones.

"How could you be so irresponsible? You can't use anything sharp on these pans," I insisted.

I was so naïve, never knowing that Lori was having friends over and letting them use the utensils and cookware with no regard for their care.

According to Effie, there was also heavy drinking; I feared what else might be going on when I was away. Lori invited everyone over to let loose in our home. My weekends at Al's came to an end.

As unbelievable as it may sound, it didn't occur to me that Lori could be following in her father's footsteps. Richie had been gone for four years, and I no longer witnessed his heavy drinking or abusive episodes. I assumed that with a new girlfriend in his life he had stopped drinking. I didn't know what his behavior was since he was away from us, so I didn't put Lori in the same category. Lori never got over her father staying away after our divorce. She talked so much about missing him, and Richie never realized what a big part he could have played in both the girls' lives. I was relieved that Debbie had Brian in her life and was stable. Lori, however, struggled with everything.

Autumn came, such a beautiful season of leaves turning gold, bright tones of reds and deep orange. They fell to the ground, covering it in a colorful carpet. I loved watching them fly up as my shoes shuffled through them when I walked. The autumn leaves and cool air were so refreshing.

This time of year didn't call for much more lawn mowing. I hated the challenge of starting the old mower. My strength wasn't always there to pull the starter cord. I had to pull it numerous times before it would start, which was exhausting. It would usually surprise me when the engine would finally start with a loud, deafening roar.

On one extremely hot day for October, when I was pushing the lawnmower, I could feel the sweat pouring off my temples. I began gasping and couldn't catch my breath. I walked slowly to the front door, went into the kitchen, and leaned on the sink. I tried to get air into my lungs. It scared the life out of me.

My brother, Albert, and I developed heart problems when we were seventeen-years old. Because of our bout with rheumatic fever when we were kids, we had to rely on heart medications. Mine consisted of Digoxin and Toprol. I was afraid the pushing and pulling of the heavy lawnmower in the heat was putting a strain on my heart. Truthfully, I feared a heart attack.

The following day I drove down the street to a house nearby where I had seen a small used riding mower for sale. I made sure it was in good working order and bought it on the spot. The man I bought it from changed the oil and delivered it to my house. He watched me run it to make sure that I could handle it. Purchasing it changed my attitude from a dreaded chore to actually enjoying it.

I was finishing the yard one afternoon when Richie drove into the driveway. He smiled and waved at me while I slowly pulled up to his car and shut the engine off. I felt proud taking the responsibility of yard work. I wanted him to see that I had become independent and could survive on my own.

"Hi, thought I'd stop by while I was in the neighborhood. You look like you're having fun," he chuckled.

"It may look like fun, but it's something that has to be done if we want to get to the front door." I smiled, getting off the rider, and walked over to his car.

It's a shame how a divorce seems to help couples become friends again. Our yelling and fighting stopped. It felt good to have smiles and respect for one another back in our lives.

I couldn't remember the last time I saw him. He seemed to be in great spirits. He got out of the car, and we both sat on the cement stairs leading to the front door. They were built into the retaining wall that ran along the long, paved driveway.

"Is there a special reason for you honoring me with a visit?" I asked him.

"No, I just felt like seeing you." He looked around the yard. "You do a great job keeping up with things."

Talking to Richie while he was sober was wonderful. There was no smell of liquor on him. I changed my thoughts real fast. It would have been so easy to get caught up in his good looks and soft manner.

I knew at that moment, looking at him, that I would always love him. Absence wasn't going to take it away.

"How have you been?" I asked.

"Okay."

Our talk didn't amount to much, just friendly joking. Finally he said, "I heard that you were dating someone. Is it serious?"

"We're just friends." I didn't want to explain my private life or actions to him. "Have you started your own business again?" I tried to change the subject.

"I don't have all my tools or equipment."

"You're welcome to come and take everything out of the shop."

"You'd give me all of it?"

"Of course, Richie, it's yours. What would I do with it? In fact, it would be helping me if you cleaned the area out. Why don't you get your own business up and running again? You've got the knowledge to be great in your field."

"I would like to come and get everything in a few months, if that's okay with you."

"Just let me know the day and time so I can be here."

"I'd like to see you, Alberta." He could see my panic. "I'm not trying to move back."

"I don't know. The person I'm seeing is nice. I don't know where it's going but I can't push him out of my life because you want in." I was trying to be honest without hurting him. "Why aren't you marrying the girl you're living with?" I asked casually, trying not to put my nose too deep into his affairs.

"I'll never marry her, I don't love her. I will never stop loving you and the girls. You're my family."

Why hadn't this conversation and his sobriety been at this stage five years ago?

I didn't want to get carried away with the conversation, and say something foolish because of emotion. I used the excuse that the mowing had to be finished. I didn't want to get too comfortable and lose my energy, or more importantly, get too deep into the uncomfortable direction the conversation was going.

Again, I stopped the discussion instead of talking it out in order to have closure. We owed each other the time to say what we felt. Throughout our marriage, I blamed him for not showing emotion and being distant. Looking back, I was the same. I was petrified of opening my heart to the hurt again. I was letting another special moment go by without talking when he seemed to want to open up. I should have asked to go for that coffee!

He gave me a long hug that sent chills through me. We said goodbye as he got into his car. He promised to call in a few days. I knew that I'd be excited waiting to hear from him.

I watched him as he backed out of the yard and drove down the street. I waved until I could no longer see him. I wondered if maybe, just maybe, he would be coming back into my life. *Would we make it this time?*

Al

Al & Alberta

Chapter Forty-Seven
No Goodbyes

"Alberta, wake up."

"Hi, Art." Paula's boyfriend was standing over me.

I looked around and became aware of my surroundings. I had fallen asleep in the chair in the hospital waiting room.

"You look exhausted."

"I am. I've been here a good four hours and you're the only one who has come over to see me."

He sat beside me and put his arm around me. "How are you holding up?"

That was all I needed, someone to show me compassion and know that I was hurting. I put my head into my hands and broke down sobbing.

Art said nothing and let me release my pain. He was so gentle and caring toward me.

Richie's sister, Lena, came into the room.

"Hi, Alberta."

"Hi, Lena, how's Richie?"

"Not good."

"Can I see him?'

"Why don't we go for some coffee?" she said.

"Is something wrong?"

"I just want to talk to you in private."

"Okay."

I hugged Art and thanked him for spending time with me. I then walked with Lena to the hospital cafeteria and we sat at a corner table away from everyone.

"What's going on, Lena? I don't understand why I'm being kept from seeing him."

"It's got to do with his girlfriend, Sara."

"Why? They're not even married, and you're allowing her to stop me from seeing him. I can't even comfort my daughters while their father is dying!"

"I'm sorry. I'm not running things."

"My God, I can't even say goodbye to him because of a girlfriend!"

"When we go upstairs, I'll see if Sara will let you see him."

"Do you know how that upsets me with you having to ask *her*? What's wrong with all of you? Debbie and Lori need me, and everyone is separating us."

We finished our coffee and headed back to the waiting room. When we got to the door, Sara came strutting down the corridor like an army general with fire in her eyes.

I was shocked at her appearance. She had dirty blonde hair that looked like it needed a good combing. Her faded jeans fit tight around her thick thighs; she looked heavy. The clothes didn't look neat or fresh. She wasn't anything like I had pictured her. I couldn't imagine Richie being attracted to her at all.

When she came upon us, Lena confronted her. "Sara, this is Alberta, and I'd like to take her to Richie's room."

A fire burned inside me when I heard her asking permission to take me. He was the father of my daughters. I had been more a part of his life than she ever could be.

She looked at me stone-faced and said, "I'll take her."

I followed behind her; there was no conversation between us. I felt insulted that the family allowed her so much control over what I could or couldn't do in this situation. No one in the family would even acknowledge me. They knew I was there. I studied the way Sara walked and could sense that she loved having this power over me. It wasn't long before she stopped at a room on the right. There were two men in it.

"He's the first one by the door."

I walked up and sat in a chair next to the man. He seemed like a stranger. I searched for something recognizable. He had the same thinning hair as Richie and the same swollen stomach. His eyes were set deep in his thin face. There were no features that resembled my ex-husband. *How could this disease have changed his features this much?*

I grew angrier every second feeling Sara's presence in the doorway. She was treating me like a child. I knew that she wanted to hear everything said between us. I held the desire to tell her to leave us alone because I didn't want to upset him. He didn't need us fighting in front of him. The vibrations were so strong that I knew she would be capable of arguing without any qualms about keeping me from having any last moments with him.

My fear wasn't about standing up to her; I feared that his family would back her in any confrontation with me, and that would wound me even more.

I put my hand gently on his. "Does that hurt you?" I didn't want to cause him any more pain. He looked up and stared at me with wonder in his eyes. He shook his head no.

I was lost for words and was shocked that he didn't talk to me. He only listened. There was no recognition in his eyes. *How could someone change this much?* I wondered. It was only six months ago that he sat with me in our yard asking me to go back to him. Why wasn't he saying anything to me? He looked at me like I was a stranger to him.

Because he wasn't talking, I thought that he might have been uncomfortable with me and Sara together in the same room. I swallowed my need to be with him, and decided to let him rest. We were denied having a moment to say anything private to each other. After another few awkward minutes, I walked out of his room toward the waiting room, and Sara went in another direction

For the next few days, I continued to go back and forth to the VA Hospital hoping to be with Debbie and Lori, although I was never allowed to be. My heart broke returning home alone, and later seeing the girls enter the house with red eyes and blotchy faces; their hearts were being torn apart.

Our daughters became the adults, making decisions about their father's life. I thanked God that I never talked bad about him to them. The compassion and love they were showing at his bedside surely had to be comforting to him.

I stayed each day in the waiting room hoping that I could have another moment with Richie. Not once did a family member come to talk with me, including my daughters. I felt so alone and was so livid that I was being ignored and not allowed to say goodbye. He needed to hear that he had been a good father and husband until he got sick. Maybe he wanted to say something to me. No one should have the right to take that away from us.

I felt that Sara was jealous and afraid of what we had together. Maybe she thought that keeping me from him could erase our memories or good times. I ached to say things to him, and he needed to know that I still loved him, before he died.

I always left before the girls. They stayed late, and I was stressed sitting in an empty room for four hours by myself. Having someone to talk to would have helped the day go easier.

As I was leaving one evening, Sara confronted me. It was as if she was waiting for me. "I want to talk to you," she said with anger in her voice and a fierce look on her face.

I continued to get my belongings and ignored her. She came up to me, and by the rage in her voice, she acted like she wanted to destroy me.

"Richie is here dying because of all the times you took him to court. The last time did him in."

"It was the court that summoned him each time, not me. He's in this hospital dying because he has been an alcoholic since he was a teen. He's now in the last stages of cirrhosis of the liver. It had nothing to do with me. If you knew anything about the disease, you'd know that. And furthermore, it's none of your business."

She tried to get me to argue with her, but I walked past her and went out the door. I left her standing in the room.

A few hours later, the girls got home, they looked drained.

"Mom, Dad went through the most terrible procedure today," Lori said.

"What happened?" I asked almost afraid to hear.

"The veins were breaking in his stomach, and he was hemorrhaging. To stop it, they had to put a balloon down his esophagus. It was held on his head by a hard helmet."

"Mom, he was so frightened that his eyes bulged. It was awful! We felt so bad for him." Debbie said in tears. "He has a tube in each nostril, and he can see the blood coming out of his body into one of the tubes."

I put my arms around the girls and tried to comfort them. My anger boiled deep within me knowing that they needed me since he had been hospitalized. Everyone selfishly took this away from us.

"This is heartless, not allowing me be with you two at the hospital."

"Mom, it would be an awful scene if you were," Debbie said.

"Sara should be stopped or kicked out for having so much authority. Other than Lena and Art, no one in his family has even spoken to me."

The girls didn't know what else to say to me. I couldn't' hold it in any longer. "Why are you girls allowing this? Aren't you telling them that you *want* me with you?"

"We don't want to cause a fight, Mom." Lori said.

I just couldn't absorb how anyone could be denied from saying goodbye to a person who was dying. Even worse, they were separating my daughters from their mother at this painful time. It seemed inhuman to me.

The next day, the girls and I arrived extremely early, and no family members were there. The doctors wanted to see Lori and Debbie.

"Mom, will you come with us?"

"I'd like that."

It was the first time that I was asked to leave the waiting room and be involved with my daughters. I felt a ton of weight leave me. No one else had arrived at the hospital, and the girls felt free to make a decision.

Once we entered a conference room, the doctor looked directly at me. "Who are you?"

"I'm their mother."

He firmly stated, "You're not allowed to make any decisions whatsoever for him since you're divorced."

"I'm only here to support our daughters."

He directed his attention to the girls. "Your father isn't going to pull through this. Do you want him put on life support if it comes to that?"

My heart sank, thinking these poor girls had to make such an important and agonizing decision at twenty-one and seventeen-years old.

Without any hesitation, both of them answered, "No."

I was so proud of them at that moment. I feared that they would have said yes wanting to hold onto him. Instead, they made the decision with love, not wanting him to suffer any longer than he had to.

After the doctor left, the girls wanted to go into his room.

"Mom, I don't think you should come with us. If Sara comes here, she'll be wild," Debbie stated.

They were scared to death, fearing she would arrive at any moment. They knew that she would make a very big scene. What a position for them to be in. I hated putting them in the situation, but I desperately wanted to see him.

"I want you to ask him if he wants to see me. Let him know that I'm here. If he says yes, no one is going to stop me."

God, I'm this close to him. Let me be able to see him. My heart skipped thinking it could happen.

Debbie and Lori went into his room. I crossed the short hallway to see if I could peek into Richie's room. The huge windows were across the whole room and went from ceiling to floor. There were white drapes that covered all of them for privacy and the heavy material made it impossible for me to see through them.

I went from drape to drape praying to see into his room. Finally, I came upon one that had parted a tiny bit. I pushed my face up against the window to see in. It was a large room with only Richie in it. I saw the three of them together. The girls stood on each side of his bed. I watched as they fed him small pieces of ice. It tore at my insides. How I wanted to run through the doorway and be a family for one last moment.

It was amazing to see how good he looked being so sick. I watched as Debbie and Lori kissed him and held his hand. The three of them smiled and laughed at their own private jokes. I couldn't get away from the window and waited for the girls to come for me. I was fighting the strongest urge to just walk inside. *Maybe he told the girls he didn't want to see me.* I was still waiting for a decision to be made, even while he lay dying. The tears fell down my face; I was aching to be with him. I hated myself for being so weak and not just bursting into his room on my own. My head spun not knowing whether to follow my heart or remain where I was in fear that I would upset everyone. As long as I knew Richie wanted to see me, I didn't care about Sara being upset.

Suddenly, I took a cold look around his hospital room. His bed was next to a large window, and he was the only patient in this huge room. This was not the same room Sara had taken me to a few days ago to see him. No wonder I felt that the man was a stranger—he was! That's why the poor man looked puzzled and didn't talk to me. I had been an unfamiliar person to him. That man wasn't Richie!

I waited for the girls to look toward the door and tell me to come into the room, but it didn't happen. I don't know if he was ever asked. My heart broke, and I walked out of the hospital crying. Our moment to say goodbye to each other never came.

The girls arrived home late, and I asked them about the room their father was in.

"Did the hospital staff ever move your father to different room?"

"No, it's the same one he's been in since he was admitted. Why?" Lori asked.

"Sara took me to see your father, only it wasn't the room he's in now. There were two men in a small room with no windows. I thought your father had become so sick that his features might have changed."

"What a horrible thing to do!" Lori said upset.

I felt like a fool. Why didn't I find it odd that family members or my daughters weren't in the room with him? How could Sara be such a bitch at a time like this? How could she do that to a sick stranger in another room to satisfy her revenge? I hated her more for being so cold-blooded. I had done nothing to this woman to cause her to act this way. Being so heartless, she must have had a good laugh over me having been so gullible.

"Mom, we had a wonderful conversation with Dad today," Lori said. "He talked about our trips to Hull and staying over. He also mentioned the fun we had in the pool, walking Nantasket Beach, and going to Paragon Park. We laughed about the crazy things that Heidi used to do."

"I'm glad he talked about them." I held her close to me.

Those times meant that much to him! He had held onto the good times together as a family. I had missed being in that conversation. The four of us would have been united in private with our fond memories. It would have been my final goodbye to him. He would have died knowing that I did love him. We were all robbed of this.

Chapter Forty-Eight
Richie's Death and Funeral

The next day, at nine in the morning, a nursed called and Lori answered the phone. Richie was in a coma. I was getting my coat on to go when she looked at me with pleading eyes. "I think it would be best, Mom, if you didn't come."

I stood in shock. My daughters didn't want to handle the stress of me being there at the hospital while the family was coming and going to say their final words in his last moments. Debbie and Lori went together. I let them know that I might be at Al's so I wouldn't be alone. For two hours, I sat home in a fog waiting to hear. I paced back and forth. Richie was dying. He would be taking his last breath, and I wouldn't be next to him holding his hand.

I couldn't stand the fright of knowing that he was leaving us for good. I thought that being at Al's might comfort me, so I decided to go.

When I arrived, Al hugged me and asked, "How's Richie doing?"

"He's in a coma. The girls left hours ago for the hospital."

"I'm sorry to hear that, are you okay?"

"I think so. I wanted to go, but no one will let me be with him."

"I can't believe his family is doing this to you," he said, upset.

I sat numb on the couch realizing that I had been completely omitted from his final moments.

Lori called a few hours later. "Dad died, Mom. It's over." She sobbed her heart out.

I felt a panic deep within me, and my insides started to race. Richie was no longer alive and breathing! I wanted to cry, but nothing was coming out of me. Nausea hit me. My hands were trembling.

Suddenly, I didn't want to be around Al or anyone. I had to go back home. I apologized to him and got in my car and left. I couldn't get it out of my mind that Richie died with us never having our private moment together so we could have closure. There was no time to show each other the love we still had between us.

Why didn't I talk to him the last time he came to the house? Why did I stop him from opening up to me and showing his emotions? Why did I hold back my feelings? I shut him off, when we could probably have finally communicated.

By now, I was bitter. I screamed out loud, "Oh, God, how could they have done this to me—to us?" I wasn't there to hold my girls in my arms when they needed me. I couldn't stop crying while I drove home.

About four hours later, the girls walked into the house looking lost and in shock.

"Uncle Sonny was sitting with Dad when we arrived. We saw him take his last breath." Lori broke down. "I wanted so badly to be alone with him in the room after he died, but I never asked."

I put my arm around her. "When someone dies, Lori, we're hurting, and there's no time to think about what would have comforted us. We were his family, and I'm sure he felt your love," I said with the tears surfacing.

My God, did he need me? Why did I allow everyone to keep me from him? Why didn't I have the backbone to go into his room?

A healing process was needed for the three of us and for everyone who felt the impact of Richie's life. The alcoholic is not the only person sick from the disease. Living separate lives and in different locations didn't erase the love in our family. It was the disease that pulled us all apart.

I sat thinking about the past and wished I had made demands on Richie in the beginning, before his drinking got out of hand. I allowed too many years to go by without seeking help for all of us. The demons took hold of him until he couldn't fight them any longer.

Maybe if I had opened up and showed him deep love and affection freely that he didn't have as a child, it would have given him strength to fight this killer. Instead of all the confusion in our marriage, I should have held him more and listened to him.

I would have to learn to forgive myself for being a teenager with no idea of what alcoholism was all about. I had to go through pain, confusion, abuse, and counseling to gain knowledge about this horrible illness. If I had shared our problems with my parents, they might have helped aim us in the right direction, but I tried to be strong and do it alone.

Richie died from a disease that he despised. Some people get help, heal and go on with life, while others have no strength or desire to fight it. He found it easier to continue down the dark road than to fight the days without a drink.

I wanted to remember the good things about him: his wonderful laugh, his enjoyment of cartoons, his love for fishing and the sea, his excitement when Heidi greeted him at the door, the times he had spent with the girls and his niece and nephews, his dreams in the beginning to build a big business. Our memories of the good quality time, hopefully, would be our healing.

The wake was in a few days, and I ran around trying to decide what to wear. I tried to help the girls pick something out, too. As I grabbed a dress, Lori looked at me in an odd way, staring at me.

"Is there something wrong, Lori?"

"Mom, Paula wants you to call her so she can talk to you before the wake."

"Why, what's wrong?"

"I'd rather she told you."

I couldn't imagine what it could be. I went to the phone and dialed her number. I wasn't sure if she or Anita would answer.

"Hi, Paula, Lori said you wanted me to call you."

"I'm afraid you can't go to the wake," she said flat and coldly.

I was absolutely floored. Not seeing him at the hospital was one thing, but not being with my daughters at their father's wake was horrifying!

"Are you serious, for what reason?"

"It was Uncle Richie's last request for you not to be there."

"I don't believe it, why not?"

"He just said he didn't want you there."

"You mean to tell me that you can't find a dark corner for me to sit in if the girls need me?"

"No."

"And if I just show up?"

"We'll have to have you removed."

"You would do this in front of Debbie and Lori?"

"It was his wish."

I hung up in a wild, violent rage. I screamed and cried, going from one room to another in the house. Debbie and Lori didn't know what to do.

I called my father and told him about Richie's death.

"What time will you be there?" he asked.

I broke down uncontrollably and told him the whole story. I never spoke to him during the time I was back and forth at the hospital. Had he known, he would have been at the hospital, himself, making a scene. Maybe that's what I should have done. I never informed my parents about any of my problems. How wrong I had been. He would have been my rock when I needed strength. As always, I had shut my family out.

"What do you mean you're not *allowed* at the wake? I don't believe Richie said that, and even if he did, a wake is for the living, not the dead. This is the worst thing for the girls to be going through, especially without their mother. If you're not allowed, your mother and I aren't going." I never heard my father so mad and disgusted.

The night of the wake came, and Anita called to pick the girls up. "Alberta, if anyone asked why you're not there, we'll tell the people at the afternoon hours that you're coming in the evening. At the night calling, we'll tell them that you came in the afternoon."

I was stunned. What a nice excuse to save their embarrassment. I couldn't breathe because of all this ungodly action against me. My God, I was the one who stuck by him until I almost had a breakdown. He still loved me and was erased off the earth and out of my life. I couldn't take it anymore. I was still angry at Lori and Debbie for not refusing to go without me. Sara was a complete stranger to them and controlled the family like puppets, but they couldn't see it. They put her before me and my daughters!

Anita came to the door to pick the girls up for the wake. There are no words to describe the pain I felt. I stayed in the kitchen doing the dishes, ignoring her. Everyone said goodbye to me, but I didn't acknowledge them. I was absorbed in so much hatred.

I spent the night sitting on the sectional alone; my stomach was in knots not having any control to be with my daughters. I was so angry at myself for not fighting at the hospital to see Richie. I didn't know what to do now. I was tempted to just get up and go to the funeral home. What an awful sight if the girls saw me being escorted out on top of the pain of losing their father.

The funeral was Monday, and I still wasn't allowed to go. I decided to go to work instead of staying home. The chief already had another dispatcher scheduled to take my shift for the funeral. Everyone was in disbelief when I came into the office. Gary Sanson was to be the officer leading the funeral procession. They had to travel right by the police station to St. Patrick's Cemetery in Somerset. Before he left the station, I talked to him.

"Gary, would you do me a favor?" I asked.

"Sure. What?"

"When you're coming down the hill by the station would you radio me and let me know?"

"That's no problem. I'll slow the procession down as much as I can when we come by," he said with a warm pat on my shoulder.

Gary left, and I waited for the call. "Cruiser 173 to 823, we're at the hill."

"Received, 173."

Janet watched the phones while I went to the front door which was all glass. I stood holding my breath.

Gary's cruiser came down the hill and hesitated just beyond the door. The funeral car carrying the casket stopped in front of me. The sides of the hearse had long, rectangular windows and I saw the casket clearly; it had a beautiful, colorful, flower bouquet placed on top of it. Richie's body was in there. I choked on tears. Gary couldn't hold the procession up and stayed at the spot for about five seconds.

This was how I said my goodbye to Richie. I looked in the family car. People were actually waving at me with huge smiles. Were they crazy? Did they realize what was taken away from me? Did they know what they put my girls and me through? I just witnessed Richie's funeral as a *drive through*. I was angry at everyone. I removed myself from the door, refusing to entertain them.

I wanted to leave work. Why didn't I at least take the day off? How was I going to get my insides together to handle emergency calls?

I went directly to my desk, grabbed a pen, and wrote my parents a letter. I knew the time to tell them how much they were loved was while they were still with me. I didn't want to wait until it was too late. I mailed it on my way home. I found that letter in Mom's nightstand after she passed away at ninety-two years old. It had meant that much to her and my father, knowing that touched me deeply.

Days went by, and I was still angry at my daughters; I couldn't stop being bitter. Years later, Lori said, "If I could live it over again, Mom, I never would have gone to the wake or funeral without you. I would have refused."

It was too late. All the pain stayed deep within me. My poor innocent daughters were forced into making a choice between their mother and their father's family. Richie was gone. Life is for the living. Our feelings and respect should be for those left behind.

Richie was buried at St. Patrick's Cemetery in Somerset, Massachusetts. Five years later, his sister, Lena, died of brain cancer. She was laid to rest across from him. His mother passed away also and was buried in another section with her husband. I never went to the cemetery to see where Richie's plot was located.

Now I prayed that my daughters, especially Lori, wouldn't follow the same alcoholic path as their father. I hoped she would find a boy to love her and make her happy. My children have had enough pain in their lives.

Little did I know then how prophetic my worries would be!